Instant
Visual Basic 5
ActiveX
Control Creation

Jakab, Gill, Homer, Jewell,
Enfield, Lhotka and Hartwell

Wrox Press Ltd.®

Instant Visual Basic 5 ActiveX Control Creation

© 1996 Wrox Press

Published by Wrox Press Ltd. 30 Lincoln Road, Olton, Birmingham, B27 6PA.
Printed in USA

ISBN 1-861000-23-5

Trademark Acknowledgements

Wrox has endeavored to provide trademark information about all the companies and products mentioned in this book by the appropriate use of capitals. However, Wrox cannot guarantee the accuracy of this information.

Credits

Authors
Stephen Jakab
Darren Gill
Alex Homer
Dave Jewell
Andrew Enfield
Rockford Lhotka
Bruce Hartwell

Technical Reviewers
Andrew Enfield
Dave Jewell
Robert Barker
Mark Harrison
Ron Picard
Bruce Hartwell
Dorai Thodla

Editor
Gina Mance

Design/Layout
Andrew Guillaume

Development Editor
David Maclean

**Proof Reading
and Index**
Wrox Team

Cover Design
Third Wave

For more information on Third Wave, contact Ross Alderson on 44-121 236 6616
Cover image by David Maclean

About the Authors

Stephen Jakab

Stephen Jakab has experience in writing custom solutions for corporate companies. He worked on the Consort II car fleet management system written in CA Clipper and the Bandit report writer. As a consultant and contractor, he has worked on various Visual Basic projects including Price Decision Support Systems, and he specialises in database programming. While he's not working, he enjoys many sports, reading and travelling. He's recently come back from a two month visit to America, and a holiday in Hungary. *Thanks Valérie Gonzales for your friendship and support over the years.*

Darren Gill

From the humble beginnings of college Pascal, Darren quickly discovered Visual Basic to help with office automation and multimedia solutions. He has since evolved from that beginning and now builds web-based intranet applications.

Alex Homer

Alex Homer is a software consultant and developer, who lives and works in the idyllic rural surroundings of Derbyshire UK. His company, Stonebroom Software, specializes in office integration and Internet-related development, and produces a range of vertical application software. He has worked with Wrox Press on several projects.

Dave Jewell

Dave Jewell is fully employed by his four children as a service engineer. His duties include the repair of broken toys, maintaining model railways and generally fixing things that have been dropped from a great height. In his spare time, he poses as a freelance journalist, consultant and Windows developer, writing technical and programming columns for many magazines in the UK. He has been involved with Microsoft Windows since Version 1.0.

Andrew Enfield

Andrew Enfield is currently finishing his computer engineering undergraduate degree at the University of Washington. He enjoys living in beautiful, green, wet, Seattle in a big house with seven roommates and a pool table. When he's not in the lab engraving circuit diagrams on his arm, he might be found reading (all kinds of things), bicycling, hiking, watching a baseball game, drinking beer, or taking a long walk in one of many parks. He recently returned from a whirlwind 2 month tour of Europe and would like to return soon, or travel to other parts of the world outside of Washington state.

Rockford Lhotka

Rockford Lhotka is a Senior Consultant and Project Manager with Born Information Services Group in Wayzata, MN. He designs and develops component-oriented client/server systems using Visual Basic, SQL Server, Oracle and Access. He is a Microsoft Certified Solution Developer and has developed study guides for the Microsoft WOSA certification tests. He regularly speaks on component-oriented and client/server design. *Thank you to my wife Teresa and son Timothy. Your love and support make everything possible.*

Bruce Hartwell

Bruce Hartwell has eight years of experience in the development, designand implementation of distributed systems. From programming Clipper DOS applications he has progressed to the development of large scale, multi-tiered, client/server systems. *To Carmen for her love.*

VB5
ActiveX
Control
Creation

Table of Contents

Chapter 3: Making Our first Control Useful 63

Chapter 4: A Custom List Box Control 93

Introduction

What Is This Book About?

Visual Basic provides one of the quickest and easiest routes to creating Windows applications. Version 5 can also create ActiveX controls which you can use in other applications, or directly in a World Wide Web page on the Internet.

In this book, we'll be focusing on a particular task—using Visual Basic 5 to create ActiveX controls of various kinds. This can be done with the special free (yes, *free*) version of VB5, which is called the **Visual Basic 5 Control Creation Edition** (CCE).

ActiveX controls (formally called OLE controls) are used increasingly in many different areas of development. Much of the growing interactivity associated with modern Web pages is down to ActiveX controls, and they are increasingly used as a basis for full-blown applications. So if you want a 'moving lights' type of marquee control which scrolls from left to right, instead of right to left like most standard ones, you just write your own. This book gives you the knowledge you need.

Who Is This Book For?

This book is aimed at anyone who needs to produce ActiveX controls. If you are an application developer, you've probably used ActiveX controls before, either as OCXs provided by other language vendors, as part of their development products, or as VBXs which were used with earlier versions of Visual Basic. Now, you can create your own OCXs to achieve exactly the tasks you want—rather than buying them from another supplier or making do with the ones that are supplied which never do quite *exactly* what you want.

So, everyone who is involved in interactive Web page development, or who builds their own applications in Visual Basic, will benefit from reading this book.

What Does This Book Cover?

In this book, we'll take you from an overview of Visual Basic 5 Control Creation Edition, right up to how you create your own highly customized controls. We'll be looking at the background to creating and using custom controls, and the structure and techniques of creating them.

First, we'll take a detailed view of the general requirements for any control. After that, each chapter will show you how we build different types of control. These include:

- A simple sub-classed list box control, based on the standard Windows ComboBox. However, this control has extra abilities, which make selecting from long lists of values much easier.

- An aggregate control, which provides a complete name and address input area in a single control. It contains methods that allow you to tailor it for UK or US use, and it can verify its own data.

- A pair of controls which, together, allow you to create all kinds of card games quickly and easily—even in a Web page. These demonstrate the way that you can create controls which bear no resemblance at all to the standard Windows controls.

- Data-bound controls, which allow you to link the information they display directly to an ODBC data source, such as an Access database. This type of control makes creating database 'front-ends' really quick and easy.

- A control created from scratch using the Windows API. We'll develop a custom slider control in this chapter.

Finally, we'll be looking at distribution. You'll see how easy it is to package and distribute your controls—either as part of your applications, as individual controls, or over the Internet as part of a web page.

By the time you've worked through this book, you'll have all the information you need to start creating your own customized controls.

Note that this book is written using the beta version of VB5 CCE so that you can have access to the information you require as soon as possible. With this in mind, there may be some small differences in the code described in the book and that of the final product. Check out the Wrox web-site for errata pages for this book: `http://www.wrox.com`.

What You'll Need to Use This Book

We won't be teaching you Visual Basic as such, in this book. We're going to assume that you have at least some previous knowledge of either Visual Basic, VBA (Visual Basic for Applications), or a similar language such as Access Basic. We will, however, show you some of the aspects of Visual Basic that are particularly important when creating controls, and which you may not have come across before.

As for software, you'll need the Visual Basic 5 Control Creation Edition, which is available free from Microsoft's Internet site. You can download it from:

`http://www/microsoft.com/vbasic/`

Where You'll Find Our Sample Controls

All the samples you'll see in this book are available from our World Wide Web site at:

`http://www.wrox.com/books/0235/code`.

From here you can download all the code for the sample controls to experiment with yourself. You can also see samples of some of the controls running by opening other pages which are referenced there.

Tell Us What You Think

We've worked hard on this book to make it useful. We've tried to understand what you're willing to exchange your hard earned money for, and we've tried to make the book live up to your expectations.

Please let us know what you think about this book. Tell us what we did wrong, and what we did right. This isn't just marketing flannel: we really do huddle around the e-mail to find out what you think. If you don't believe it, then send us a note. We'll answer, and we'll take whatever you say on board for future editions. The easiest way is to use e-mail:

feedback@wrox.com
Compuserve 100063,2152

You can also find more details about Wrox Press on our web site. There, you'll find the code from our latest books, sneak previews of forthcoming titles, and information about the authors and editors. You can order Wrox titles directly from the site, or find out where your nearest local bookstore with Wrox titles is located. The address of our site is:

<code>http://www.wrox.com</code>

Customer Support

If you find a mistake, please have a look at the errata page for this book on our web site first. The full URL for the errata page is:

`http://www.wrox.com/Scripts/Errata.idc?Code=0235`

If you can't find an answer there, tell us about the problem and we'll do everything we can to answer promptly!

Just send us an email to `support@wrox.com`.

or fill in the form on our web site: `http://www.wrox.com/Contact.htm`

All About ActiveX Controls

Visual Basic is one of the quickest and easiest ways to create Windows applications. It's also one of the most popular and widely used tools for prototyping new applications, and building the trial elements of more extensive projects. However, it still has a place in mainstream application design. Millions of projects have been realized in VB, and these are regularly used in commercial and industrial environments, as well as in homes, schools, and colleges. As the power of the average PC has increased, VB's sluggishness has disappeared—and even considering the extra weight each new release brings to the party, it still has speed on its side.

So where are we going with this chapter, and the book as a whole? We will be showing you how VB has changed from a way of creating simple Windows applications, into a development tool capable of creating fully functional ActiveX controls that you can use in a web page, or as part of another application.

This chapter introduces a lot of concepts, without going into too much detail. It also covers some background and some of the programming techniques that you may not be familiar with. In particular, you're going to need to be comfortable using class modules, so we've included a broad overview here in case you've been sitting on the OOP (object-oriented programming) fence for the last few years. Our main aim, though, is to introduce you to some of the aspects of VB which are particular to the creation of ActiveX controls. These, after all, are the focus of the whole book.

In this chapter, you'll see:

- An overview of VB5 Control Creation Edition.
- Why we might want to create our own controls.
- The different kinds of controls, and what they can do.
- How classes act as the basis for ActiveX controls.
- An outline of the structure of a control.
- How we interface our controls with developers.

So, to start, what actually is the Visual Basic Control Creation Edition?

What is VB5 CCE?

The long-awaited version 5 of Microsoft's Visual Basic has several editions. One of these, the Control Creation Edition, is specifically tailored for just one task—that of creating ActiveX controls. And it's a lot cheaper than earlier versions—Microsoft is actually giving it away free over the Net.

The Need for Controls

So what's behind this sudden generosity? Well, like most things today, the Internet is part of the problem (and in our case, the whole solution). When you want to create objects to be used in a web page, you need to be able to compile them into some kind of insertable form, so that the browser can work with them right there in the page. Unlike the scripting languages that you use in a web page, such as VBScript and JavaScript, objects can actually execute within the page. In other words, they can do something visually—such as display a moving ball, a 'moving lights' text streamer, or a steaming coffee cup.

The first language primarily used for creating these objects was Java. Java is a C++ style language that was originally developed by Sun Microsystems for use in micro-controllers, and even in household appliances. This is now a widely accepted standard for creating objects—or applets, as they are referred to in Java terminology. Unlike Visual Basic, however, the language is not immediately intuitive, and is somewhat limited in the effects it can directly produce. Java is a 'sand-boxed' language, which means that it has only limited access to the host computer's operating system, although add-ins such as the Java APIs and Java Beans are extending its capabilities.

Visual Basic, Come On Down

Even though Microsoft's browser, Internet Explorer, supports Java applets, it was unlikely that they would allow this language a totally free run in the marketplace. The existing OLE technology that has long been part of Microsoft's strategy was ideally suited, with only some minor changes, for use in web pages.

Along with the technical changes, came a new image and a new name. All of a sudden, everything is ActiveX, not OLE, and the new types of OLE controls are ActiveX controls. In a rush of development, there emerged a huge number of new controls that are specially tailored for use in web pages. And, of course, you can still use existing OLE controls as well.

The big problem was that to create an ActiveX control, or a fully functional OLE control, realistically required something like C++ or Delphi. Neither of these offers the same level of introductory ease of use as Visual Basic. While VB4 could be used to create executable (out-of-process) OLE Automation Servers and (in-process) OLE DLLs (Dynamic-link Libraries), it couldn't create true ActiveX controls as OCXs (OLE Control Extension) files that included things like property pages, events, or a Windows interface.

Of course, Visual Basic 5 is the answer. It can create full blown ActiveX controls as OCXs. In this book, you'll see how we use it to create these controls.

Note that the Control Creation Edition, which we're using in this book, cannot create normal executable files or DLLs. It can only create ActiveX controls.

Why Create Controls?

If you aren't 'into' the Internet (well, there must be somebody who isn't), then the previous few paragraphs might have you thinking 'So, what?' It's just possible that creating ActiveX controls for web pages isn't top of your agenda. If you use Visual Basic for anything more serious than small application development, however, you're sure to have come across OCX and VBX controls before.

VBX (Visual Basic Extension) controls were developed for use with 16-bit versions of Visual Basic. They provided a way for the application developer to buy in specific functionality that could be dropped into any application. While many of these were graphically improved versions of the standard controls, such as 3D text boxes and panels, some were truly useful tools such as the Graph or Grid controls. In fact, many were bought in by Microsoft and supplied with VB in the Professional and Enterprise Editions.

As we started to move towards 32-bit operating systems, Microsoft developed the **OCX** control. The VBX technology is a very proprietary standard that only works well with Visual Basic, and in 16-bit operating systems. It can't be used to build true 32-bit Windows 95 or Windows NT applications. The OCX standard is based on the 32-bit Component Object Model (COM) technology, which is the basis for all kinds of new application and operating system inter-operability. It's also well suited to a multiplatform environment, supporting different types of operating system. While some OCX controls *are* available in 16-bit form, VB5 CCE can only create 32-bit OCX files.

So, the application developer can drop OCX controls into any project, whether it's written in Visual Basic, or one of many other languages. We're only interested here in Visual Basic, but of course the increased market for controls means that many more varied, and hopefully high quality, controls will be available. And you'll have a bigger market in which to sell your own controls when you move from being just an application programmer to a tools and controls developer.

Who is the Developer?

So, having mentioned developers, lets briefly define the people you'll be meeting in this book. The people who actually get the pleasure of using our finished VB applications or web pages, we'll be referring to as the **users**. The people who write these applications or web pages, which may well include you, we'll call the **developers**. Finally, the people who design and create the components, tools, add-ins, and (of course) ActiveX controls that the developers use in their applications, we'll refer to as the **control developers**. If you like, you can call yourself a **tools vendor**—we're pretty relaxed about these things.

How Controls are Used

Assuming that you fill the slot of developer, then, you'll probably have used various controls before. We've created a pair of controls that make creating a card game very easy. You just drop one of each of the objects into your application or web page, set the relevant properties, and then at run-time you manipulate the objects to display the hands and deck of cards.

Over the page you'll see how these controls look when used in a test VB application.

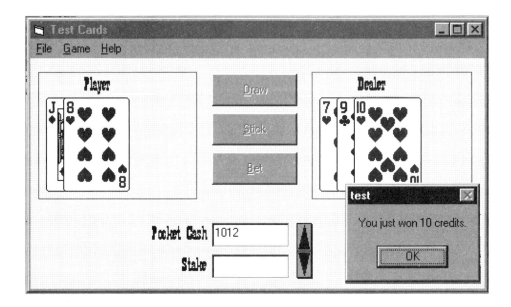

And for those of you who are building exciting web sites, you might like to add a games room. Here are the controls being used in a web page:

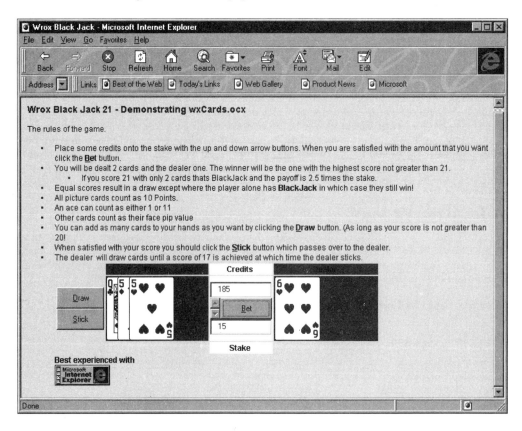

To use the controls in code, we just manipulate them like any other object. For example:

```
'-----------------------------'
'Buttons
'-----------------------------'
Sub cmdDraw_Click()

    Dim objCard
    Dim blnRet
    Set objCard = Deck.TopCard
    objCard.DrawStyle = 0        'deal these face up
    blnRet = hndPlayer.AddACard(objCard)
    Call CheckGameResult
End Sub
```

Types of Controls

Having seen some background to ActiveX controls, and VB5 CCE generally, it's time to get down to some serious study. Before we can go off creating controls, there's quite a lot we need to know about their structure. OCXs are quite complex beasts inside, and if you haven't been introduced to their structure before, it's easy to get lost on a sea of technical jargon.

We're going to take you through all the building blocks of a control in this section of the chapter, so that you are really at home when you come to getting your hands dirty and building some real controls. If you've been involved with Visual Basic 4, and used class modules, some of it will be revision. But we do suggest that you make sure you are familiar with the topics covered. First, what types of controls can we create with VB5 CCE?

Simple, Sub-classed Controls

The simplest type of control is one that uses a single subcontrol as its base. For example, in Chapter 4, you'll see how we have used a standard Windows ComboBox control as the basis for a new control. In effect, we **subclass** the control by placing it inside a new class of our own and then connect the subclassed control to our new class 'wrapper', so that it behaves just like a normal ComboBox control.

Of course, there's no point in subclassing a control like this if it only behaves the same way as the standard one. The point is that we can then change particular facets of its behavior, while the rest will continue to work like the standard control. And if we don't change the physical appearance of the control, the developer will think that they are working with a standard control.

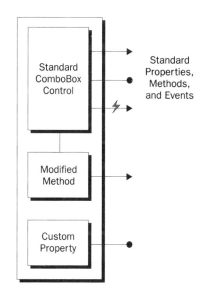

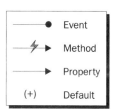

As an example, we could create a text box control that looks, and generally behaves, just like a standard one. But when clicked, the background color could change to, say, green. We could even arrange for the color to change to one that the developer selected in design mode, while developing the application that uses it.

Aggregate Controls

Subclassing a standard control is a very useful technique. Often, however, you have a group of controls that need to act together. This could be a set of option buttons, or a custom toolbar. In this case, we can create a control that contains all the subcontrols we need. The complete package behaves like a single control when used in code, but looks like several different ones.

Because all the subcontrols are packaged in a single control, we can also include code which links them together. For example, we can examine, combine, and validate the values of each one, inside the control, as required. We can even provide a single combined result to the application that is using the control, if required.

You'll see an example of an aggregate control in Chapter 5. We've created a custom Address control, which contains several text boxes. This is useful when you want to include a 'contact' section in any application.

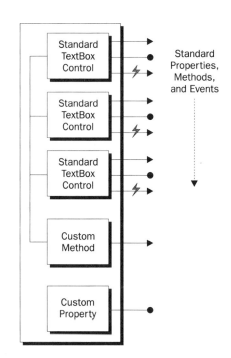

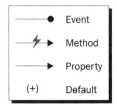

User-draw or Owner-draw Controls

The third option is to create a control that doesn't display any constituent controls (although it may still use them—it's just that they're not visible). This is the method we choose if we want to create a control for which no standard control gives the appearance we need.

For example, we may want a 'moving lights' text display (rather than just a normal marquee control), like the ones you see above an airline check-in desk. There is no obvious control we could use as the base for this, so we would have to build it ourselves by using drawing methods to place the dots of light on the control's form or in a picture box. Now, there's no limitation to the way we display the results. We can have every letter in a different color and scroll it in either direction.

User-draw controls have to create their own physical appearance when the project that uses them is in both design-time and run-time modes. However, some types of controls don't actually appear on the screen at run time—for example, the standard **Timer** control. In these cases, we set the **InvisibleAtRunTime** property to **True**, and we just have to create a design-time appearance so that developers can manipulate it while they're building their applications.

The hang-up with user-draw controls, of course, is that they normally take a lot more effort to build. However, they are also the most eye-catching and individual, and so provide a great way to make your applications or web pages stand out from the crowd. In Chapter 8, we'll describe how we created the Cards controls you saw earlier in this chapter. These are, of course, user-draw controls.

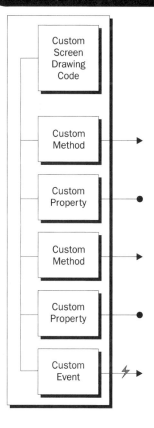

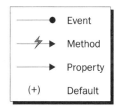

What Do ActiveX Controls Look Like?

Before you dash off and start creating your own controls, you need to consider how and where they'll be used. This affects how they should behave and what they should look like. For example, if you are creating controls to sell to developers, you need to make sure that they have an interface which makes them as useful as possible. In other words, you should consider all the different situations in which they could be used, and hence which properties, methods and events you need to make available to the developer.

If you are creating specialized controls just for your own use, you can tailor them exactly to your needs. This may mean making them as compact as possible for use in a web page, or using fixed colors which match your requirements.

In some cases, you may not want a physical appearance. Perhaps your control carries out some processing task, but doesn't appear on the screen. This means that it can be used on an unattended network server. But if it keeps popping up dialog boxes, it's quite likely to be unsuitable for this task.

11

So generally, controls fall into two categories:

 Controls that primarily provide a physical appearance and are used to build an application's interface. An example is the Windows TabStrip or Slider control.

 Controls that are primarily task-oriented, and carry out some kind of background processing. Examples are the Windows Timer and MAPI controls.

What Can ActiveX Controls Do?

Inside an ActiveX control, we write the code that manipulates any constituent controls, and otherwise carries out the tasks that we want our control to perform. That's a bit like saying that a computer works because it's got wires and chips inside. The point is that a control can do anything that's possible with the language that's used to write it. Anything we can do directly in Visual Basic, we can do in a control. And if we can't do it directly, we can plug in someone else's controls, or use external DLLs and the Windows API (Application Programming Interface).

However, just because we *can* do it doesn't mean that we *should*. It's wise to follow the principle of keeping the controls as simple as possible, in line with achieving the tasks required. It's better to create small, compact, and fast controls than huge monoliths, especially if they have to be downloaded over the Net. This will also mean that there's more chance of them being generic and reusable in other projects, and less chance of them having bugs.

One interesting feature of ActiveX controls, is that you can create them as **container controls**. In other words, they can themselves act as a run-time container into which the final user of the application can insert other elements, such as pictures and sound files. Of course, how well this works will depend on the way your custom control is being used, and whether the host application it's running in can provide its share of the functionality required. It may well not work in a web page, for example.

Understanding Controls

Having seen some of the types of controls we can create, and the kinds of tasks they can achieve, we need to look inside a control to understand how we go about building one. All controls are based on **classes**. In Visual Basic, this means using **class modules**.

Classes

You may have been writing applications in Visual Basic in the past, without ever having seen or used a **class module**. When you come to create controls, however, it's time to start. You have to use them to create any kind of ActiveX control object. The mention of classes and objects stirs up all kinds of uncertainty in the minds of some programmers. Well, don't panic. It's not *that* different from other ways of structuring your code, as you'll see in this book. In many cases, it actually makes the task easier, once you're familiar with the basic principles.

In this section, we'll give you the background you need to get started using VB5 CCE to create **control classes**. If you're well versed on class modules in VB, you might want to skip to the next section.

What are Classes?

Think of how you create a complex application using traditional methods. You probably isolate sets of tasks that you know will be repeated regularly, and then define the types of data you'll need to store. To connect the data to the actual application, you write code routines that manipulate it— perhaps to write a line of text to a file, or format a record from a database in a particular way.

We look for these related elements of a complete application, and separate them into different blocks of code. However, there is more to it than just writing separate functions and subroutines. We actually remove them to a different module within the application. In the past, you've probably done this by using a VB code module to store all your regularly used routines.

But classes give us more than this. As well as separating code routines, we can use them to hold the data as well. By placing the data and the code that is connected with it into a separate class, we allow the class to be reused in other applications where we have the same (or similar) tasks to achieve.

What Do Classes Do?

OK, so it doesn't sound like a great breakthrough. But it starts to give us the benefits that have long been sought after by programmers using all kinds of languages. Once we have a class we can create an object based on that class. The object stores its own data, and it can manipulate that data itself. The benefits we get are:

Reusability—when we want to use the same object again in an application project, we can just include it by adding the corresponding class module, or attaching the separate compiled OLE server DLL that incorporates the class.

Encapsulation—by designing it carefully, we can hide the details of how the data is stored and manipulated. All the user of the class (in this case our application) sees, is the **interface** (i.e. the properties, methods and events) that is exposed in that class module. The code that underlies the interface isn't important to the developer. All they need to know is what methods are available, what parameters they need, and what will be returned.

Another thing that we can get from using a class, depending on the way it's implemented and the language in use, is **inheritance**. Inheritance broadly means that we can use a class as a basis for another class. The new class inherits the behavior of the original class, but we can then add to or change that behavior in the new class. This, of course, makes the likelihood of being able to reuse it even higher. Visual Basic 5 handles inheritance from the point of view of the interface. This is a little different from the way it works with other languages like C++ where you inherit the code implementation. However, we will not dally on this subject as the intricacies of what inheritance is and is not are well beyond the scope of this book.

This leads on the last object-oriented concept, **polymorphism**. Essentially this is the ability for one type of object to be used in place of another. With Visual Basic this is again based around the interface. Consider where you have two types of object, A and B. If the class of B inherited an interface from that of A, then you could use an object of type B everywhere that an object of type A is required.

Neither polymorphism or inheritance will play a great part in the controls that we will generate in this book. The most important feature is that of encapsulation of the data and procedures.

How Do Classes Work?

So a class can store its own data, and contains the code routines necessary to manipulate the data, and communicate it to the outside world. Of course, it's all right laying down grand schemes like this, but we have to be able to make them work in the 'real world'. To do this, we create classes to a pre-determined pattern that allows them to communicate with other parts of an application. These classes can then form the basis of the various applications we use.

As an example, consider the Equation Editor that comes with Microsoft Office. This is an application in its own right, that can store and manipulate its own data. We can use it to insert an equation into a Word document. However, Word knows nothing about equations. It just blindly accepts the data that Equation Editor produces, and stores it in its own document file. When we want to edit the equation, Word starts up Equation Editor and hands the data over to it.

Of course, there are all kinds of messages being passed back and forth here. Word tells Equation Editor what the data is, and Equation Editor displays the equation you create, in the document. Equation Editor tells Word when it's finished, and hands the data back again. All this happens behind the scenes, as part of COM's defined standards.

The message-passing mechanism is implemented in Visual Basic behind the scenes. We, as Visual Basic programmers, can generally escape from being involved in message passing, and use the abstracted form in terms of **properties**, **methods**, and **events**.

Properties are attributes of a class, and are usually represented as data that is maintained within it. For example, a custom MyTextBox class could have a **Width** property. Some properties can be changed from outside the class, while others might be read-only. And different ones may be available at project design-time than at run-time.

Methods are just routines within a class that carry out some task. There can be more than one method in a class, and they can accept parameters. For example, our custom MyTextBox class may have a **ClearToZero** method that we could execute with no parameters, which just sets the contents to a string of zeros and a **ClearToChar** method that accepts a character as a parameter and sets the contents to a string of that character.

Events are occurrences of something happening to, or within, an object. For example, our custom MyTextBox class might have a **TextChanged** event that occurred each time the user changed the text in it. The developer can decide whether to respond to these events with code in their application, outside the object, and specify what to do at that point.

The Class as an Object

A **class** is a just blueprint for an **object**, and an object is just an instantiated class. That is, it's a copy (or instance) of a class that's been executed (instantiated) and is running in memory.

We'll be looking at how, and when, a control class is instantiated later on in the book.

To create an ActiveX control, we write the definition of a class, such as MyTextBox, as a **UserControl** class, and then instantiate it. This class has properties defined within it, methods that can be executed by an application (or another object), and events which can be handled by an application or another object. There are likely to be several of each of these in all but the very simplest control:

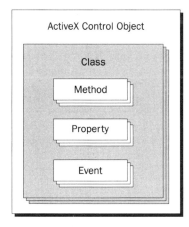

The UserControl Class File

Visual Basic can create the empty control class file when it starts up, as you'll see later. Then, the ActiveX Control Interface Wizard can be used to do all the repetitive background work of creating an outline of the code required for the control. These files are stored in text format with the file type of **.ctl**. If there are any elements in them that can't be stored as text, such as bitmaps, these are placed in separate **.ctx** files for that class. VB also creates a project file for the control, with the extension **.vbp**. This stores details about which files are used in the project, and other project-specific information.

When we come to compile the code to create our control, VB gives it the extension **.ocx**. At this point, it can be used in our applications or web pages. The standard class that we use to create an ActiveX control is called **UserControl**, and it has a set of default properties and events. You'll be seeing more of these later on.

When we start a new ActiveX control project, Visual Basic creates the **.ctl** file that defines the **UserControl** object, and opens a window that looks just like a normal borderless VB form. Here, we can design the physical user interface for our control by, for example, placing standard controls on the form. And, like a VB form, this interface will look and behave differently when the control is in run mode. The grid on the form disappears and any constituent controls behave like they would in a normal VB project during execution.

If we are building a control which won't be visible at run time, and won't contain any user interface elements, we set its **InvisibleAtRunTime** property to **True**. Then, we only need to worry about creating the visible design-time interface. This is what the developer will use to place our control on a project's form in design mode and move it around. It simply acts as an indicator to show that the object is, in fact, available in that project.

Design and Run Modes

Once we've designed and built a control, we will want to insert it into various projects or web pages. We can set the properties we've defined for it at project design time, then run the project and change the control's properties at run time. At the same time, we will call the control's methods, and respond to the events that are defined in it.

Running at Design-time

What's difficult to come to terms with at first, is that the definition of when **run time** and **design time** occur is different for the *control* and for the *project* it's being used in. To make more sense of this, look at what happens when we use a pre-built control in our projects. We set the properties for it while our project is in design mode, and we expect the control to do two things: first, we expect it to remember the settings we make to the properties; and second, we expect it to change its appearance where this is applicable. The figure shows our card hand control in design mode (you can tell it's in design mode because it's full of aces!)

Think about this for a moment. Our application's project is in design mode, so it's not going to be much like a running program. We won't expect it to respond to events, as it will when we execute it. If our ActiveX control was in this mode, we certainly couldn't imagine inserting it into another project as it is. It's only when we switch to run mode that an application actually *does* anything. However, we're expecting the control to do things while our project is in design mode (such as draw some aces). This is only possible because the control is actually *running* (i.e. executing) while the main application project is not.

Running at Run-time

Of course, our control is also running when the project is in run-time mode. But now it may have to behave differently. For example, the cards control has a property to display a certain number of cards. When our project is in design mode, we would expect to be able to change this value in the **Properties** window. We'd also expect to be able to set the **BackColor** of the control . Both of these changes should be immediately reflected on screen, in the control that's inserted in our application.

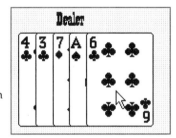

When we start the application running, however, we expect a mouse click on the control to cause an event that the developer can write some VB code to handle, perhaps highlighting the card. So the control has to behave differently, depending on which mode the containing application is in. But the control is always in run-time mode when it's being used in another project.

Saving the Property Settings

Remember what else we said earlier? We expect a control to remember the settings made to its properties once it's been inserted into an application. Again, this is pretty obvious when you think about it. If we set the number of cards to show in our example control to five, we wouldn't be very pleased if, each time we switched our project from design-time to run-time, the number changed back to the default value of, say, three.

A control has to save its property values after they've been set by the developer, and then retrieve them each time the project is switched from design mode to run mode. Why each time it's switched? Well, that's because the control is actually destroyed and re-created each time this happens. The initial action of inserting a control into a project, by drawing it on a form, for example, creates an instance of that control which is actually running while the containing application's project is in design mode.

When you click the Run button to start the application, the instance of the control on the form first saves its property settings within the design-time copy of the form. This control instance is then destroyed, but the design-time copy of the application's form that is in memory contains the latest settings made to its properties. Then a new instance of the control is created in the application's run-time mode, and it retrieves the property settings and sets them inside this instance.

When you click the Stop button, the control is again destroyed, and a new instance created inside the design-time environment of the containing application. This reads the original property settings again. Notice that the run-time instance of the control *doesn't* save its property settings. When you change the properties of a control using code, from within a running application, you don't expect this to have changed the settings you made to the properties at design time.

The next diagram lays out the whole cycle, from inserting a control into the application's project for the first time. When placed on a form and first created, the control must set some sensible default values for its properties, and this is done in the **InitProperties** event. This is one of the three events that VB supplies for handling property values. The other two, **ReadProperties** and **WriteProperties**, occur after the control has been added to a project, each time it's switched from design to run mode.

The application that's actually hosting our control supplies a location to store the values—imaginatively named the PropertyBag. Property changes made in design mode will be saved as part of the file that defines the form on which the control is placed, so the property values we set for it are saved when the form is saved, and written into the executable code when the application is compiled. If you are creating an active web page, then the properties will be saved as **<PARAM>** tags in the HTML file.

Defining Properties, Methods and Events

To create the control, we have to write a class definition for it. The class has to define all the properties, methods and events for the control, and contain the code necessary to make them work. The properties, methods and events are the **interface** that the application developer or web page creator sees and works with. Think of the interface to a standard type of control, such as a ComboBox, that you regularly use in VB. This has properties such as **Font**, **ForeColor**, and **Width**. There are methods, such as **AddItem** and **SetFocus**, and events such as **Click** and **MouseDown**.

An Outline View of Properties

To define a property for a control class, we declare a variable within the class to hold the value of that property. However, we don't normally want to allow the developer who uses the control to access these variables directly, so we don't define them as being global or **Public**. If we did, they could assign any old value to them—which could prevent our control from working correctly. Instead, we provide a way for them to set and retrieve the values using **property procedures**.

```
'Retrieve the value of the 'Text' property
Public Property Get Text() As String
   Text = txtInternalText.Text
End Property
```

```
'Set the value of the 'Text' property of contained Text box
Public Property Let Text(ByVal strParam As String)
   'accept strings of length 1 to 255 only
   If (Len(strParam) > 0) And Len(strParam) < 256) Then
     txtInternalText.Text = strParam
   End If
End Property
```

In an application we're developing, we can create an instance of the control on a form, and name it **txtMyControl**. Then we can use the property:

```
strTheText = txtMyControl.Text            'use Property Get procedure
txtMyControl.Text = "This is some text"   'use Property Let procedure
```

An Outline View of Methods

The methods that a control makes available to developers are just procedures, stored within the class module code. These can accept parameters if required, and within the code we carry out all the necessary actions. For example, the **ClearToZero** method of the custom MyTextBox control we mentioned earlier might look like this:

```
Public Sub ClearToZero()
   txtInternalText = "00000000"
End Sub
```

Alternatively we might implement the **ClearToChar** method which accepts a character as a parameter, and sets the value to a string of that character:

```
Public Sub ClearToChar(strCharacter As String)
   txtInternalText = String(8, strCharacter)
End Sub
```

When developing an application, we can create an instance of the control on a form and name it **txtMyControl**. Then we can use these methods:

```
txtMyControl.ClearToZero
```

or

```
txtMyControl.ClearToChar("X")
```

18

It's just like using a normal text box, but now it has methods that aren't available in the standard variety.

An Outline View of Events

Lastly, we'll probably need to respond to events in our control, and also be able to raise events which are then passed back to the host application. An event occurs when the user, another application, or the operating system, needs to notify the control that something is happening. As an example, consider what happens when you change the system colors in the Windows Display Properties dialog. If it needs to look like other standard Windows objects, the control must change its colors to match.

The control could continuously check to see if the system colors have been changed, but this is an incredibly wasteful use of processing time. Windows sends a message to all running applications to tell them that the colors have changed, so all our control has to do instead is respond by updating the colors when it receives this message. It's like getting someone whose phone is engaged to ring you back, rather than having to keep trying their number.

A control can send notifications of an event back to the application in which it's being used. Then, in the application, we write code for the events that we actually want to respond to directly. For example, we might want to respond to an event named **OpCompleted** which occurs in a control named **MyControl** which we've placed on our form. We create a subroutine in the application that is executed when this event occurs:

```
Private Sub MyControl_OpCompleted()          'in the application
  ...
  MsgBox "The operation is now complete"
  ...
End Sub
```

To cause the control to pass this event back to the application, we write a routine in the control's class. In this example, it will be executed when the user clicks on the control:

```
'Declare the User control events
Event OpCompleted()

Public Sub UserControl_Click()               'in the control
  RaiseEvent OpCompleted
End Sub
```

To cause the event, we use the **RaiseEvent** statement. This effectively passes an event back to the container (i.e. the application or web page which is hosting the control). The event is identified by the name we provide—in this case it's **OpCompleted**. Of course, we can also pass on the **Click** event from our subclassed controls, by responding to their **Click()** event procedure directly:

```
'Declare the User control events
Event OpCompleted()

Public Sub txtInternalText_Click()
  RaiseEvent OpCompleted
End Sub
```

19

If we don't include a **RaiseEvent** from the subclassed control's event procedure like this, then the developer will not be able to respond to the click at all. Of course, this might be what you want. You may want to do all the work yourself, and not let on to the developer that anything has happened.

Stock and Custom Members, and Mapping

We can use the term **members** to refer to the properties, methods and events for a class. These fall into two broad categories. The ones that are supported by default for all controls are called **stock members**, and those that you create yourself are called **custom members**. The members that *are* actually supported and available, are said to be **implemented** by that control.

When we create a class, we have access to all the stock members of the constituent controls, plus the members for the control class itself. However, our control doesn't have to implement all the available stock members. There are some that are implemented anyway (by the container), and some that are generally implemented because they are expected by applications. For example, we would normally expect to implement the **Visible** property, or the **Click** event.

Also, we don't always have to write code for those that we *do* implement. Assuming that our control uses subclassed constituent controls, we can **map** our control's properties, methods and events to the standard ones for the constituent controls. Mapping a member means that we link the property, method or event for the control itself directly to a matching member from the constituent controls. In other words, if we have a custom control which contains a normal text box control, we can map our control's **Click** method directly to the **Click** method of the contained text box. So, although part of the custom control's interface, the various mapped members are actually implemented by the standard properties, methods and events of the constituent controls.

When we add custom members to a class, we can still map them to existing members of the constituent controls. For example, we can map the **MouseMove** event to a constituent control's **Click** event. Then, when the mouse moved over the control, the subclassed control would act as though it had been clicked. We can also write our own code for a method, and then call a standard method of the subclassed control afterwards. And, lastly, we can write our own code to map a member for the control to more than one of the constituent controls. For example, the **Click** event for a control, that itself contains four text boxes, could be mapped to all of these text boxes.

Using the Paint and Resize Events

There are a couple of events that we'll generally want to create our own code for. If we create a control that uses constituent controls, we often need to change the way that these are displayed in response to changes in the size of our control. For example, the custom list box control we describe in Chapter 4 changes the width of the standard ComboBox (on which it's based) to match the width of the control. We do this in the control's **Resize** event.

However, if we've created a user-draw control that has no constituent controls, we can't expect Windows to know what our control is supposed to look like. We have to draw the details ourselves, and we do this by responding to the **Paint** event. When it occurs, we know that we must calculate the requirements for the control's visible appearance, based on its size, and then go ahead and draw it in code. The **Cards** control in Chapter 8 takes this approach, although it gets help to do the actual drawing from elsewhere—as you'll see later.

For controls with no run-time appearance (i.e. where the **InvisibleAtRunTime** property is **True**), we can create the design-time appearance by drawing directly on the form using VB's **Line**, **Circle** and **Box** methods. Alternatively, we can simply place a bitmap on the control designer form. In both cases, we can enter code in the **Resize** event that makes sure the size can't be changed:

```
Private Sub UserControl_Resize()
   UserControl.Size 200, 200
End Sub
```

Our **CardDeck** control exhibits just this behavior. At project design time, the developer sees a bitmap that we've assigned to its **Picture** property. At run time, it's invisible.

Enumerated Types

When we come to implement properties that the developer can set and manipulate in code, we often need to limit the values that they can apply. Standard properties are usually a number or text value, and we might want to limit these to a particular maximum or minimum value, or number of characters. We saw how this could be done with the **Text** property earlier in this chapter.

However, Visual Basic also implements **enumerations**, and we can use these to help implement properties that have enumerated values, which makes setting an appropriate value much easier. We see this with the **Alignment** property of various standard controls. It can usually be set to values like **0 - Left, 1 - Right, 2 - Center**, etc. We can do the same thing with our custom properties.

As an example, our **InfiniteImprobability** control could have an **OverloadResponse** property, for which we only want the user to be able to set the values **0 - NoProblem, 1 - Monitoring, 2 - KnownIssue**, and **3 - Panic**. We could do this by declaring an enumeration in our control's code:

```
Public Enum enOverloadResponse
   iiNoProblem
   iiMonitoring
   iiKnownIssue
   iiPanic
End Enum
```

If we need special values for the members of the enumeration, we can also specify this as we declare it. For example

```
Public Enum enOverloadResponse
   iiNoProblem = -1
   iiMonitoring = 10776
   iiKnownIssue = 16419
   iiPanic = 99999
End Enum
```

This enumeration can then be used in a property procedure to ensure that only valid data is applied to the property.

```
Public Property Let OverloadResponse(enuResponse As enOverloadResponse)
   m_enuOLR = enuResponse
End Property
```

The string names for the values of the enumerated properties will then be made available in the Properties window, and can be set directly in code when the **InfiniteImprobability** control is used in an application's project. We'll be coming back to this subject in later chapters.

```
MyObject.OverloadResponse = iiNoProblem
```

*Notice that the members of the enumeration are prefixed with a couple of characters that reflect the control's classname. This reduces the likelihood of other types of controls clashing with our control if they implement enumerated properties with the same names for the members. For example, a **WarpDrive** class may have a **NoProblem** property as well. Placing one of each of these objects on a form, where they both used a property enumeration member called **NoProblem**, would render one of the controls properties unusable. If one is **iiNoProblem** and the other **wdNoProblem**, then there really is no problem.*

Setting the Procedure ID, or DISPID

Although we usually use the text name of properties and methods when referring to them in our code, Visual Basic also provides for the use of numeric **procedure identifiers**, generally referred to as a **DISPID**. Using the **DISPID** makes the execution of the code faster, because VB doesn't need to look up the text name in its internal tables to find where the routine is located in the file.

There are five **DISPID**s that are of interest when we create controls, and each control can specify just one of its methods or properties for each of these. The five are:

(Default) The default property of the control

AboutBox The method that's called to display your control's 'About' box

Caption Tells VB that this property should behave like a Caption

Text Tells VB that this property should behave like a Text property

Enabled Links the Enabled property of your control to its container

The one **DISPID** that's almost always implemented is the **(Default)** property for a control, such as the caption of a label, or the text value of a text box. When you refer to the control without specifying a property name, the application uses the **DISPID** named **(Default)** to discover which property you actually want. This is why referencing these properties without using the actual property name creates code that runs faster. For example:

```
strTheResult = txtMytextBox          'the default property is 'Text'
```

executes faster than:

```
strTheresult = txtMyTextBox.Text          'specifying the property by name
```

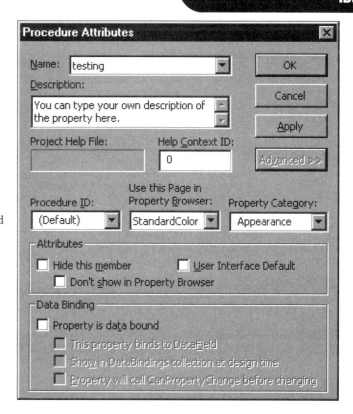

The Procedure Attributes dialog allows us to select the particular **DISPID** we want to set to refer to any of the properties or methods in our control, including the **(Default)** property. Once we've set it, that property or method will be called automatically when that particular standard **DISPID** is called in the application or control's code. For example, we can set the **DISPID** for our **Enabled** property and the **AboutBox** method. You'll see what this means, and how it's done, a little later.

One important use of Procedure IDs is for the **Text** and **Caption** properties of our controls. Both of these change the way the Properties window behaves for the properties that are assigned the **DISPID**'s **Text** or **Caption**. Normally, the value of a property is updated on the form only when the user has entered all of the value, and moved to another property or pressed *Return*. However, the properties that are specified for the **Text** or **Caption DISPID**s have their **Property Let** procedures called for each keystroke in the Properties window. This means that the control will display the new text or caption as it's typed.

The Minimum Interface for a Control

At a minimum, our control should implement the set of properties that is supported for all standard controls. For all controls are visible at run time, and where otherwise appropriate, this is:

Appearance	**BackColor**	**BackStyle**	**BorderStyle**
Enabled	**Font**	**ForeColor**	

On top of this, it should implement the same properties as similar controls, though here the choice depends on exactly how the new control is designed to behave. For a drop-down list control, the user will expect to find properties for the contents of the list, and the selected item, for example.

Setting User-defined Access Keys

It's an accepted practice in Windows to allow 'hot keys', or access keys, to be set up so that the end-user can move to a control, or click a button, just by pressing *Alt* plus the letter underlined in that control's caption. For example, pressing the key combination *Alt-D* will be equivalent to clicking a button with the caption <u>D</u>elete.

If we include labels, frames, or buttons in our custom control, we need to allow the developer to set the captions for these, by setting properties for our control. If we hard-code the captions into the control, they will not be able to change the access keys when they come to use our control in their applications. This is particularly important if they use two instances of our control on the same form. Both will have the same access keys, so the second one will be effectively isolated except for use with a mouse.

It's easy enough to provide user-defined captions. We just create a custom property for any caption in the control, and the developer can set this in the Properties window when they place the control on their application's form at design time.

Interfacing with the Developer

The main reason for creating a control is, obviously, to be able to use it in other projects, or in web pages. To do this, it offers a developer interface, made up of the design-time appearance plus the various properties, methods and events we define for it. The developer sees our design-time interface when they place an instance of our control on their project's form.

We can make the task of working with our control easier for the developer in several ways. At application run time, we have to ensure that it implements sufficient, and useful, members for them to use. For example, a custom text box control isn't likely to be much use to anybody unless they can access the **Text** property to get the text it contains. In design-time mode, they won't be very pleased if they can't change the background color to match their application's form.

On top of this, we can make design-time a more enjoyable and productive experience by implementing **property pages**. These can help to make setting the properties of a control easier, by displaying them in a way that's defined by the control developer, rather than in the standard Properties window. We'll look at this in more detail next.

Creating Property Pages

When we come to use our control in Visual Basic, when building an application around it, we will see and work with the Properties window. In it, all the properties we've included in our class will be visible. Typing new values, or selecting from drop-down lists, can set those that are read/write.

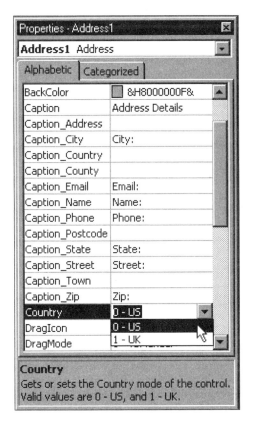

Some controls, however, especially if they are not fundamentally similar to standard controls, have one or more separate property pages. These can be implemented for any control you build. In these pages, the developer can see, and work with, the properties in a way that's specially defined just for that control. These pages are part of the control itself, and are created when we build the control.

We can take advantage of VB's 'standard property pages' to create these. What this means is that we can use three types of property page that are standardized in the VB environment. These are the pages for selecting a control's font (**StandardFont**), color (**StandardColor**), or a picture (**StandardPicture**).

Our Address control, which you'll see in more detail in Chapter 5, contains a custom property page that allows us to change all the design-time property values.

This property page provides us with an alternative way of changing property values. By creating custom property pages for your controls, it's possible to lay out the properties in a more natural way to how they're displayed in the Properties window.

In addition to this, we can also add extra code that allows them to behave like a miniature application. In Chapter 7, we'll show you how we can create complex property pages like these, and how you'd go about attaching them to your controls.

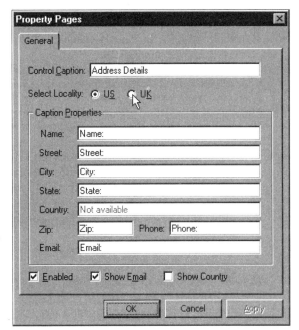

Grouping Properties by Category

There are two tabs in the standard Properties window shown on the previous page. The first one lists all the properties by name, in alphabetical order. The second one lists them by type, or category. As we create custom properties for our control, we can add these to any of the categories in the second tab, making it easier for the developer to find the one they want. Just select the Name of the property in the top list, open the dialog with the Advanced>> button, and select the Property Category:

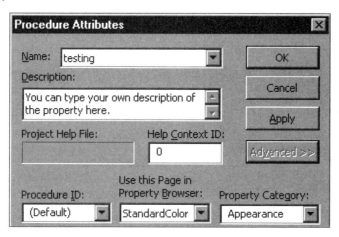

We can also create new categories, which is especially useful if we are producing a control that implements many non-standard types of property. We define all the settings for the property grouping in the Procedure Attributes dialog.

Adding an About Box

Most custom controls implement an **About** property, which displays details of the control and its creator in a dialog window. We can add these to our controls easily. We just include a normal VB form, containing the information in standard controls, in the control project. To connect it to the VB environment, we set the procedure attribute named **AboutBox** to point to a routine that displays our dialog. Then, when the developer clicks the **(About)** property in the normal Properties window, they'll see our dialog.

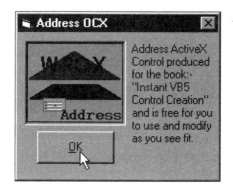

Adding a Toolbox Bitmap

Once our new control is built, tested, and installed on a machine, it can be added to the VB environment using the **Components** dialog. Here, we select which of the various controls installed on the system we want to make available for use in VB. Again, we'll be coming back to this later in the book.

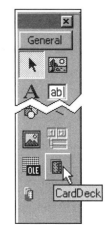

When a control is listed and selected in the **Components** dialog, its icon appears in the toolbox. There is a default toolbox icon for ActiveX controls included in all VB5 CCE projects, but we can create our own and use it instead. We simply assign it to the **ToolboxBitmap** property of the **UserControl** object we are creating. When the mouse pointer pauses over the icon, the name that we gave to our control is displayed as a tool-tip. We'll deal with this in more detail in the next couple of chapters.

Providing Help for a Control

A good control will include sufficient help features to make it easy for the developer to make the most of it. How much help you provide depends on how complex the control actually is. There are three main ways of providing help.

- Create a separate Help file, using Windows Help compiler, and link it to your control.
- Create hypertext Help pages, most useful if you are creating ActiveX controls for use in web pages.
- Create browser strings, which are displayed in various places within VB as the developer works with your controls.

In this book, we won't be going into how you create Help files or hypertext Help pages. However, we will look at how you connect them to your controls. We'll also see how you add browser description strings to your project.

> *Microsoft have a technology called HTML Help available for download from their web site at* **http://www.microsoft.com**. *This is specifically designed to make creating web-based Help pages easier. To find out more, look out for the book 'Instant HTML Help' from Wrox Press.*

When we create a Help file, the first step is to identify it to our control by placing its name in the **Project Properties** dialog. Here, we could also specify the ID for the topic that's to be shown when the developer clicks the 'What's This?' button in the **Object Browser** window while our control class is selected. Object Browser is an important center of information for the developer—you'll be seeing it used regularly in the coming chapters.

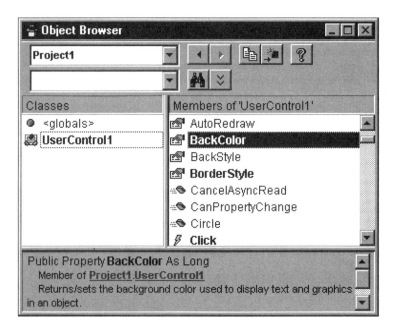

In the Object Browser window, we can also enter a browser description string for each property, method and event (i.e. each **member**) that will be shown as the user selects them in the various parts of the VB environment—as they work with our control. This is a useful way to offer a brief description of what that member does, or the kinds of values that are acceptable. It is supplied automatically for the stock members that we include in our control.

The Control Container

Throughout this chapter, we've talked about the application or web page that will host our control—in other words, the application form or the browser window where the developer will actually use it. We call this the **container**, and it's pretty obvious that our control will need to communicate with it at both design time and run time. To do this, VB defines two objects, the **Extender** and **Ambient** objects. Once again, we'll cover these important objects more extensively in the following chapters, but we'll give you a brief overview here.

The Extender Object

The **Extender** object contains a set of properties that are set by the container, and relate to our contained custom control. The list of properties will be different for different containers, but will normally include such things as **Name** and **Visible**. It may also include additional properties such as **Left**, **Top**, **Width** and **Height**.

Our control can read these properties, and in some cases set their values. For example, it can normally change the **Extender.Visible** property to tell the container application to hide it. The **Extender** object's properties are visible in the Properties window for our custom control, as well as the ones we've defined for the control.

*If you refer to a non-existent property, the **Extender** object just returns an empty string or zero value.*

The Ambient Object

Our control also implements an **Ambient** object, which holds information about the environment which the control is running in. These properties are again provided by the container in which the control is placed, and there is also a method named **AmbientChanged** which (as you've probably guessed) runs when any of the property settings change.

Amongst the most used **Ambient** properties is **UserMode**, which tells us if the container project is running in design-time or run-time mode. This is how we know what behavior our control should exhibit at any moment. As well, we can use the **Ambient** object's **ForeColor**, **BackColor**, **Font**, and **TextAlign** properties to make sure our control matches its environment's display. There is also the **LocaleID** property that allows us to tailor our control to match the International setting of the target system. Lastly, the **Ambient.DisplayName** property is assigned a value to ensure that any error messages our control creates reflect the name of our control.

Summary

In this chapter, we've taken a fairly brief look at what VB5 Control Creation Edition can do, and how you need to understand the whole basis of the way controls are created and interfaced with the developer. Your completed controls can be used in any application, in web pages, or anywhere else that an ActiveX control can find a home.

The most important points to remember in this chapter are:

- The amount of work saved by reusing a control increases with the generality of the control, and the number of times the control is used. Providing options to make the control non-specific to a particular environment is the key way of increasing the generality, and hence reusability of the control.

- All controls fit into one of three broad categories: simple, subclassed and user-draw controls.

- Classes provide reusability and abstraction, and they are the cornerstone of creating controls in VB5 CCE.

- Controls can only respond to their environment when their code is executing. Control code executes both at project run time and design time.

- In VB, we allow developers to interact with controls by providing properties, methods and events.

Visual Basic 5 is a complex environment in that there are a lot of things you have to think about as you develop both full applications and controls. In the next chapter, we'll be introducing two topics. We'll show you the main features of the new VB5 development environment, concentrating mainly on how it differs from earlier versions. Then, we'll walk through the first steps in designing and building a simple control. You should now have a reasonable understanding of some of the concepts of involved with control creation. One thing that will become apparent is that a little time spent designing your control up front (especially its interface) will have real benefits.

So, it's time to power up the beast that's sitting on your desk, and let's get our hands dirty...

Getting Started with VB5 CCE

In the previous chapter, we took an overview of the various issues that you need to face when you come to build ActiveX controls with VB5 CCE. It's quite different from writing normal applications, in that you have to understand the underlying structure of a control class, and manage the properties, methods and events that it needs to implement.

In this chapter, we're going to spend some time looking at how the new development environment differs from earlier versions of Visual Basic, so that you'll feel more comfortable when you start to develop controls. Then, later in the chapter, we'll start the process of developing our first control. This is the Converter control, which will convert decimal numbers to binary format and vice-versa. It will form the basis for the next two chapters and is designed to show you most of the ways that the ActiveX Control Interface Wizard can make the process much easier than coding from scratch. It allows you to knock out basic controls in next to no time.

There are many things to think about when writing a new control, and we'll introduce you to concepts that you won't have been concerned with when you were just a control *user*.

So, in this chapter, you'll see:

- The new features of the VB Integrated Design Environment
- How we can create project groups to assist in control development
- Some tips on designing the interface and functionality for a control
- Starting to build the control with ActiveX Control Interface Wizard
- How we can easily add an About box and a toolbox bitmap

We'll get started right away with a stroll around the new Visual Basic 5 environment.

The Visual Basic Environment

We've talked enough about the background to control development, and you're itching to fire up VB5 CCE to see what it can really do. The rest of this book is aimed at making that discovery process as productive as possible. We'll start this chapter with a quick look at the parts of Visual Basic's Integrated Development Environment (IDE) which are most concerned with the task of creating controls.

Using the IDE

The VB5 IDE presents a complete system designed to help you with all aspects of creating ActiveX controls, ActiveX DLLs, and complete applications. We're only concerned in this book with ActiveX controls, because in the free Control Creation Edition this is all you can do. However, most parts of the IDE are designed to assist in all kinds of project development.

The IDE presents a single screen window, with several contained and floating windows which allow you to work with different elements of the project. It has the same overall interface appearance as Microsoft Office 97, and later versions of Internet Explorer, with the new look 'flat' buttons. As soon as you start it, the New Project dialog appears, where you can specify the type of project you want to create, or select an existing one.

Although the dialog shows a Standard EXE option, you can't actually create executable programs with the Control Creation Edition. However, you can create an EXE project and run it inside the IDE. What you *can't* do is compile the project into an executable file. The other option, CTLGROUP, is a control project group—a special type of project option which is designed for building and testing ActiveX controls. You'll see more of this later.

The Main Window

Selecting the ActiveX Control option creates a new control project, together with the **UserControl** object outline that we met in Chapter 1. The next screen shot shows the main IDE window, with the various default windows rearranged so that you can see them.

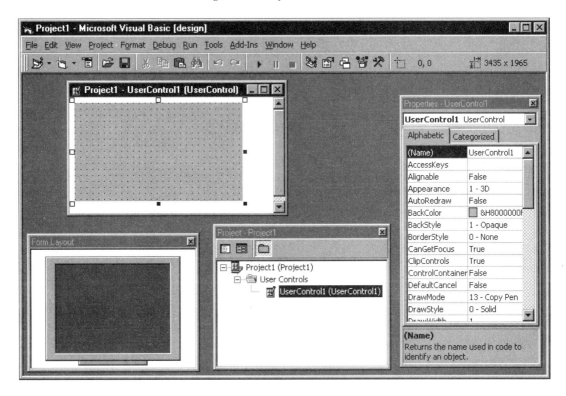

If you've come from VB4, or earlier versions of Visual Basic, you'll immediately notice two differences in the IDE. There's a single overall window which contains most of the other windows, in a similar way to a normal application, and the various floating windows have a habit of attaching themselves to the edges of this main window when you try to move them around.

To get control of your windows is easy—select Options from the Tools menu, and open the Docking tab. Here, you can tell VB which should be amalgamated into the 'overall' window, and which can be free standing.

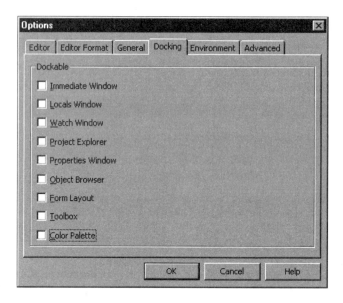

If you prefer to be able to see the desktop and access other programs and windows while VB is in use, as with earlier versions of VB, you can open the **Advanced** tab in the **Options** dialog and select the **SDI Development Environment** option.

> *The term SDI actually means* Single Document Interface, *while the default in VB5 is* MDI
> (Multiple Document Interface).

The Subsidiary Windows

The windows that appear when you start a new project are (by default) the **Project** window, which shows the new control's 'form', the **Properties** window showing the properties for this control, the **Project Explorer** window which shows the hierarchy of the project and the objects within it, and the **Form Layout** window which shows how the control's form will appear on the user's display.

There are several other windows which can be opened as you work on a project. We'll take a quick look at each window in turn.

The Project Window

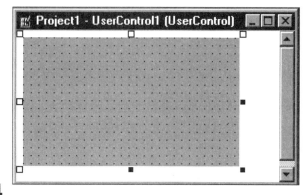

This shows the way that the control will look in design mode, and it's here that you actually create the visible appearance of the control. When the control project is put into run mode, as it would be when used by the application developer, you see the run-time visible appearance. Otherwise, it's just like the normal forms that you work with in VB, and you can add controls by 'drawing' them on to the form in the usual way.

The Properties Window

This shows the properties that are applicable for the selected control or controls, taken from both the control itself and its surroundings (through the **Ambient** and **Extender** objects). Here, you set the design-time values for the properties as you build the control. Again, it's used just like the Properties window in previous versions of VB, but you also get a choice to view the properties sorted by category. When creating controls, it's possible to assign your own categories for properties.

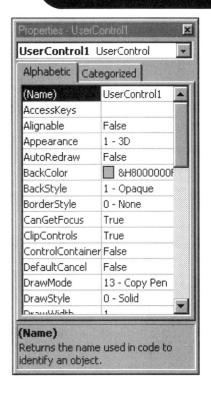

The Project Explorer Window

This window shows the various parts of the current project and the objects that it contains, displayed in a tree view. For example, in our new ActiveX control project we have the main project called **Project1**, and the control itself, called **UserControl1**. As we add more objects to the project, they appear here. It provides a useful place for switching between the parts of your project. When you select the different entries, you'll see the available properties change in the Properties window.

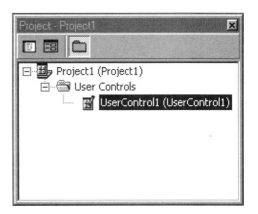

The Project Explorer window is also a handy nerve-center for navigating around your project as you work. For example, you'll need to change the name of the control from **UserControl1**, and the name of the project from **Project1**, to something more indicative of its purpose. By selecting them in turn in the Project Explorer window, you can edit both of their **Name** properties in the Properties window. The first two toolbar buttons in the window allow you to view the form or the code behind it, bringing these windows to the front if they're hidden. When it comes time to enter some code for the objects, you just click the View Code button.

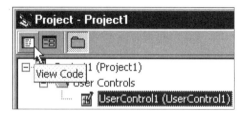

The Form Layout Window

This window allows you to see how the final project will appear. It's displayed on a picture of a monitor, which may seem a little like overkill. However, the window has other uses, as you'll see when we come to build a control. For example, right-clicking it allows you to specify where on the screen, and how, the dialogs or forms should appear. You can also get an idea of how your finished project will look in different screen resolutions.

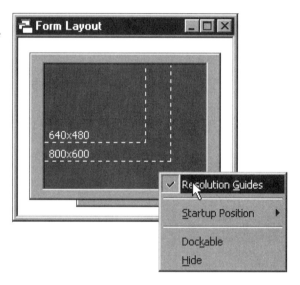

The Toolbox

The other window you'll see, which will immediately be familiar, is the toolbox. Here are the different types of controls that can be inserted into our projects. We can add more controls to it as required, on a project-by-project basis, using the Components... option in the Project menu.

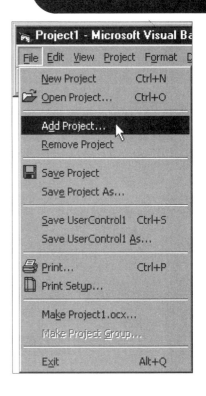

Because VB5 can manage more complex kinds of projects, the main menu has changed. The File menu has the usual options to start and open projects, print the code, and Make (or compile) the control. However, notice the Add and Remove Project options. In Visual Basic 5, including the Control Creation Edition, it's possible to have more than one project open at a time—something that wasn't possible in earlier versions. Why would we want to do this? Well, remember in the previous chapter we talked about how a control has to be running when the application project that uses it is in design mode. This gives us a way to solve the problem without having to run two copies of VB. We use a **project group**.

Project Groups

One of the things that is difficult to understand until you've worked with VB5 CCE for a while, is how you actually debug and test a control, and how you can see it working in another project. In VB4, you could only open one project at a time. When building an OLE Server, for example, you had to start a second copy of VB to run the application that used the services provided by it. Then, you switched back to the original copy to edit the OLE server and run it again.

In VB5 CCE, you can create a project group, which contains a normal executable-type application project, plus one or more ActiveX control projects. This means that you can add running controls to a project and see the effects, all in one environment. It's also useful as you build the control, because you can easily test each new piece of control code in the test project.

The CTLGROUP Project Group

To create a project group, you just select CTLGROUP from the New Project dialog. A project group consists of a normal **UserControl** project, like we started with, plus a standard VB executable project which can act as a container for the control we're building.

Once we've built the control, we can insert a copy of it into the executable application project. To do this, we must first close down the code of the control to ensure that it's in run mode. This will make the bitmap associated with the control appear on the toolbox, and we can then add the control to the application project in the usual manner. At this stage, we can see the end results by running the current project.

If we switch back to the *control's* project and edit its code, the control will stop running. In this case, in the application project, the control has hatching covering it—to show that the control will not respond to actions. Once we've completed the changes, we can use the new version of the control, in the form where it's been added, by simply right-clicking on the form and selecting Update UserControls. This puts the control back into run mode, reflecting the changes that have been made. When developing our own controls, we've used this technique extensively.

More Windows

The View menu is used to display or hide all the main floating and subsidiary windows. The first two repeat the options available in the Project Explorer window, showing the object's 'form' or the code stored in it. There are also several windows which you use as you run and debug a control. These include the Immediate, Locals, Watch, and Calls windows, which are very similar to those in earlier versions of VB.

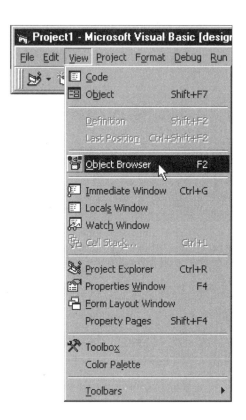

Other options open the windows we've already seen, plus the Color Palette dialog where you can quickly set the colors for the various standard controls you place on your custom control's form.

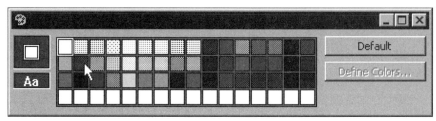

The Object Browser

There is one other window, which we mentioned in Chapter 1, that will form the core of your activity when you come to create code for a control, or manage various parts of its behavior. Object Browser shows the objects that make up the whole project, plus the various methods, properties and events that they support. It also provides a description of their use, and shows where they come from—allowing you to follow through the object hierarchy to find the objects or attributes you need.

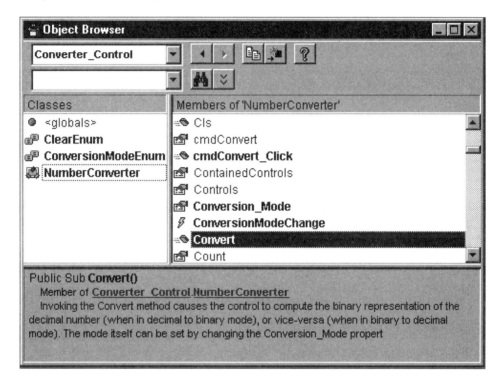

Object Browser also performs several other tasks. Using its toolbar buttons, you can search for objects or their members, and copy their definition into the clipboard ready for pasting into a code module. As anyone who's developed OLE automation servers will know, the Object Browser is an invaluable tool.

Projects and References

The Project menu allows you to add and remove various elements from a project. Remember that a project can be part of a project group, so the menu will refer to the current project in this case. You can add a Form, Module, or Class Module in the same way as in VB4. However, there are also options to add a User Control or a Property Page.

Adding a User Control is useful where you need to create an application that uses more than one user control. You can design and build several controls inside the IDE at any one time, using them all in one containing application project. And, as you've already seen, these controls can contain Property Pages which you design yourself. You'll see these used in the next chapter.

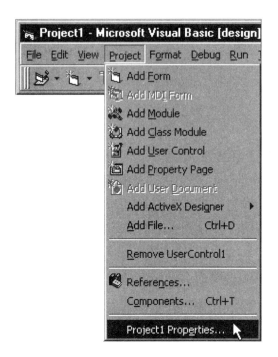

Near the bottom of the menu are the options that show the Components dialog (where you specify the components to be included on the toolbar) and the References dialog. This is where you can add in functionality from OLE Automation servers (including those written in VB4), data access using **Data Access Objects** (DAOs) which come as part of VB4 Professional and Enterprise Editions and MS Office Professional Edition, and the many other libraries that you've become accustomed to using in VB4 projects. In fact, by adding a reference to the DAO library, we can use database access within VB5 CCE! We'll show you how to make data bound controls in Chapter 6.

Add-ins and Wizards

The final menu we'll look at here is Add-Ins. This contains the options to run the various Wizards and Add-ins installed with VB5. In the Control Creation Edition, there are just the two you'll see used in this book—the ActiveX Control Interface Wizard and the Property Page Wizard. Other versions of VB5 have further add-ins available, and there are many available from other vendors. The Add-In Manager option allows you to select which ones are installed, and are therefore available on the Add-Ins menu.

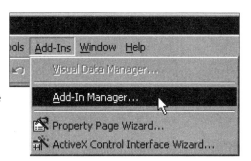

So, having had a quick stroll around the new surroundings of the IDE, let's get a start and do something with it. We'll design and build our first control.

Designing Our Control

As Visual Basic developers, we have all used controls in the projects we have worked on. Back in the days of Visual Basic 2.0 and 3.0, developers used VBXs custom controls designed specifically for the Windows 16-bit platform. Then along came the inclusion of Object Linking and Embedded (OLE) technology into these controls. At this point, they were no longer know as VBXs, but as OCXs. These new OCXs were designed for both the 16-bit and 32-bit Windows platforms. So why are OCX controls better than the older VBX variety? Since OCXs are based on an open, proven, and strategic technology, they have additional advantages: the architecture scales well; they generally behave better, since they're based on a standard technology; and any improvements in the OLE implementation (such as performance increases) provide direct improvement in the control with little or no code rewriting.

When we create controls in VB5 CCE, we're creating 32-bit, OLE based ActiveX controls. ActiveX controls are very similar to the OLE OCX controls used in VB4, but they're slightly lighter because they're also aimed for use across the Web. However, we still need to get involved with issues that didn't concern us as a control user.

Looking at the Tasks Ahead

To give some sort of overview of the control creation process, we're going to outline the main steps necessary to create and distribute a control. We're going to show you how to:

- Determine the features your component will provide

- Determine what objects are required to divide up the functionality of the component, in a logical fashion

- Create a component project and test project

- Design any forms your component will display

- Design the component interface—the properties, methods and events—for each class provided by your component

- Implement the forms required by your component

- Implement the interface of each class, provide browser strings for interface members, and add links to help topics

- Debug and test your control incrementally

- Compile your component and test it with all potential target applications

- Deploy your control

We'll start by introducing the Number Converter control—which will just convert decimal values to the binary equivalent, and vice-versa. This is a relatively simple control, so it allows us to concentrate on the actual process of creating controls, without having to spend too much time on the functionality that the control itself will provide.

Determine the Features It Will Provide

Considering the features that are part of the control is an important issue. As well as those that distinguish our Number Converter control from any other, we also need to provide a standard set of stock properties, methods and events which are present in practically every control.

In this section, we're not going to incorporate every stock member into our control, but we will provide the more common ones which will serve to illustrate the concept. Later in the chapter, we'll also list the full range of members that you should include—where applicable—in your own controls. Let's start off with some stock members.

Stock Properties, Methods and Events

Since we want our controls to behave in a consistent way, we can include some stock members that have the usual effects associated with them. In most cases, we can get the ActiveX Control Interface Wizard to make these members do what we'd expect, but sometimes we have to define some extra code when we want our control to treat them in a particular way.

In the Number Converter control, we'll be including the following stock members:

```
Appearance      AutoRedraw      BackColor          BorderStyle
Caption         Enabled         Font
```

However, if we just include these, then our control—while different in appearance to others—won't have any custom functionality defined for it. Once we've decided what our control should do, it's time to pay attention to the custom properties, methods and events which will provide the features of our control that we're really interested in. Here's a list of the custom members for the Number Converter control:

Properties	Methods	Events
Conversion_Mode	Convert	InputChange
Input_Value	Clear	OutputChange
Output_Value		ConversionModeChange

As you'll recall, **properties** are items of data that are contained within the control, and which can effect the state of the control when they're set to a new value. **Methods** are procedures that can operate on objects, and are defined to cut down the amount of work required for a developer to effectively use the control. They often encompass sets of common operations that may alter the control appearance and/or state, and so they can provide a clearer and simpler interface by reducing the number of other properties and methods we need to support.

With event driven programming, where the operations of each part of the application are initiated by an event such as a mouse click or key press, we have to be able to execute code when a certain condition or set of conditions is met. This has given rise to **events**—in effect an empty code routine that is called by the control in certain circumstances. By filling in the body of the routine, developers can extend the functionality of the control and make it interact with code and other controls as required.

Let's have a quick look at each of the above members, so that you can see why we've included them:

Property	Description
Conversion_Mode	Allows developers to determine which mode of operation the control is currently operating under, and also provides a mechanism to set it through code.
Input_Value	The **Input_Value** property can be used to retrieve or set the number on which the conversion process should operate.

Table continued on following page

Property	Description
`Output_Value`	This property will provide the converted result, obtained when the decimal value is translated into its binary equivalent, or vice-versa.

Method	Description
`Convert`	Instigates the conversion process.
`Clear (optional)`	Clears the control values (input and output). We're actually going to implement it so that, if specified, we'll allow the developer to clear either the input or the output value.

Event	Description
`InputChange`	This event will fire when the value of the input number is changed, either by the user, or when new values are assigned in code to our control's `Input_Value` property.
`OutputChange`	Fires when the conversion is completed and the new value is displayed.
`ConversionModeChange`	The conversion mode can be set by the user or programmatically via the `Conversion_Mode` property. When either of these happen, the `ConversionModeChange` event fires and the parameter `ConversionMode` indicates the new mode of operation.

Now that we've defined all the members for our control, we'll introduce the concept of an **interface diagram**.

The Interface Diagram

An **interface diagram** is a really useful tool for instantly showing developers the interface—the properties, methods and events—that the control provides. We can abstract the level of detail so that the diagram provides the most important features, without showing a lot of irrelevant details. Here's what our interface diagram looks like for the Number Converter control:

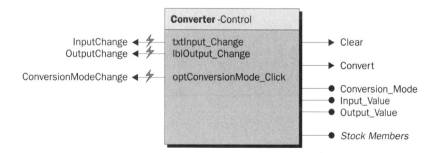

Now that we've covered our custom members, let's proceed to the control's appearance.

Implementing Our Control's Appearance

Using VB5 CCE, we can quickly put together the appearance of our control by adding **constituent** controls (standard VB controls or other ActiveX controls) to the **UserControl** class, just as though it was a normal Visual Basic form.

> *The* **UserControl** *class acts as a template for the creation of control instances, and is the base object used to create an ActiveX control. It's much like the way that a normal class is a blueprint of the object it represents, and a form is a template for the form objects that it creates.*

So, let's create the control. Select File | New Project and select CTLGROUP. The first step is to assign the names we want to use for the various elements in our project group.

Setting the Control and Test Project Names

In the Project Explorer window, click on the entry for **Project1**, and change the **(Name)** entry in the Properties window to **Converter_Control**. If you can't see the Project Explorer or Properties windows, select them in the main View menu. Then open the User Controls folder in the Project Explorer window, and double-click on **UserControl1** to open the control's form. Change the **(Name)** entry in the Properties window to **Number_Converter**.

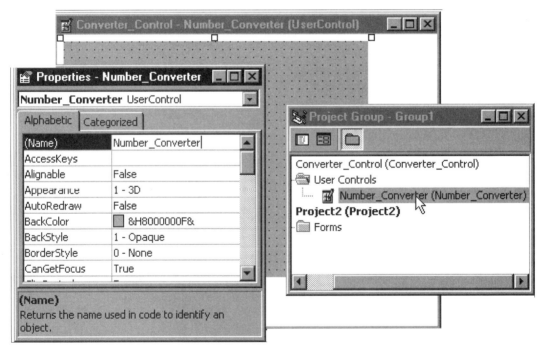

Now we can set the names for the test container application and its project. Change the **(Name)** from **Project2** to **Converter_Tester**, then open the **Forms** folder, double click on **Form1**, and change the **(Name)** of the form to **frmTestForm**. Then click the Save button on the main toolbar, select a folder for your project, and save the files that VB5 has created. Finally, click the folder button on the toolbar to hide the folder icons in the list, which makes it easier to see the contents of the whole project group.

Adding the Constituent Controls

Next, we must add the constituent controls that we need to our custom control's form. To bring the window to the front, click on the control in the Project Explorer window and click the View Object icon, or just double-click on the control in the list.

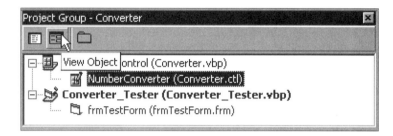

Now you can add controls to it, so that your **UserControl** form looks the same as the one in this diagram:

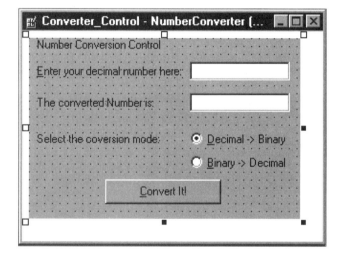

This is the design-mode view of the control. The label **lblCaption** at the top of the control has two purposes. In project design-mode, we can make it display the name of the control so that users can easily distinguish one instance from another. The textbox **txtInput** becomes the source number for our conversion. Next to this, we have the descriptive label **lblCapInput**. The caption of this label should change depending on whether decimal to binary conversion is selected (via the option button control array **optConversionMode**), or vice-versa. The conversion is actually achieved by clicking on the command button **cmdConvert**. This displays the converted value in the label **lblOutput**.

The **lblOutput** label looks like a text box, because we've changed the **BackColor** and **BorderStyle** properties. In addition, we've set the **BackStyle** of all the labels to **0 - Transparent**. This reduces the amount of work we have to do later when we come to change the **BackColor** of our control.

We'll also want some way of standardizing the appearance of the controls in our **UserControl** class. We can do this by setting the **BorderStyle** and **Appearance** properties for the constituent controls based on the property values defined for the **UserControl** class.

Using The ActiveX Control Interface Wizard

Once the appearance and form elements of our control have been put into place, we can then add properties, events and methods to this shell. One of the quickest ways to do this is by using the ActiveX Control Interface Wizard. The number of steps will vary depending on the properties, methods and events you define for your control.

Bring the control's Project window to the front, then start the wizard by choosing ActiveX Control Interface Wizard... from the Add-Ins menu. Remember, you can activate a control's Project window by double-clicking it in the Project Explorer, or by selecting it and clicking the View Object button.

After a bit of disk whirring, the introductory window pops up. Once you've read it, you can stop it appearing when you invoke the wizard in the future by setting the checkbox at the bottom of the dialog. Then click Next to proceed.

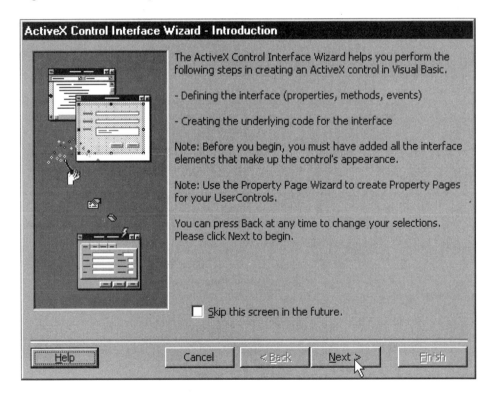

We now have to select which of the globally available stock properties, methods and events we want to include in our control. We're referring to them as *stock* members, because we can always include them and their representative functionality in our control. It's at this stage that we add the properties that are common to most controls. For our Converter control, we need the following stock properties:

Appearance	**AutoRedraw**	**BackColor**	**BorderStyle**
Caption	**Enabled**	**Font**	

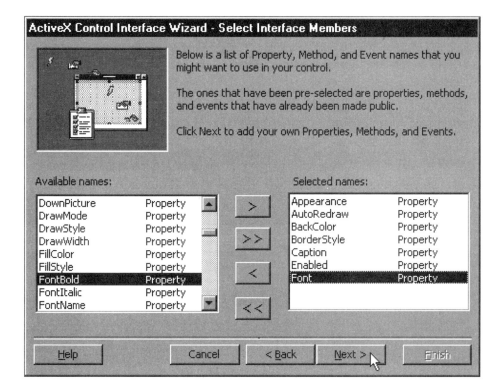

Once we're happy with our selection of stock properties, methods and events, we can click **Next** to move on to the next stage.

We now need to add members that will provide the custom functionality we need for the control. These are as follows:

Properties	Methods	Events
Conversion_Mode	**Convert**	**InputChange**
Input_Value	**Clear**	**OutputChange**
Output_Value		**ConversionModeChange**

To add the first of our custom members, we need to select the **New** button.

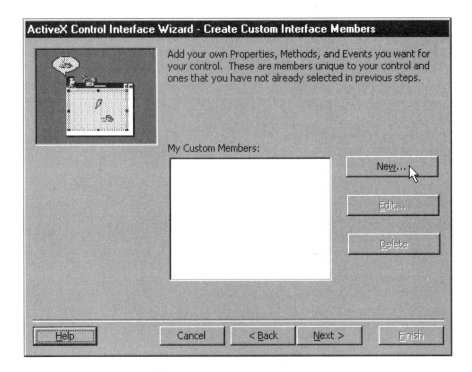

We can then proceed to enter the names of all our properties, methods and events, making sure to select the correct type.

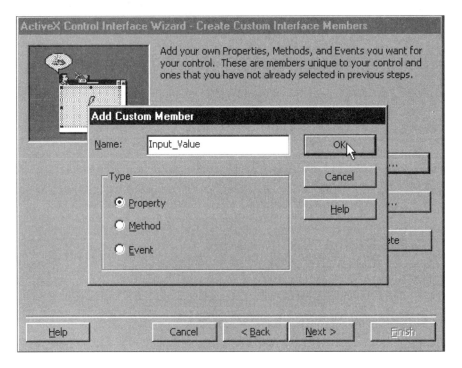

Once that's been done, we can view the full list of our custom members. Then select Next to carry on to the next stage.

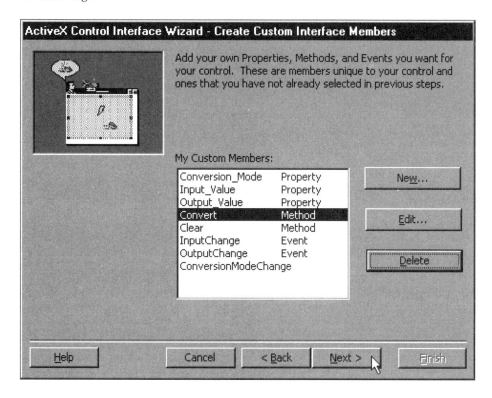

Once we've added the stock members and defined our custom members, it's time to use the facilities of the wizard to set up logical mappings. These define the behavior of our control members by connecting them to the members of the constituent controls. For example, connecting the **Input_Value** property to the **Text** property of our **txtInput** text box ensures that the **Input_Value** property reflects the value in the text box. The wizard doesn't automatically differentiate our stock members from the ones we've entered ourselves, so we need to help it out by setting the mappings. We can also set custom mappings for our own members. Here's the window that's presented for this purpose:

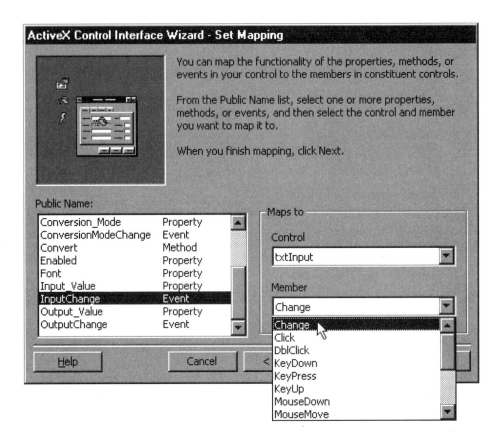

The wizard is clever enough to know that a property can only be mapped to a property, a method can only be mapped to a method, and an event can only be mapped to an event. Because this is so, only the members of the same type will be displayed in the Member drop-down list.

For standard stock members, we want to map many of them to the **UserControl** class, so that our control will behave like a standard Windows control for the tasks it doesn't need to manage itself—without us having to worry too much about how it will do this. Here's a list of the mappings we'll be using and that need to be set in this page of the wizard:

Member Name	Member Type	Maps to Control	Member
Appearance	Property	(None)*	
AutoRedraw	Property	UserControl	AutoRedraw
BackColor	Property	(None)*	
BorderStyle	Property	UserControl	BorderStyle
Caption	Property	(None)*	
Clear	Method	(None)	

Table continued on following page

Member Name	Member Type	Maps to Control	Member
Conversion_Mode	Property	(None)	
ConversionModeChange	Event	(None)	
Convert	Method	(None)	
Enabled	Property	UserControl	Enabled
Font	Property	(None)*	
Input_Value	Property	txtInput	Text
InputChange	Event	txtInput	Change
Output_Value	Property	lblOutput	Caption
OutputChange	Event	lblOutput	Change

Note that we've defined properties which have words separated by the underscore character '_', but we don't use this convention for events. This is because the event name for our control will be defined as **ControlInstanceName_EventName** *and including an underscore in the event name will lead to a syntax error in our code. We'll cover this in more detail later.*

You may be wondering why we've marked some of the control items above with an asterisk (*). This is because we've decided not to map these stock properties to their equivalent **UserControl** class property. When these properties change, we want to update the appropriate **UserControl** class properties ourselves, as well as the properties for our controls. By adding custom code that we'll show you later, we can ensure that the effects are propagated down as we would expect.

After we've set the mappings for our members, we have to define attributes for members that we've mapped to (None) i.e. that we haven't mapped to anything. The wizard provides the **Set Attributes** stage for this purpose, so that we can tailor these members to our liking:

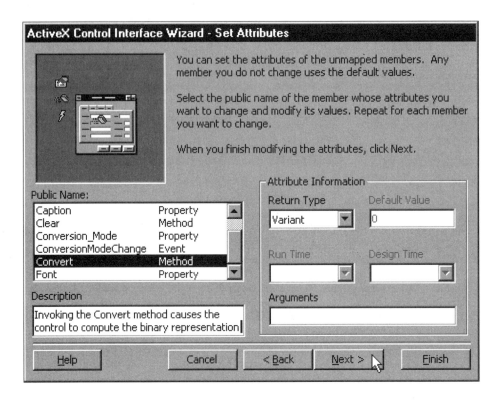

We may not be able to get exactly what we want using the wizard, but we can certainly go a long way towards it. Here's the list of mappings we'll be using for our control:

Public Name	Type	Data Type	Default Value	Run Time	Design Time	Arguments
Appearance	Property	Integer	0	RO	R/W	N/A
BackColor	Property	OLE Color	0	RO	R/W	N/A
Caption	Property	String		R/W	R/W	N/A
Conversion _Mode	Property	Integer	0	R/W	R/W	N/A
Conversion ModeChange	Event	N/A	N/A	N/A	N/A	intChangedTo As Integer
Font	Property	Font		RO	R/W	N/A

Public Name	Type	Return Type	Default Value	Run Time	Design Time	Arguments
Convert	Method	Variant	N/A	N/A	N/A	
Clear	Method	Variant	N/A	N/A	N/A	Optional strItem

*In the tables above, **RO** means Read Only, and **RW** means Read/Write.*

At this stage we can also add custom descriptions for our methods, but we also get the chance to change them later, if we wish. These descriptions will show up in the Description section of the Properties window, as well as in the Object Browser for the project where we're using the control. They are a great way of helping developers to know what each member does, and how it's to be used. Here's how our member descriptions appear in the object browser:

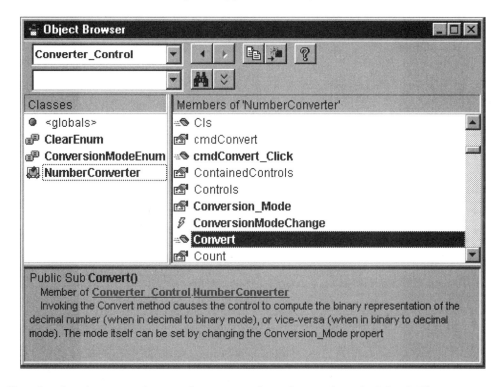

You'll notice that there are other members present here that we haven't defined. These are automatically included as part of our control; we'll talk more about them later in this chapter. Getting back to the wizard, though, the last screen that's displayed allows us to create a report which outlines the actions we've still got to do in order to complete our control.

53

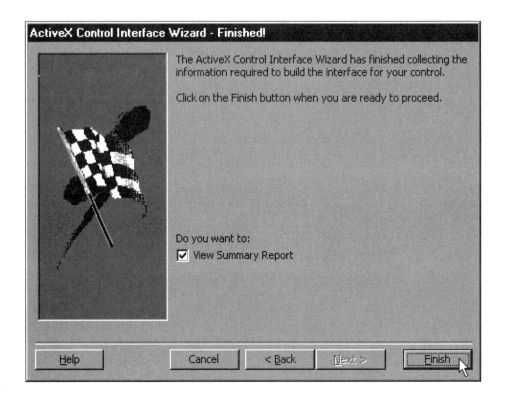

This report can be saved for future reference.

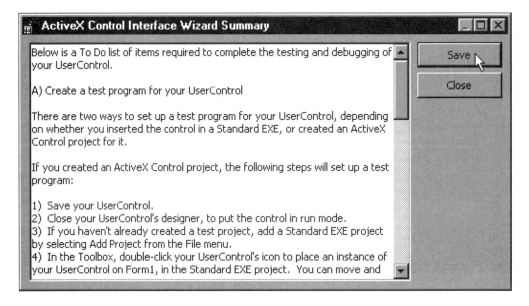

We now find ourselves with a basic control that has all the interfaces that we'll need in our finished version. From the events that we've defined, one of them works already—namely, the **InputChange** event. Let's test this out in our test project.

Open the control that's been created using the Project Explorer window (as explained previously) and then close it. Once it is closed, its bitmap is enabled on the toolbox, and you can add the control to the test form in the usual way. To test the **InputChange** event, we need to add some code—double-click on the instance of our control on the test form to bring up the code window. Our control, called **NumberConverter1**, will automatically be shown in the Object list, but we'll need to select the **InputChange** event from the Procedure list. In this list, we can also see the other events that have been made available to the test project through our control.

To test out the **InputChange** event, just add some code which presents a message box:

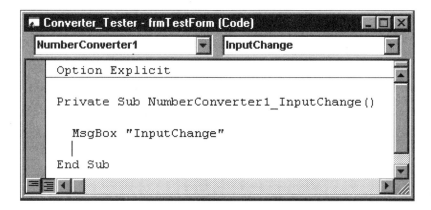

Now, right click on the control's Project window and select UpdateControls. Switch to the test project form, click the new control's icon in the toolbox, and draw an instance of the control on the form. Then, press F5 to run the project, and type a value into the input textbox.

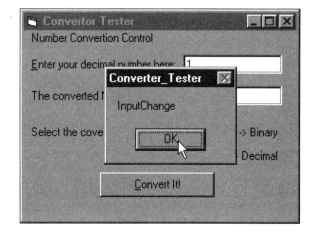

What we must do now is add our own custom functionality to make this control genuinely useful. Before we go into this, though, let's have a look at the various components that we can use in our control, and see how we can use them in developing our design.

Standardizing Our Control

Now that the wizard has helped create the outline of our new control, we need to think about what else is required to finish the job. In the next chapter, we'll look at the code that carries out the main functions of the control. Before we leave this chapter, however, we'll see some of the other niceties that make our control appear a lot more professional, and make it fit into VB5 like a standard control.

Here we'll consider a couple of the properties that the users sees in the Properties window, how we can add an 'About' box, and how we change the default picture of our control in the toolbox.

Enumerated BorderStyle and Appearance Properties

In the next chapter, you'll see how we implement enumerated types for the **Conversion_Mode** property of our control. We can also extend our control by making it behave even more like a standard control. For example, we can use enumerated types for the stock properties like **BorderStyle** and **Appearance** that are currently defined as **Integer**.

At the moment, we can attempt to set these properties to any integer value, but an 'Invalid property value' error message will be generated when an illegal value is entered. For example, here's the result of setting the **BorderStyle** property to the value 2:

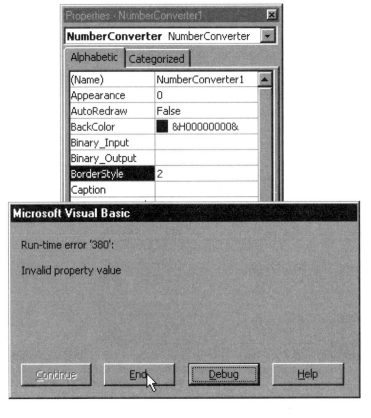

Clearly, it's much better to only provide the possible alternatives and allow the developer to select one from this list.

Consider a standard Windows control that has a **BorderStyle** property—just like in our control. In the drop down list in the Properties window, we can see that there are two member values defined for it, **0 - None**, and **1 - Fixed Single**.

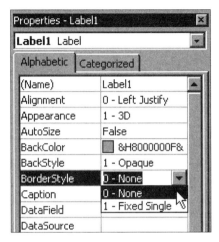

We want to provide the same choice of property values for our control. We can do this by using an enumerated type, with the same members, so that our **BorderStyle** property behaves in an identical manner. The first part of the process is to define the member values of the enumeration. In the case of the **BorderStyle** property, we'll need to define two member values:

```
Public Enum BorderStyleEnum
  None = 0
  Fixed_Single = 1
End Enum
```

One really neat aspect about using enumerated types like this is that the member values, as well as the names of the members, are displayed in the format we require when they're used as a return type in a **Property Get** property procedure. This is all we need to do, to give us a list of alternatives, as shown above, when someone inspects our **BorderStyle** property in the Properties window:

```
'MappingInfo=UserControl,UserControl,-1,BorderStyle
Public Property Get BorderStyle() As BorderStyleEnum
   BorderStyle = UserControl.BorderStyle
End Property

Public Property Let BorderStyle(ByVal New_BorderStyle As BorderStyleEnum)
   UserControl.BorderStyle() = New_BorderStyle
   PropertyChanged "BorderStyle"
End Property
```

We can do a similar thing with the **Appearance** property and implement our own drawing effects. We'll see some clever ways of doing this in Chapter 9.

Note that once this has been done, the ActiveX Control Interface Wizard will not recognize any enumerated types and will thus not work properly. You should therefore only do this when you've finished using the wizard and you are ready to take over control development by hand.

Adding the About Box

Everyone wants to be given credit for their work, and you also need to make sure that your legal copyright is brought to the user's attention. An 'About' box provides the de-facto way of easily providing this important information. If you want to provide an About box for your control, then read on.

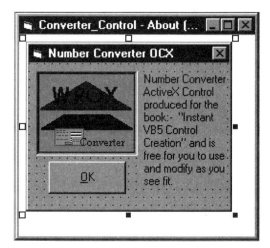

The first step is to add a new form for your control. For the conversion control, we've called ours About. Here's the control design-time view of our About window:

It's customary for About windows to appear in the middle of a user's screen. We can do this for our About window by selecting our About form (as shown above), and then right-clicking on the Form Layout window—the one that displays a monitor. The Startup Position option on the context menu allows us to make the form appear in the center of the user's display.

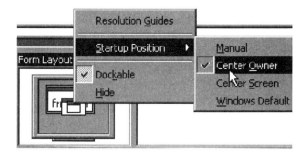

So far, we've got the About window, but no way to access it through our control. What we need to do now is add a method (public subroutine) to our control code that will display our About box.

```
Public Sub About()
   Dim frmAbout As New About
   frmAbout.Show vbModal
   Set frmAbout = Nothing
End Sub
```

This method is special in that we want it to be invoked from the Properties window, when the developer selects the (About) property and clicks the button with three dots.

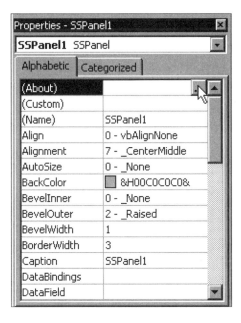

We can get this type of behavior in our control by mapping this method to the 'About' category that's provided specifically for this purpose. In order to do this we'll have to bring up the Procedure Attributes window, which is accessed via the Procedure Attributes menu item found on the Tools menu:

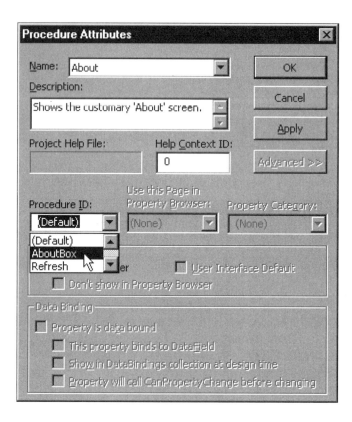

We just select the name of our **About** method from the list and click the Advanced button so that we can get at the features we need. Then, from the list given under the Procedure ID heading, we choose the AboutBox item. This will include the (About) property item in the Properties Window.

Creating the Toolbox Bitmap

When you used the custom control in the test project, you'll have noticed that a toolbox icon is displayed, and that when the mouse pointer is kept on it, a small tool tip displays the name of the control class:

The bitmap that's used by default is the same for all custom controls we create, but you'll be glad to hear that we're not stuck with this image. You can create your own 16 x15 pixel, 16 color bitmap using your favorite paint package, and then simply assign it to the control using the **ToolboxBitmap** property:

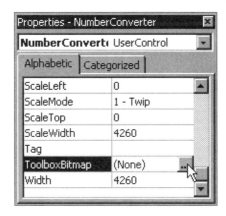

The new image will then be used the next time we start our control executing.

Summary

In this chapter we've looked at the VB5 IDE and started the process of creating a new control from scratch. We've talked about using the ActiveX Control Interface Wizard for quickly knocking up the shell of our control, and we've looked at what it does as well as what else we need to do to make the control work. Along the way, we've shown you more of the general structure and workings of an ActiveX control—something that will be increasingly useful as you develop your own, more complex, controls. We've also shown how you can create the customary About box, and the process used for assigning a toolbox bitmap image for your control.

The most important points in this chapter are:

- Don't underestimate the design that the control deserves. A 'hack and code' approach to coding controls is totally unsuitable.

- The special **UserControl** class is used as a core component when building controls using VB5 CCE.

- We can quickly put together the shell of our control using the ActiveX Control Interface Wizard, which can be used to define the properties, methods and events that our control will exhibit.

- Properties, methods and events are known collectively as members. These members can be of two types—stock members and custom members.

- Always use your control in a test project as you're coding it. Building the control incrementally means testing new control features in the test project before adding others.

So where do we go next? Well, as you've seen, the current performance of the control could best be described as disappointing. It doesn't actually do anything at the moment, other than display a message box. In the next chapter, we'll fill in the missing functionality.

61

Making Our First Control Useful

In the previous chapter, we used the ActiveX Control Interface Wizard to create the bare bones of a simple control. When we left it, it looked the business, with a fancy About box and a custom toolbar bitmap. The only problem was that it didn't actually do very much, other than display a less than helpful message when you tried to use it. In this chapter, we'll be filling in the gaps, and making it work as it was designed to do.

Much as in structured programming, where we have many building blocks that help us build our programs, so we have a variety of different mechanisms to help us build our controls. In our VB5 CCE control project, we must have a control class—**UserControl**. But after this, we can include one or more **class modules**, **standard modules** and **property pages**. We're not going to cover the advantages and disadvantages of using classes and modules. Suffice to say that they can be used in the normal way in control projects—you'll see examples of this in the chapters that follow.

We'll also define a couple of simple property pages using the Property Page Wizard. This is a subject we'll be covering in more detail later in the book, but we'll show you the basics towards the end of this chapter.

So we'll be covering:

- What ActiveX Control Interface Wizard has done
- What the underlying **UserControl** class actually looks like
- How we add the custom members we need to the class
- How we resolve design-time and run-time issues
- How we add the extra functionality required
- How Property Page Wizard is used, and what it does

First, then, let's take a more detailed look at what we need to do to fill out the functionality of our first control.

The UserControl Class

Although we've used the **UserControl** class like a kind of Visual Basic form on which we place our controls, the behavior is not identical—and there are some properties, methods and events that you probably won't have come across before.

New Properties

The **UserControl** class has some specific properties defined for it. Using these, we can tailor the behaviour of the control instances that will be created from it. Here's a quick run down:

Property Name	Description
AccessKeys	Returns or sets a string containing the keys that will act as the access keys (or hot keys) for the control.
Alignable	Returns or sets a value determining if a control is alignable, and can use the extender **Align** property.
CanGetFocus	Returns or sets a value determining if a control can itself receive the focus. If the control contains constituent controls which can themselves receive the focus, the control itself will be unable to receive the focus, regardless of the setting of **CanGetFocus.**
ControlContainer	Returns or sets a value determining if a control can contain other controls placed on it, in the same way the **PictureBox** control can contain other controls.
EditAtDesignTime	Returns or sets a value that determines if a control will have the Edit option on its context menu.
ForwardFocus	Returns or sets a value determining which control receives focus when one of the access keys for the control is pressed.
InvisibleAtRunTime	Returns or sets a value determining if a control should not have a visible window at run time.
PropertyPages	Returns or sets a string member of an array, that holds the name of a property page associated with the control that is represented by a **UserControl** class.
Public	Returns or sets a value determining if a control can be shared with other applications.
ToolboxBitmap	Returns or sets a bitmap that will be used as the picture representation of the control in the toolbox. The size of the space for the bitmap in the toolbox is 16x15 pixels; the bitmap specified by this property will be scaled to these dimensions if necessary.

For our control, the defaults of most of the property values will suffice, but we're going to be changing the **PropertyPages** and the **ToolboxBitmap** property values later on.

Control Objects

When we're using our controls within other projects, the controls need to know about the environment in which they're used. This immediate environment is the container in which they reside, which may often change as the host project executes. Our controls need to be aware of any such changes, so that they can react accordingly. VB5 manages the changes through the **Extender** and **Ambient** objects.

The Extender Object

The controls that we'll be creating in VB5 CCE automatically have certain properties provided for them by the container rather than by the control. These are known as **extender** properties. Quite often, we'll want to access an extender property, and we'll also want to change one. The **Extender** object allows us to do this, by making these properties available for use with the **UserControl** class.

Some extender properties, such as **Name**, are standard—and will therefore be available to every control we create. Others, like **Height** and **DragIcon**, are non-standard—and are dependent on the properties provided by the container. Here's a list of the standard extender properties:

Property Name	Description
Name	A read only string that contains the user-defined name of the control.
Visible	A read/write Boolean that specifies if the control is visible or not.
Parent	A read only object that represents the container of the control, such as a form in VB5 CCE.
Cancel	A read only Boolean that indicates that the control is the Cancel button for the container.
Default	A read only Boolean that indicates that the control is the Default button for the container.

In our simple Converter control, we'll be accessing the **Name** property of the **Extender** object, so that we can set the caption of the label, **lblCaption**, to provide for easy identification of our control in a project.

The Ambient Object

In addition to the **Extender** object, the **UserControl** class can access the **Ambient** object (often referred to as the **AmbientProperties** object). The purpose of the **Ambient** object is to hold information about the current state of the container application, such as the host window's **BackColor**, and to suggest behaviour to controls within the container. The **Ambient** object's properties are read-only. Just like the **Extender** object, some of the properties provided are standard, while others are particular to certain containers. Accessing non-standard ambient properties will make the control we're designing container specific.

We've already used the **Ambient** object via the ActiveX Control Interface Wizard. As an example, we included **BackColor** and **Font** properties through the Select Interface Members stage of the wizard. These are examples of standard ambient properties, or stock properties, and we should make them available to developers who use our controls.

65

Understanding the Control Lifetime

There's a lot more to the lifetime of a control than you may think. It's not just a simple case of the length of time it exists in a given project. Controls are destroyed and recreated each time a developer switches between the host application project's design-time and run-time modes, as we saw in Chapter 1. The design-time instance of the control is destroyed, and replaced by a run-time instance, and vice-versa.

If this is the case, why does it seem that we're just using the same instance of a control and not a different instance altogether? The reason is that the control uses **data persistence** to 'remember' the design-time values that were set, and the new instance uses them when the control is re-created. Even though controls allow you to change the values of properties at run-time, they don't keep these changes once that particular control instance has been destroyed and recreated (i.e. once the developer returns to project design-mode). Controls therefore have to behave differently depending upon which context they are used in.

This is something that we must think about when we write our own controls, but the ActiveX Control Interface Wizard has already helped us quite a lot in this respect. We'll go into this in more detail later, and show you what the ActiveX Control Interface Wizard has produced in way of code. Of course, we'll need to modify and extend this code so that our control functions as we originally intended.

Control Creation and Termination

In order to write code that makes our controls behave like other standard ones, we have to understand exactly what our control is doing when it's being used by a developer in a project. Fortunately, the control's properties and events provide us with this information.

When we first place any control on to another application's form, which is in design mode, the control is created and the code behind the control starts executing immediately. Based on events and properties that occur within the control, it can set itself up appropriately for project design-mode operation.

When the project is run by the developer, that instance of the control saves any information that will be needed by the new instance, and is destroyed. Then, as the project starts running, the control is recreated and the new instance loads the previously saved information. When project execution is halted, this control instance is destroyed, but before this occurs, it saves any data required.

UserControl Specific Events

As the control author, it's our responsibility to decide when control property settings are to be stored for later use, and when we can just ignore any changes and start the control up using some default values instead. For this, we can use the following **UserControl** events:

Event Name	Description
AccessKeyPress	Occurs when the user of the control presses one of the control's access keys, or when the *Enter* key is pressed and the developer has set the **Default** property to **True**, or when the *Escape* key is pressed and the developer has set the **Cancel** property to **True**.
AmbientChanged	Occurs when an ambient value is changed by the container of a user control.
AsyncReadComplete	Occurs when the data that is requested by the **AsyncRead** method is available.
Initialize	Occurs when an application creates an instance of a user control class.
InitProperties	Occurs the first time a user control is created.
ReadProperties	Occurs when a user control is asked to read its data.
Terminate	Occurs when all references to an instance of a user control class are removed from memory.
WriteProperties	Occurs when a user control is asked to write its data.

In addition to these events, all the usual methods and events, such as **Click**, **DblClick**, **Resize** etc. are provided—just like with standard forms. You may have noticed that we've included the **UserControl_Initialize** and **UserControl_Terminate** events in the list, even though they're not particular to the **UserControl** class. We've done this because, although controls are drawn on a form-like area during design, we are not furnished with the events **Form_Load** and **Form_UnLoad**.

The **InitProperties**, **ReadProperties**, and **WriteProperties** events are fired when the control is created and terminated. These events provide a mechanism so that, where necessary, the property values are initialized, read and saved at the appropriate times. When the **UserControl** object is first created, the **InitProperties** event is fired. It's within the subroutine we create for this event, that default values for the control are assigned. The control then continues to execute until the host application's form is destroyed. When this happens, the control fires its **WriteProperties** event to save the current property values. Subsequently, whenever the control is re-created, the **ReadProperties** event is fired (instead of the **InitProperties**). In the subroutine for this event, we write code that retrieves the stored properties from the **PropertyBag** object, and alters the state of the control to that which it was before termination.

> *The **PropertyBag** object is a mechanism that provides a convenient means to store and retrieve persistent property values across the lifetimes of a control instance. It's actually part of the container.*

Back to the Converter Control

In the previous sections, we've talked quite a bit about control lifetime, and how controls are destroyed and recreated on a frequent basis. We're now going to discuss the basic structure of a control, so that you'll understand how we going to cover the control lifetime issues with our Converter control. We'll be examining code fragments produced by the ActiveX Control Interface Wizard to see how they apply to our control.

When writing our control, we must ensure that every control instance based on the **UserControl** object has default property values. This is because we have to ensure that the property values of our control instance at any point in time are defined to be within the range of permissible values. Also, by setting sensible default values for our properties, we'll be cutting down on the amount of work required for developers. They will be able to leave many of the settings pretty much alone.

When we're writing controls, we use constants that define the default values. In this way, it's easy to change the default value if we're required to do so. If we have a look at the code that the wizard has produced, we can see that it's already done this for us:

```
'Default Property Values:
Const m_def_Caption = ""
Const m_def_BackColor = 0
Const m_def_Appearance = 0
Const m_def_Conversion_Mode = 0
```

Of course, we're not actually making use of these values yet, but we'll come on to that in a moment.

Exposing Properties, Methods and Events

The public properties, methods and events that our control will supply to developers, are known collectively as the **interface** of the control. It's through this interface that our control is used and all valid operations are carried out. We've already seen part of the interface in use—namely the **InputChange** event which we wrote code for at the end of the previous chapter. While the wizard has helped us set out the interface in the control's code, we've still got to determine *what* the control needs to do, and *how* it should do it.

Using Property Procedures

Property procedures provide the standard means of accessing and updating values stored in a control. There are three types available: **Property Get**, **Property Let** and **Property Set**. Whenever we want to retrieve a value from a control, we use **Property Get**. Looking at some code that the wizard has produced, we can see how such a property procedure is defined:

```
Public Property Get Conversion_Mode() As Integer
   Conversion_Mode = m_Conversion_Mode
End Property
```

When we make a request to inspect the **Conversion_Mode** value of our control, at project design-time or run-time, our control executes the public property procedure of the same name—**Property Get Conversion_Mode**.

You'll notice above that the procedure is acting like a function, since it returns a value. In addition, an extra variable is referenced within it, namely **m_Conversion_Mode**. This variable name is based on the corresponding property we've created using the wizard, with the 'm' standing for *member*. The variable is a member of our control, and contains the actual value of the property we want to access. If we look through the code of our control, we'll see that the wizard has declared this value:

```
Dim m_Conversion_Mode As Integer
```

By default, if we just supply a **Property Get** for one of our properties, then that property won't be displayed in the properties window when we select a control instance. This is because we haven't supplied a route for updating the property. When we used the wizard, we specified that the **Conversion_Mode** property should be available for access and updating at both project design-time and run-time. The wizard has therefore kindly provided us with the appropriate **Property Let** procedure for this purpose:

```
Public Property Let Conversion_Mode(ByVal New_Conversion_Mode As Integer)
   m_Conversion_Mode = New_Conversion_Mode
   PropertyChanged "Conversion_Mode"
End Property
```

There are some interesting things to note here. First, the new value of the property is passed by value instead of by reference. This way, if we were to change the value of the parameter (whether on purpose or accidentally), the new value wouldn't be propagated back to the user of the control. If it was, they could spend a lot of time looking for bugs in their code!

Second, the wizard has included a call to **PropertyChanged** with a string parameter. Remember how we talked earlier about data persistence between instances of a control? Well, by calling **PropertyChanged**, we've let VB know that the value of the property has changed, and that we'll want to keep that new value when we next recreate the control instance.

> *On reading this section you may think that we could have just defined a global variable to achieve the same effect as the **Property Get** and **Property Let** procedures. You'd be right, but this is considered very poor practice as it allows developers free access to the variable, which means they'll be able to set it to whichever value they choose. By using **Property Let** to update the value, we can introduce constraints and validation as required.*

There's one last form of property procedure—**Property Set**. This is similar to **Property Let**, in that it's used to update a variable. The difference here is that its purpose is to update a variable that refers to an **object**, rather than a normal 'value'. The wizard has used this form of property procedure to update the **Font** property:

```
Public Property Set Font(ByVal New_Font As Font)
   If Ambient.UserMode Then Exit Property
   Set m_Font = New_Font
   PropertyChanged "Font"
End Property
```

When we used the wizard in the last chapter to create the shell of our control, we specified that the **Font** property should be read-only at run-time. The wizard has added code which checks to see if it's being called at run-time. If it is, it just exits without updating the property variable. Otherwise, it sets the new value of **m_Font**, and calls the **PropertyChanged** routine.

> *You can think of the value of **Ambient.UserMode** as being **True** when the control is being run by the **user** (rather than the developer). In other words, the host application is in run-time mode.*

Before we look at how the **ReadProperties** and **WriteProperties** events are used, we'll see how the other methods and events are specified for our control.

Defining Methods

Defining **methods** for our control is quite a simple process. All we have to do is write a **Public** routine that can accept parameters. Here's the definition of the **Clear** method that the wizard has created for us:

```
Public Function Clear(Optional strItem) As Variant
End Function
```

When we use a function in VB, we can ignore the value it returns. In this way, we are using it like a subroutine. For purposes of clarity in our control, and because we don't need to return a value anyway, we're going to change this function to a subroutine:

```
Public Sub Clear(Optional strItem)
End Sub
```

When we define a subroutine like this, we make the method available to the developer who can then invoke our method for the control instance. Assuming we're using an instance of the control called **NumberConverter1**, then we can call the method from the test project. In order to get a positive affirmation that our method works as expected, we can enter some code into the **Clear** subroutine:

In the control:

```
Public Sub Clear(Optional strItem)
   If IsMissing(strItem) Then   'No parameter used.
      MsgBox "Clearing all values..."
   Else   'A parameter given.
      MsgBox "Clearing value represented by " & strItem & "."
   End If
End Sub
```

Within the confines of our test project, we've decided to test the method by creating two command buttons, and entering this code in their respective **Click** events:

In the test project:

```
Private Sub cmdClearAll_Click()
   NumberConverter1.Clear
End Sub
```

```
Private Sub cmdClearAValue_Click()
   NumberConverter1.Clear ("First")
End Sub
```

We can test our method by running the test project. Clicking the two command buttons produces appropriate message boxes. Obviously, this isn't very useful, as neither the input or output field values are cleared, but it does show how we can test our control in a client project environment. From now on, we won't be showing you how we test each piece of code as it's added, but that's not to say you shouldn't be testing as you go along!

Creating Events and Firing Them

The process of defining new events for our control is fairly quick and painless, and we can easily augment the standard events that are automatically defined for our control.

We've all used events, whether it be **Timer1_Timer**, **Text1_Change**, etc. Events fire when a certain condition or set of conditions occur. The process of defining an event in our control is therefore a two stage process: we first have to somehow declare the event so that it's accessible to developers; and then we have to ensure that it's fired under the right conditions.

To start with then, let's have a look at how the events are declared:

```
'Property Variables:
...
'Event Declarations:
Event InputChange() 'MappingInfo=txtInput,txtInput,-1,Change
Event OutputChange() 'MappingInfo=lblOutput,lblOutput,-1,Change
Event ConversionModeChange(intChangedTo As Integer)
```

You'll notice that there are some strange looking comments in the code created by the wizard. These are actually read and used by the ActiveX Control Interface Wizard to determine mappings defined in the 'Set Mappings' stage. They have no real use when it comes to the functionality of the control. The wizard can only do what we can through code and the IDE. But, as we've seen, it can significantly reduce the amount of work we need to do, initially, to create a new control.

Next, we have to define the conditions that will cause the events to fire. Naturally, we should have at least one condition, otherwise that event declaration is superfluous—it will never add to the functionality of the control. Events are fired by using the **RaiseEvent** keyword and supplying the name of our declared event as a parameter. We've already seen that the **txtInput_Change** event fires when the **Text** value of the **txtInput** textbox changes. Now you know how it works!

```
Private Sub txtInput_Change()
  RaiseEvent InputChange
End Sub
```

```
Private Sub lblOutput_Change()
  RaiseEvent OutputChange
End Sub
```

There is one restriction that you need to remember when declaring and raising events. You must only do this in a **UserControl** class, as you'll get errors if you try this anywhere else.

Now that we've covered some of the basics, it's time to introduce an outline that we can work to when developing our control.

A Workable Control Outline

In this section, we'll show you a suitable 'pseudo template' for the **UserControl** code that we'll be building upon. It demonstrates the general layout for code in a **UserControl** class. You've already seen some of the fragments of the code, but it's always nice to see how this fits into the larger picture (or code listing, in our case).

```
Option Explicit
'Default Property Values:
Const m_def_PropName1 = ""
Const m_def_PropName2 = 0
...
'Property Variables:
Dim m_PropName1 As Type
Dim m_PropName2 As ObjectType
...

'Event Declarations:
Event CustomEvent1() 'MappingInfo=ControlName1,ControlName1,-1 ControlEvent1
Event CustomEvent2()
Event CustomEvent3(SuppliedParameter As Type)
...

'Initialize Properties for User Control:
Private Sub UserControl_InitProperties()
  m_PropName1 = m_def_PropName1
  Set m_PropName2 = Ambient.AmbientPropName
  ...
End Sub

'Load property values from storage:
Private Sub UserControl_ReadProperties(PropBag As PropertyBag)
  m_PropName1 = PropBag.ReadProperty("PropName1", m_def_PropName1)
  UserControl.PropName2 = PropBag.ReadProperty("PropName2", m_def_PropName2)
  Set PropName3 = PropBag.ReadProperty("PropName3", Value)
  ...
End Sub

'Write property values to storage:
Private Sub UserControl_WriteProperties(PropBag As PropertyBag)
  Call PropBag.WriteProperty("PropName1", m_PropName1, m_def_PropName1)
  Call PropBag.WriteProperty("PropName2", UserControl.PropName2, m_def_PropName2)
  Call PropBag.WriteProperty("PropName3", PropName3, Value)
  ...
End Sub

'Declare any Property Gets, Lets and Sets:
Public Property Get PropertyName1() As ReturnType
  'Any suitable validation if necessary.
  PropertyName = m_PropertyName
End Property

Public Property Let PropertyName1(ByVal New_PropertyValue As PropertyType)
  'Any suitable validation if necessary.
  m_PropName1 = New_PropName1
  PropertyChanged "PropName1"
  'Any custom programming to update control state if necessary.
End Property

Public Property Set PropName2(ByVal New_PropName As ObjectType)
  'Any suitable validation if necessary.
  Set m_PropName2 = New_PropName
  PropertyChanged "PropName2"
  'Any custom programming to update control state if necessary.
End Property
```

```
'Declare methods:
Public Sub MethodName1([Parameter1 As Type,...][Optional Parameter2])
  'Code that uses Parameter1.
  [If IsMissing(Parameter2) Then   'No parameter used.
    'Process this case.
  {Else   'A parameter given.
    'Process case when parameter given, and use value Parameter2 somehow.}
  End If]
  'Can also raise events in methods:
  RaiseEvent CustomEvent2
End Sub

'Any simple custom RaiseEvent calls:
Private Sub ControlName1_ControlEvent1()
  RaiseEvent CustomEvent1
End Sub

Private Sub ControlName1_ControlEvent()
  RaiseEvent CustomEvent3(ControlName1.PropertyValue)
End Sub

'Any private subroutines and functions.
...
```

While the template provides us with a recommended framework, we can also see how the various constructs covered so far fit together, and how properties, methods and events are declared and used. The names of the control and its members are in italics—you'll need to insert the relevant names when writing code for your own controls.

While this is a good starting point, we'll need to flesh out this template and insert our own functionality. However, before we do this, let's see how our control can distinguish between design-time and run-time use. This is very important, as will become more apparent shortly.

Design-Time and Run-Time Issues

We've already mentioned that when we create an instance of a control, the control code is actually executing. It doesn't matter whether the control is being used in the design-mode or run-mode of the host application's project. However, we need to set up the control differently, depending on the actual project mode.

In the host application's design-mode, we want the control to display its name (via **lblCaption**), and also display the string literals Input_Value and Output_Value as the **Text** and **Caption** properties of the **txtInput** and **lblOutput** controls respectively. In this way, we'll be helping the developer who uses our control to be able to quickly locate the correct control instance, and see the main property names—without having to look them up in the Object Browser.

During project run-time, we're going to change this arrangement and have **lblCaption** display the current value of the **Caption** property. We're also going to blank out the **Text** and **Caption** properties of **txtInput** and **lblOutput** controls. In order to do this, we'll need to inspect the **Usermode** property of the **Ambient** object. When this value is **True**, we know that the project that's using our control is in run-mode.

Let's start by tackling the caption of the control. We've already have the **Property Get** and **Property Let** property procedures:

```
Public Property Get Caption() As String
   Caption = m_Caption
End Property
```

```
Public Property Let Caption(ByVal New_Caption As String)
  m_Caption = New_Caption
  PropertyChanged "Caption"
End Property
```

As it stands though, changing our caption won't change **lblOutput** at all, and neither do we currently have any way of assigning the name of the control. The property procedures shown above are only called when we assign or retrieve the **Caption** property value. We must therefore add code to the **InitProperties** event so that we can set the control up as we want.

> You may wonder why we won't be doing this in the **Initialize** event. This is because the container for our control only becomes available (and so accessible via the **Ambient** and **Extender** objects) when all the controls within it have been successfully created and placed. Referencing the **Ambient** or **Extender** objects in the **Initialize** event causes a run-time error.

If you recall from our description of the **InitProperties** and **ReadProperties** events, it is **InitProperties** that is fired on the creation of the first instance of the control, and **ReadProperties** that is fired thereafter. We'll therefore have to include code in *two* places to ensure that the control caption is displayed as required. Since we'll be using the same code in each case, it's reasonable to declare it within a subroutine that we can call:

```
Private Sub UpdateCaption()    'Updates the display caption of the control.
   If Ambient.UserMode Then    'Project run-time mode.
     lblCaption.Caption = m_Caption
   Else
     lblCaption.Caption = Extender.Name
   End If
End Sub
```

Changing the **InitProperties** and **ReadProperties** events is then really easy:

```
'Initialize Properties for User Control
Private Sub UserControl_InitProperties()
   ...
   UpdateCaption
End Sub
```

```
'Load property values from storage
Private Sub UserControl_ReadProperties(PropBag As PropertyBag)
   ...
```

```
      UpdateCaption
   End Sub
```

We have another alternative when coding this functionality: we can make the **Property Get Caption** procedure return the appropriate value:

```
Public Property Get Caption() As String
   If Ambient.UserMode Then    'Project run-time mode.
     Caption = m_Caption
   Else
     Caption = Extender.Name
   End If
End Property
```

And then simply assign the result straight to the **Caption** property of the label. Using this approach, we don't need the subroutine **UpdateCaption** at all:

```
'Initialize Properties for User Control
Private Sub UserControl_InitProperties()
   ...
   lblCaption.Caption = Caption
End Sub
```

```
'Load property values from storage
Private Sub UserControl_ReadProperties(PropBag As PropertyBag)
   ...
   lblCaption.Caption = Caption
End Sub
```

Whichever method we choose, we will also specify a default caption for the run-time instance of this control by changing the constant that's used:

```
Const m_def_Caption = "Number Converter"
```

Now consider what happens when the name of the control is changed in project design-mode. We need to update the view of the control so that this new name is reflected by the caption. How do we detect when the name of our control has changed?

The **UserControl** object provides an event that helps us out here. Whenever an ambient property is changed (by whatever means), the **AmbientChanged** event fires and gives us a parameter that indicates which property has changed. We can try this out by entering some simple code into this event:

```
Private Sub UserControl_AmbientChanged(PropertyName As String)
   MsgBox "The ambient property " & PropertyName & " has changed."
End Sub
```

When we change the name of the control instance, we now get a message box which informs us that The ambient property DisplayName has changed. There are several ambient properties that can change, but we only want to act when the **DisplayName** changes. So, once again, we update **lblCaption** accordingly:

```
Private Sub UserControl_AmbientChanged(PropertyName As String)
   Select Case PropertyName
   Case "DisplayName" 'Update control caption.
```

75

```
        lblCaption.Caption = Caption 'Works as gets current new Extender.Name.
    End Select
End Sub
```

Looking at the code created by the wizard, there's another place where the **Ambient** object is used. In our design, we specified that certain properties, such as **Appearance** and **BackColor**, are to be read only during project run-time, and read/write during project design-time. Here's the code that achieves this:

```
Public Property Get Appearance() As Integer
    Appearance = m_Appearance
End Property
```

```
Public Property Let Appearance(ByVal New_Appearance As Integer)
    If Ambient.UserMode Then Exit Property
    m_Appearance = New_Appearance
    PropertyChanged "Appearance"
End Property
```

We'll always be able to read the property, and so no validation is incorporated into the **Property Get** procedure. However, when setting such a property, we need to test to see if attempts are being made to change the property at project run-time, i.e. when it's supposed to be read only. If this is the case then we simply exit out of the **Let** property procedure. By doing this, the new value is never propagated to the member property variable (**m_Appearance** in this case), and we skip over the code that informs VB that the value has changed. The property value isn't stored when the control is destroyed.

Instead of just skipping over the rest of the code, we can inform the user that an invalid attempt was made to update the property value at project run-time. By doing this, it's easy for developers to spot and correct problems in their project. So, an alternative to the above would be:

```
Public Property Let Appearance(ByVal New_Appearance As Integer)
    If Ambient.UserMode Then
        Err.Raise Description:= "Appearance is read only at run-time!", _
                Number:=vbObjectError + 512
    End If
    m_Appearance = New_Appearance
    PropertyChanged "Appearance"
End Property
```

Note that we can only raise errors like this in project run-mode. If we raise an error in project design-mode, the error will not be displayed.

The constant **vbObjectError** is available in VB5, and specifies where our own object error number should start from. We've added **512** to this as well, because some other object errors have been introduced after this number, and we don't want to overwrite them with our own. We can also use some of the standard error numbers like **383**-Set not supported (read-only property), and **393**-Get not supported at runtime. We'll also be raising errors later, when we introduce validation for the updating of property values.

Filling in the Blanks

There are a number of things that we need to do to complete our control. They are:

- Introduce enumerations where appropriate, instead of using integers.

- Change the value of **m_Conversion_Mode** to a value depending on the current conversion mode, and raise the event **ConversionModeChange**.

- Update the caption properties of the labels **lblCapInput** and **lblCapOutput** appropriately, and update the option buttons when the **m_Conversion_Mode** property is changed.

- Check for valid input when converting binary numbers to decimal.

- Complete the **Clear** and **Convert** methods.

Conversion Mode

Developers frequently need to change property values when using our controls. When there is a small number of choices, they are often displayed in the Properties window as a drop-down list, as we saw in the previous chapter. We can achieve the same sort of effect by using enumerated types instead of just making do with integers. As an example, let's give the property **Conversion_Mode** this treatment. We'll change the type to **ConversionModeEnum**, which is declared later:

```
'Property Variables:
Dim m_Conversion_Mode As ConversionModeEnum
...
```

The actual declaration of the enumeration is just a mechanism that assigns integer values to its members:

```
'Type Declarations:
Public Enum ConversionModeEnum
   DecimalToBinary = 0
   BinaryToDecimal = 1
End Enum
'Event Declarations:
```

Notice how we've made this enumeration **Public**. We've done this for two reasons. Firstly, **Public** properties can now return values of the enumerated type, instead of just integer, and it's this that gives us the drop-down list of alternatives that we've become accustomed to. In our case, we will get two items in the list: 0 - DecimalToBinary, and 1 - BinaryToDecimal.

Secondly, the member values defined within the enumeration are automatically available to the client project, and so the more meaningful member names can be used in preference to the integer values they represent.

We can now update our **Conversion_Mode** property procedures like this:

```
Public Property Get Conversion_Mode() As ConversionModeEnum
   Conversion_Mode = m_Conversion_Mode
End Property
```

```
Public Property Let Conversion_Mode(ByVal New_Conversion_Mode As _
                                               ConversionModeEnum)
    m_Conversion_Mode = New_Conversion_Mode
    PropertyChanged "Conversion_Mode"
End Property
```

We'll also change the parameter type of the event **ConversionModeChange** that we've already defined:

```
'Event Declarations:
...
Event ConversionModeChange(enConversionMode As ConversionModeEnum)
```

Since the parameter name and type are shown in the client project code, we are making the developer's life easier by letting them know the enumerated type name. They can then lookup the member values using the object browser.

> *If we change the parameter types for an event or method like this, we need to delete the event or method definition from the client project. We can always establish the new form by selecting our control from the object list, and then the event or method from the procedure list. This ensures that we are using the right declaration.*

What we haven't done is raise the **ConversionModeChange** event when the conversion mode changes, so this is our next job. We can do this in a variety of ways. For instance, recall that we've defined members of the **ConversionModeEnum** enumerated type as shown:

```
Public Enum ConversionModeEnum
    DecimalToBinary = 0
    BinaryToDecimal = 1
End Enum
```

We could just use the fact that the numbers 'tie up'. In other words, the **index** value of the option button associated with converting decimal to binary is **0**—the same value as the corresponding member of the enumeration. We could therefore change the conversion mode using the new index value, and raise the **ConversionModeChange** event when the other option button is selected:

```
Private Sub optConversionMode_Click(Index As Integer)
    m_ConversionMode = Index
    RaiseEvent ConversionModeChange((Index))
End Sub
```

This, however, is bad design. For a start, our code is unclear, and we have specified in the design that the conversion mode can be changed by code in the client project. In such a case, the **ConversionModeChange** event would not be raised.

Another thing that you'll notice is that we're raising an event from an *interface object*—in this case an option button. This is fine if there are no methods which change the member value **m_ConversionMode**, but this isn't the case here. A better approach is to use the appropriate **Property Let** procedure to raise the event instead. Here's how this is done:

```
Private Sub optConversionMode_Click(Index As Integer)
    Conversion_Mode = IIf(Index = 0, DecimalToBinary, BinaryToDecimal)
End Sub
```

By changing the public property value **Conversion_Mode**, we're using the appropriate **Property Let** procedure to carry out any additional functions that are necessary. We've also shown that an index value of **0** indicates that the **Conversion_Mode** property should be **DecimalToBinary**, and that another value indicates that the new property value is to be **BinaryToDecimal**.

When we update the conversion mode, we also have to change the captions of **lblCapInput** and **lblCapOutput** to represent their function. This is easily achieved, depending on the new conversion mode. Here's the final **Property Let Conversion_Mode** procedure:

```
Public Property Let Conversion_Mode(ByVal New_Conversion_Mode As _
                                                    ConversionModeEnum)
   If New_Conversion_Mode <> m_Conversion_Mode Then
     RaiseEvent ConversionModeChange(New_Conversion_Mode)
   End If
   m_Conversion_Mode = New_Conversion_Mode
   If m_Conversion_Mode = DecimalToBinary Then
      lblCapInput.Caption = "&Enter your decimal number here"
      lblCapOutput.Caption = "The binary representation is"
      If optConversionMode(0).Value = False Then
        'Conversion mode changed by call to this Let routine, rather than
        'by clicking the option button. We must update the buttons.
        optConversionMode(0).Value = True
      End If
   Else
      lblCapInput.Caption = "&Enter your binary number here"
      lblCapOutput.Caption = "The decimal representation is"
      If optConversionMode(1).Value = False Then
        'Conversion mode changed by call to this Let routine, rather than
        'by clicking the option button. We must update the buttons.
        optConversionMode(1).Value = True
      End If
   End If
   Clear
   PropertyChanged "Conversion_Mode"
End Property
```

We're only raising the **ConversionModeChange** event if the new property value differs from the existing value. We've also called the **Clear** method within our code. (We'll define the **Clear** method later.) There's nothing stopping us from using the methods we've defined for the control as ordinary subroutines. Such methods are simply **Public** subroutines. As usual, we can add code to our test project to check the operation of our control.

In the test project:

```
Private Sub NumberConverter1_ConversionModeChange(enConversionMode As _
                                       Converter_Control.ConversionModeEnum)
   Select Case enConversionMode
   Case DecimalToBinary
     MsgBox "The conversion mode has been changed to Decimal -> Binary."
   Case BinaryToDecimal
     MsgBox "The conversion mode has been changed to Binary -> Decimal."
   Case Else
     MsgBox "Unknown conversion mode!"
   End Select
End Sub
```

The input parameter to this subroutine has been declared as of type
`Converter_Control.ConversionModeEnum`. *When events are exposed in this manner to a client project, any* **`Public`** *user-defined types declared in the control will be referenced by pre-pending the name of the class where that type is defined. We needn't concern ourselves with this because, as a developer using the control, we shouldn't tinker with event interface provided by the control.*

You'll probably be glad to hear that there's only one aspect that we've missed out when changing the conversion mode, and that's in the control startup. The wizard has created the code shown below:

```
Const m_def_Conversion_Mode = 0
```

We can set this to **DecimalToBinary** or **BinaryToDecimal** as defined in the **ConversionModeEnum** enumeration. If we do this, we have to move the line below the enumeration declaration so that the values of the members are defined:

```
'Type Declarations:
Public Enum ConversionModeEnum
  DecimalToBinary = 0
  BinaryToDecimal = 1
End Enum
Const m_def_Conversion_Mode = DecimalToBinary
```

However, if we change **m_def_Conversion_Mode** to **BinaryToDecimal**, what would happen? Well, the conversion mode property member value (**m_Conversion_Mode**) would be set to the correct value, which can be seen in the code below, but the view of the control wouldn't reflect this:

```
'Initialize Properties for User Control
Private Sub UserControl_InitProperties()
    . . .
    m_Conversion_Mode = m_def_Conversion_Mode
    . . .
End Sub

'Load property values from storage
Private Sub UserControl_ReadProperties(PropBag As PropertyBag)
    . . .
    m_Conversion_Mode = PropBag.ReadProperty("Conversion_Mode", _
                                              m_def_Conversion_Mode)
    . . .
End Sub
```

Clearly, this isn't a desirable outcome. Even though the wizard sets up the default values like this, it doesn't take into account any of the functionality of the control, including how the control draws itself. We can easily put the situation right by setting the **m_Conversion_Mode** property value using the **Property Let Conversion_Mode** procedure. Here's how we do it:

```
'Initialize Properties for User Control
Private Sub UserControl_InitProperties()
    . . .
    Conversion_Mode = m_def_Conversion_Mode
    . . .
End Sub
```

By assigning to the property procedure **Conversion_Mode** on the left hand side of the assignment, we can change the value of the property member variable **m_Conversion_Mode** *indirectly*, and use the code provided by the property procedure to effect any appearance changes as necessary. We can also use this method of assignment in the **ReadProperties** event:

```
'Load property values from storage
Private Sub UserControl_ReadProperties(PropBag As PropertyBag)
   . . .
   Conversion_Mode = PropBag.ReadProperty("Conversion_Mode", _
                                          m_def_Conversion_Mode)
   . . .
End Sub
```

In general, whenever your **Property Let** procedures do anything more than just update the property member's value, it's a good idea to use this technique to ensure that your control behaves properly.

Converting the Numbers

Now that we've completed the conversion mode coding, let's move on to actually performing the conversion. To keep things simple, we're going to perform validation when a number is to be converted. In a more complex version of the control, we could introduce input validation on the **txtInput.Change** event and only accept legal values. Our starting point, however, will be the empty **Convert** function that the wizard has set up for us:

```
Public Function Convert() As Variant
End Function
```

Just like in the case of the **Clear** method earlier, we've converted the function to a public subroutine for clarity:

```
Public Sub Convert()
End Sub
```

In Visual Basic, it's common practice to invoke a subroutine on an event. This technique is extremely useful when we're writing controls. In our design, we've acknowledged that we'd provide a **Convert** method that can be accessed through client project code. In our control, we created the button **cmdConvert**, which can be used to invoke the **Convert** method from the user interface. All we need to do is put the method name within the **cmdConvert_Click** event like this:

```
Private Sub cmdConvert_Click()
   Convert
End Sub
```

Our **Convert** method then just takes the input value and converts it to the appropriate value depending on the conversion mode. It's important to test that the input numbers are valid. Here, we've simply stated that any number is a valid decimal number, and any number comprising just **0**s and **1**s is a valid binary number. If an invalid input is detected, we raise an error.

Remember, we can only raise errors at project run-time. However, methods can also only be invoked at project run-time, i.e. when the project is executing. So we don't need to check that the **Convert** method is being invoked at project run-time.

```
Public Sub Convert()
  Dim strConverted As String
  If IsNumeric(Input_Value) Then 'OK so far as we've just got numbers.
    If m_Conversion_Mode = BinaryToDecimal Then
      If Not IsValidBinary(Input_Value) Then
        Err.Raise Description:="Invalid binary number", Number:=vbObjectError + 513
        Exit Sub
      End If
      'Calculate decimal representation.
      strConverted = CStr(GetDec(txtInput.Text))
    Else
      'Calculate binary representation.
      strConverted = GetBin(CLng(txtInput.Text))
      strConverted = IIf(Len(strConverted), strConverted, "0")
    End If
    'Now update the output.
    lblOutput.Caption = strConverted
  End If
End Sub
```

The **Convert** method updates the caption of **lblOutput**, which in turn triggers the **lblOuput.Change** event if the new value is different from the previous value. When this happens, the **OutputChange** event is raised:

```
Private Sub lblOutput_Change()
  RaiseEvent OutputChange
End Sub
```

When we used the wizard for mapping this event, it created both the **Property Get Output_Value** and **Property Let Output_Value** procedures. In the context of our control, we only want to retrieve the value of the property **Output_Value**. We must therefore delete the **Property Let Output_Value** procedure so that the property value can't be changed directly.

We've also used some access functions—that is functions that help to break down the complexity of the tasks into manageable units. Here's the function we've used to determine whether a valid binary number was input:

```
Private Function IsValidBinary(strProposedBinary As String) As Boolean
  Dim intIndex As Integer
  Dim chrTestChar As String * 1
  For intIndex = 1 To Len(strProposedBinary)
    chrTestChar = Mid$(strProposedBinary, intIndex, 1)
    If chrTestChar <> 0 And chrTestChar <> 1 Then
      'Invalid binary number detected.
      IsValidBinary = False
      Exit Function
    End If
  Next intIndex
  IsValidBinary = True
End Function
```

We've also used a couple of recursive functions for calculating the binary equivalent of a decimal number, and the decimal representation of a binary number:

```
Function GetBin(ByVal lngX As Long) As String
  If lngX > 0 Then
    GetBin = GetBin(lngX \ 2)
    GetBin = GetBin & IIf(lngX Mod 2 = 1, "1", "0")
  End If
End Function
```

```
Function GetDec(ByVal strX As String) As Long
  Dim lngPower As Long
  lngPower = 1
  While Len(strX) 'While strX is not = "".
    GetDec = GetDec + IIf(Right$(strX, 1) = 1, lngPower, 0)
    strX = Left$(strX, Len(strX) - 1)
    lngPower = lngPower * 2
  Wend
End Function
```

When using recursion like this, remember to always pass parameters by value so that new variables are used in each call.

Now that we've effected the **Convert** method, we can use this in the test project, together with the **InputChange** event, to calculate and display the converted number each time the input number is changed.

In the test project:

```
Private Sub NumberConverter1_InputChange()
  NumberConverter1.Convert
End Sub
```

Coding the Clear Method

The **Clear** method allows the developer to clear either the input, output, or both input and output values. By *clear* we mean set to **0**. As before, the most convenient way to allow a parameter to be passed into this method is to use an enumeration:

```
Public Enum ClearEnum
  ClearInput = 0
  ClearOutput = 1
End Enum
```

The coding of **Clear** is then relatively straightforward. All we really need to watch out for is the **Optional** argument:

```
Public Sub Clear(Optional ClearItem)
  If IsMissing(ClearItem) Then  'No parameter supplied
    'Clear all the values.
    txtInput.Text = "0"
    lblOutput.Caption = "0"
  Else  'A parameter supplied
    If ClearItem = ClearInput Then  'Clear input field only.
      txtInput.Text = "0"
```

```
      ElseIf ClearItem = ClearOutput Then 'Clear output field only.
         lblOutput.Caption = "0"
      Else
         'Some other invalid parameter supplied
         Err.Raise Description:="Invalid ClearItem!", Number:=vbObjectError + 514
      End If
   End If
End Sub
```

Using the Working Control

So far, we've covered control design and creation. Let's now have a look how it can be used in an application. We'll demonstrate the control in an example application that's designed to hone your powers of conversion. Here's a screenshot; you'll instantly recognise our Converter control:

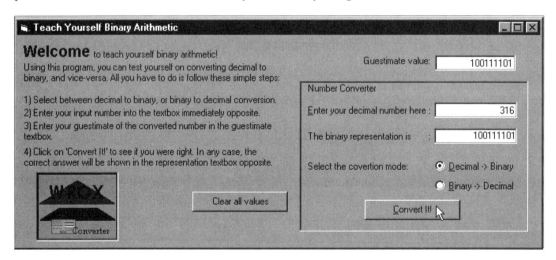

Remember you can download the sample controls described from our web site. Just browse to **http://**
www.wrox.com/books/0235/code/.

Let's kick off with the Clear all values button. Here's the code that is defined for its **Click** event:

```
Private Sub cmdClearAll_Click()
   txtGuestimate.Text = "0"
   NumberConverter1.Clear
End Sub
```

As an aside, we can test the value of the **Input_Value** property within the **InputChange** event, which allows us to detect immediately when an invalid input is submitted. In this case, we can alert the user, and just keep the valid part of the input. It's also customary to set the focus back to the control that caused the problem. By doing this, we can stop the **Err.Raise** statement being executed within the control when an invalid input value is fed into the **Convert** method:

```
Private Sub NumberConverter1_InputChange()
   Dim strMsg As String
   If NumberConverter1.Conversion_Mode = BinaryToDecimal And _
```

```
        Not IsValidBinary(NumberConverter1.Input_Value) Then
            strMsg = "Invalid binary input number." & vbCrLf _
                & "The last number will be used."
            MsgBox strMsg, vbInformation
            With NumberConverter1
                .Input_Value = Left$(.Input_Value, Len(.Input_Value) - 1)
            End With
        End If
    End Sub
```

The rest of the code is in the **OutputChange** event for the **Converter** control. Here is where we'll compare the computed and entered results for equality:

```
    Private Sub NumberConverter1_OutputChange()
        Dim strMsg As String

        If NumberConverter1.Output_Value > 0 Then
            'Event occured for other than the 'Clear All Values button being selected.
            If NumberConverter1.Conversion_Mode = BinaryToDecimal Then
                If Trim$(txtGuestimate.Text) = Trim$(NumberConverter1.Output_Value) Then
                    strMsg = "Well done, you've got the correct decimal equivalent!"
                Else
                    strMsg = "Hard luck. The correct decimal representation " _
                        & " of " & NumberConverter1.Input_Value & " is: " _
                        & NumberConverter1.Output_Value & "."
                End If
            Else
                If Trim$(txtGuestimate.Text) = Trim$(NumberConverter1.Output_Value) Then
                    strMsg = "Well done, you've got the correct binary equivalent!"
                Else
                    strMsg = "Hard luck. The correct binary representation" _
                        & " of " & NumberConverter1.Input_Value & " is: " _
                        & NumberConverter1.Output_Value & "."
                End If
            End If
            MsgBox strMsg
        End If
    End Sub
```

So now that we've persuaded our new control to do something useful, and seen it working, we'll go on to show you how we add property pages to it. These can make it a lot easier for developers to work with your control.

Property Pages

Property pages provide a more natural and friendlier environment for changing the design-time property values of a control than that provided by the Properties window. For complex properties, the one value in the Properties window is often inadequate to cope with changing the required attributes. We looked briefly at property pages in Chapter 1. The good news is that VB5 CCE lets you create property pages for your own controls, and what's more, it provides the Property Page Wizard to help you on your way. In this section, we'll take you through the process of using the wizard to create a set of property pages for the Number Converter control like you can see over the page. You'll be amazed how easy it is.

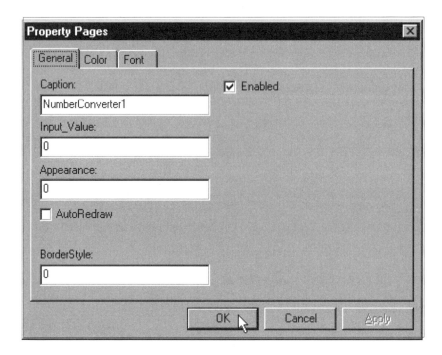

Using the Property Page Wizard

The first step is to select your control from the Project Group window. Then select Property Page Wizard from the Add-Ins menu, and you are greeted with this screen:

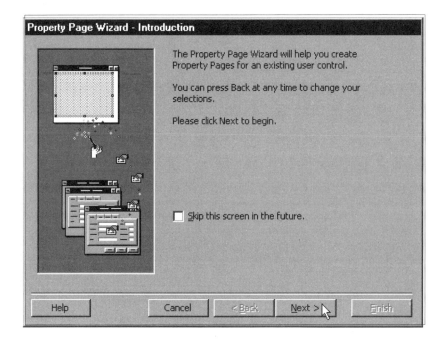

Click on the checkbox so you won't see this screen again. Then select **N**ext to proceed.

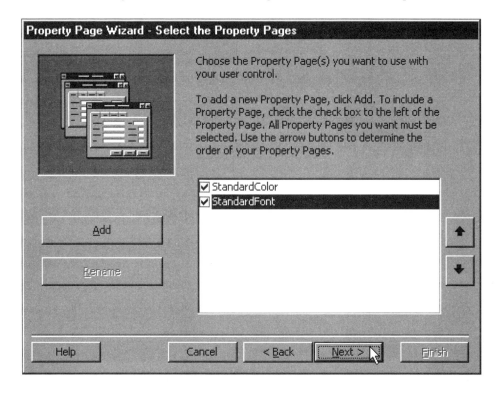

The wizard has detected that the stock properties **BackColor** and **Font** are already defined in our control. We actually added these with the ActiveX Control Interface Wizard the first time around. Leave these checkboxes set, and click on the **A**dd button since we want to define a general property page for our custom properties.

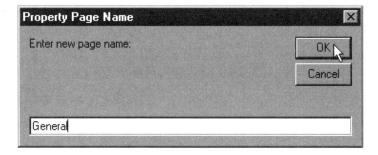

For our simple control, we'll just define a General page, which we'll use to display our custom members. If you're developing a more complicated control, it's worth defining several property pages, and splitting up your properties by category.

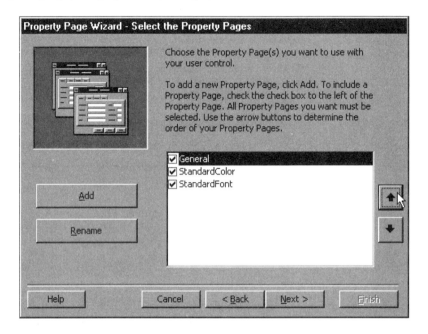

We want to make our General property page appear first in the tab sequence, so we move it up by selecting it and clicking on the 'Up' arrow to move it to the top of the list. Then click Next again.

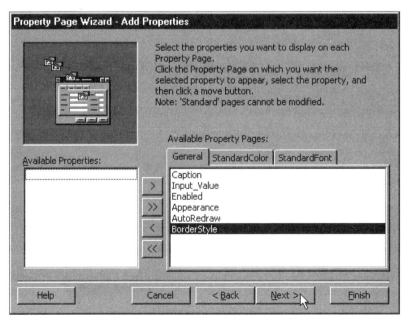

We now have the option of adding any or all of our properties to the appropriate property pages. The order of the properties on the property page is determined by the order in which they're added. Once all properties have been added as shown, select the Next button.

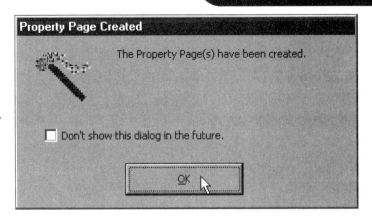

Our property pages have been created and we now get the chance to view a summary report.

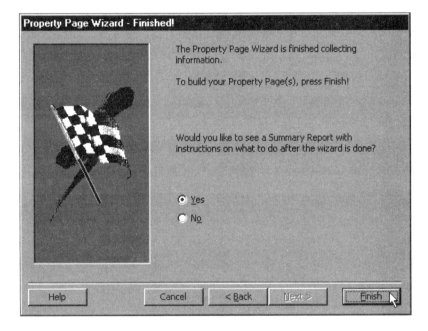

This summary report gives us information on how we can take the design and functionality further. For such a simple control, the property pages created are complete. However, this information can be useful where the control is sufficiently complex, and so we'll save a copy of the summary report for future viewing.

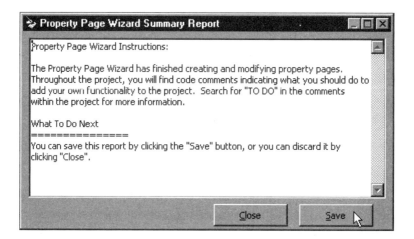

After the process of creating the property pages is complete, we can test them out by right-clicking on an instance of our control, and selecting the Properties menu item on the popup menu. Alternatively, we can choose the (Custom) property from the Properties Window and click on the button with the three dots.

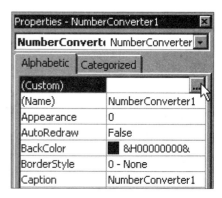

Here's what our property pages look like:

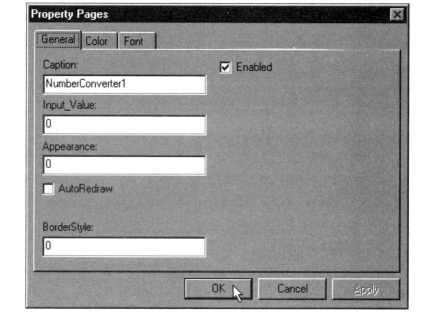

You'll notice that the wizard has taken into account the property *types* used in our control. For instance, the **Caption** property accepts string values and the **Enabled** property accepts a Boolean value—which is reflected by the use of a checkbox.

There is, in fact, one property missing from those we've defined for our control—the **Conversion_Mode** property. We've actually changed the type from **Integer** to the enumerated type **ConversionModeEnum**, but the wizard hasn't picked it up. The wizard is good at picking up *standard* types, but doesn't know how to deal with our *user-defined* types. Don't worry too much about this, because in later chapters we'll be looking at coding property pages by hand. In this way, we can add whatever functionality we desire.

Summary

As you've seen in the last couple of chapters, VB5 CCE makes creating controls relatively easy. However, there's still an inherent amount of work that we just can't get away from.

We've taken you through the whole process of creating a control. In the previous chapter, we used the ActiveX Control Interface Wizard to quickly knock out the basic shell of our control, and in this chapter we've shown how you proceed from there by adding your own custom functionality. We've also shown you how we can include other features in our control, such as adding property pages by using the Property Page Wizard.

The most important points in this chapter are:

- Controls are created, destroyed and recreated as we switch between design and run-time project environments.

- We can write code in the **InitProperties**, **WriteProperties** and **ReadProperties** events to ensure that data is saved and restored as controls are destroyed and recreated.

- By using the **Ambient** object, it's possible to access stock members that are always defined for standard controls.

- The **Extender** object provides information regarding the *container* rather than the control. This is very useful when you need your control to interact with its environment.

- Simple property pages can be put together very quickly using the Property Page Wizard, but this only works satisfactorily for properties using *basic* types. Property pages allow developers to access properties of a control through an alternative, more natural way than provided by the Properties window.

We'll build on this knowledge in the following chapters when we take you through the design and implementation of a variety of controls. In the next chapter, we'll go back and create a simple control from scratch, just to show you how quickly and easily this can be done once you know what's happening inside the control.

A Custom List Box Control

The previous three chapters have looked at what an ActiveX control is, and how VB5 CCE helps us to create them. We also took you steadily through the whole process of creating your first control. Chapter 1 talked about the three different kinds of ActiveX controls that you can create: simple controls, aggregate controls, and user-draw controls. In this chapter we'll go back to the first of the three types, to build a simple sub-classed control. And, as you'll see, we can knock out a control like this in a matter a few hours. Now that you appreciate the background and the terminology that's involved in creating controls, we'll spend more time on the mechanics of making the control do something useful.

Visual Basic programmers are provided with a number of ways to work with lists of information, including the ListBox, ListView and ComboBox controls. These controls make the programmer's job very easy when presenting lists of information to the user.

The primary limitation of these controls is that they become hard to use, from the user's viewpoint, when the lists of data become very long. Imagine a ListBox or ComboBox with over a thousand entries. The user can page down or use the mouse to scan the list, but this can be very awkward. It's true that if you set the list's **Sorted** property to **True**, the user can press the first letter of a word and jump to the first instance, but there may be hundreds of entries with that same first letter, so this hardly improves the situation.

Other environments have controls which allow the user to enter the first few characters of a word and then scroll the list to any matching entry. This allows the program to present hundreds or thousands of entries to a user in a simple but effective manner. The good news is that we can achieve the same effect by creating a new type of list box control as an ActiveX control. This is done by effectively subclassing the existing one. Then we can change its behavior to achieve exactly the effect we want, and use it just like a normal control in our applications. This is what we will do in this chapter.

So, you'll see how we:

- Decide on the requirements for our new control
- Design the way it will look and work
- Implement the design and build the control
- Test the final product to ensure it meets our original requirements

The first step, then, is to look at what our new control needs to achieve.

The Requirements for the Control

Let's start by laying out the requirements for our enhanced combo box control. To begin with, our control will allow the user to enter any number of characters and then search its list of items, looking for the first match. Obviously, our primary requirement is that the user can easily choose an entry from a large list of items. We are going to allow the user to enter any number of characters into our control, and have the control attempt to match those characters against the items in the list. We'll have it match from the beginning of each item, although you could easily change the control to match any part of the list entry that you wish.

We'll make our control similar in look and use to the standard ComboBox control. This will make things easier for both users and programmers, since they will be dealing with something that's already familiar. The easiest way to achieve this is to work from the ComboBox standard control itself. It already mixes the best of text entry with list management all in one control, and so we will just 'subclass' it within our control.

To make our control as easy as possible for developers to use, we should support an interface that's very similar to the standard ComboBox. This means that we'll want to expose the same set of properties, methods and events with which Visual Basic programmers are already familiar.

We also want to make the control more powerful where possible, so let's allow the developer to set a property indicating whether the user can enter an item that isn't found in the list of entries.

Lastly, we want our control to operate in as similar a way as possible to the ComboBox in the design and run-time environments. This will simplify things for our developers. To the end user, our control will appear just like a regular ComboBox—there are no visual cues to indicate that it has extended functionality. It isn't uncommon for controls to look the same and act differently throughout Windows applications, and so we won't alter the appearance of our control.

The Design of the Control

While we want to mimic the ComboBox control interface as much as possible, there are some properties, methods and events that we may not want, or be able, to carry over into our new control.

Appearance

In terms of general appearance, we need to design our control to look just like a normal ComboBox both at design time and at run time. The easiest way to do this is to actually use a ComboBox control inside our own control. This means that when we are designing our control we will physically place a ComboBox control from the Visual Basic toolbox into our custom control design window, and then base our custom control around that ComboBox, supplying the extra code which adds our custom functionality to that already provided by the ComboBox. The ComboBox is then considered to be a 'subcontrol', because it's really a subordinate part of our custom control.

Programming Interface

The normal ComboBox has a **Style** property which allows the programmer to decide on the appearance and behavior of the control. We'll set the **Style** property of the ComboBox when we add it to our control. Since we want to allow the user to enter text into the control, our **Style** setting will be **0 - Dropdown Combo**; the control will then allow text entry and also provide full ListBox functionality.

We will be relying on the ComboBox to provide events to trigger our code. However, when a ComboBox has a **Style** of **0**, the **Click** and **DblClick** events never fire, and so we can't support these events in our control.

There are other interface elements which are also inappropriate for our control, and we need to remove these. For instance, our control will not be a data bound control, and so the **DataSource**, **DataField** and **DataChanged** properties and methods don't make sense.

Custom controls created using Visual Basic CCE don't allow the programmer to change properties of subcontrols that are read-only at run time. This is because when a CCE-created control is in design time, all the subcontrols it contains are *running* inside it. Therefore, a number of properties in our control will be read-only at design time whereas they would be read-write at design time on the normal ComboBox. We will still support the properties as read-only so that we can maintain as much compatibility with the original control as possible.

One property we will *add* to our control is the **LimitToList** property. This property will allow a developer to tell our control whether or not the user can enter text values which don't match any of the items in the list.

So in the end, our control will have the following interface.

Properties:

Appearance	BackColor	Container	DragIcon	DragMode
Enabled	Font	FontBold	FontItalic	FontName
FontSize	FontStrikethru	FontUnderline	ForeColor	Height
HelpContextID	hWnd	Index	ItemData	Left
LimitToList	List	ListCount	ListIndex	Locked
MouseIcon	MousePointer	Name	NewIndex	Parent
SelLength	SelStart	SelText	Sorted	Style
TabIndex	TabStop	Tag	Text	ToolTipText
Top	TopIndex	Visible	WhatsThisHelpID	Width

Methods:

AddItem	Clear	Drag	Move	Refresh
RemoveItem	SetFocus	ShowWhatsThis	ZOrder	

Events:

Change	DragDrop	DragOver	DropDown	GotFocus
KeyDown	KeyPress	KeyUp	LostFocus	

Implementing the Control

Now that we know what we want our control to do, and we've determined how it will look and feel, we can move on to creating it.

Creating the Control

First, we need to bring up CCE and open a new ActiveX Control project.

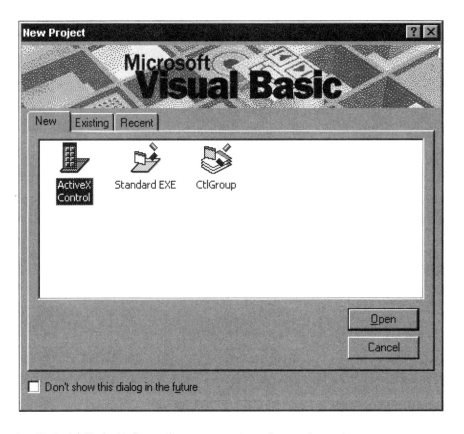

Using the Project | Project1 Properties menu option, change the project name to WComboBoxControl.

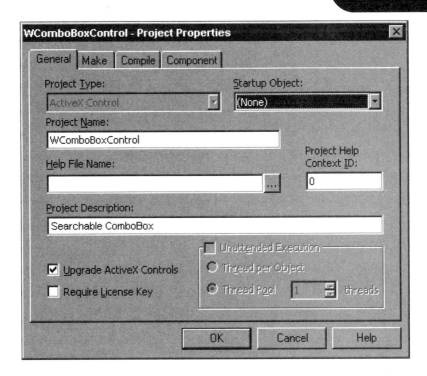

While we're here, let's also make the Project Description read 'Searchable ComboBox'. This description will show up in the Component list and Object Browser, providing a more readable description of our control.

Next, in the Project window, click on UserControl1 to select it. Now click on the (Name) property in the Properties - UserControl1 window and type **WComboBox**. This is the control name that will be seen by developers who use our control in their projects.

Adding a ComboBox

Now that we have the basics set up, let's add a ComboBox control to our custom control. Just double click on the ComboBox icon in the toolbox to add a ComboBox control.

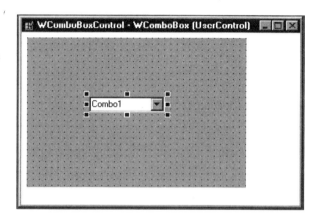

We won't worry about where it appears in the design window, as we'll be repositioning and re-sizing the ComboBox within the code. We want it to respond to the programmer just like a regular ComboBox control, and so we'll need to create some code to handle that requirement.

First though, let's give the ComboBox a decent name and set up the control's properties.

Click on the (Name) property in the **Properties - Combo1** window and type **cboCombo**. This will be the name we'll use for this control. The ComboBox we've added is *inside* our control. Since we are defining our control's programming interface, our ComboBox subcontrol won't be directly accessible to a programmer unless we allow it. They will only see **WComboBox**, the name of our control.

The ActiveX Control Interface Wizard

Before we add any of our own code, we will use the ActiveX Control Interface Wizard which largely automates the process of adding properties, methods and events to our custom control. You saw this wizard used in Chapter 2. The wizard won't do everything for us, but it will at least create the skeleton of our interface.

To bring up the wizard, choose the **Add-Ins I ActiveX Control Property Wizard** menu option. The first panel of the wizard is an introduction containing an overview of the wizard's capabilities. Read this, then click on the **Next** button to move on.

This next panel is where the real fun begins. The wizard has already made a number of guesses about the interface for our control. Most of them are fine, though there are a few where it guessed wrong.

98

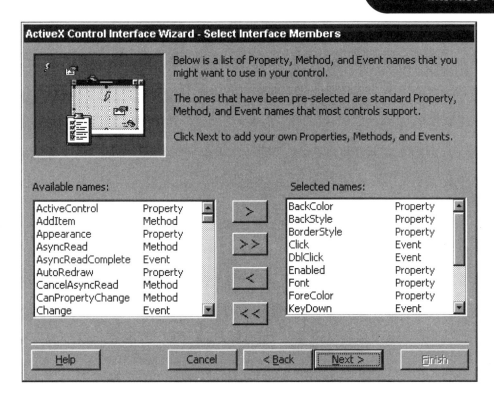

On the left, the wizard automatically lists all of the available properties, methods and events from the user control itself and from any subcontrols we've added to our user control. In this case, it has added all the interface elements for our ComboBox subcontrol.

Off to the right, the wizard lists all the properties, methods and events which it will include in the final control. To start, the wizard creates a default list of items that are typical in most controls. This is the list we need to modify, removing those items we don't want and adding those that we need.

Removing Unnecessary Properties

Let's start by trimming out the properties that we know we don't want. The wizard's default list contains some interface elements which are not appropriate for our control. In particular, there are some elements which aren't supported by a normal ComboBox control with its **Style** property set to **0**:

BackStyle   **BorderStyle**   **Click**   **DblClick**   **MouseDown**
MouseMove   **MouseUp**

To remove an item from the list, select it and then click the '<' button.

Adding Custom Properties

Once these are removed, we can add in the missing interface elements from the left-hand list. The ones we need to add are those that are specifically supported by the ComboBox control, so we can have an interface that matches as closely as possible:

AddItem	Appearance	Change	Clear	DropDown
FontBold	FontItalic	FontName	FontSize	FontStrikethru
FontUnderline	hWnd	ItemData	List	ListCount
ListIndex	Locked	MouseIcon	MousePointer	NewIndex
RemoveItem	SelLength	SelStart	SelText	Sorted
Style	Text	ToolTipText	TopIndex	
WhatsThisHelpID				

To add an item to the list, select the item and click the '>' button.

The LimitToList Property

At this point, we have all the normal properties, methods and events we will support for our control. We still need to add our new **LimitToList** property, so that the programmer can instruct our control to only allow the user to enter items that are in the list. Since this is an entirely new property, it's not in the list on the left, and so we'll have to add it ourselves.

Clicking on the Next button will bring us to the next panel of the wizard, which provides a way to add our new property.

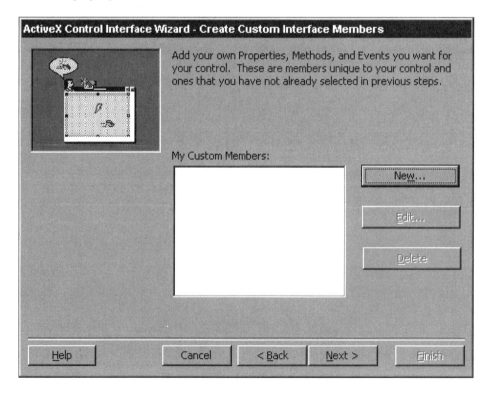

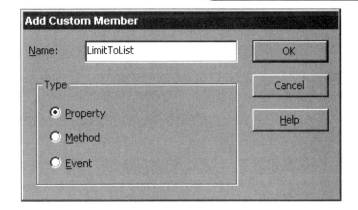

Clicking on the New... button will allow us to add our **LimitToList** property:

We can, of course, add as many properties, methods or events as we need.

Mapping the Interface

The next panel in the wizard lets us map our properties, methods and events to our control or subcontrols. Mapping means that we tell the wizard to automatically make each property, method or event be handled by a property, method or event which is supported directly by our control, or our ComboBox subcontrol.

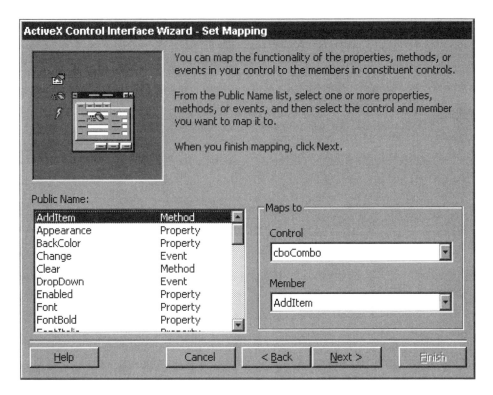

In our control, the entire interface will be mapped to **cboCombo** except for the **LimitToList** property, which we'll talk about later. Since **cboCombo** doesn't have a matching **LimitToList** property, we can't map this property to the subcontrol. The wizard helps us out here, in that custom interface elements aren't even listed on this panel.

Since we want our entire interface to be mapped to our ComboBox control, we can use a shortcut technique on this panel. Select all the items in the list on the left, then click in the Control box on the right and choose **cboCombo**. The wizard will automatically map all the items to the properties, methods and events from **cboCombo** since they all have the same name.

You can check this by clicking on any item in the Public Name list—the Member box shows that each property, event or method is mapped to the **cboCombo**'s property, event or method of the same name.

> *This technique can be very useful to identify which interface elements are supported by a given subcontrol. You can do a global mapping, and then arrow down through the items in the* Public Name *list. If any of the items in the list have no corresponding match in your subcontrol, they will show up as being mapped to* Control '(None)' *with the Member field being blank.*

Setting Attributes

All of the properties, methods and events that we mapped in this last panel are pretty much done at this point: the wizard will see to that. However, the wizard still needs information about any elements that aren't mapped (in this case our **LimitToList** property).

In particular, the wizard needs to know the data type of our property, what its default value will be and whether it is read-write, write-only, read-only or unavailable at both design and run time.

We can also specify a description for the property. This description will be used in the various help windows and browsers throughout CCE's IDE.

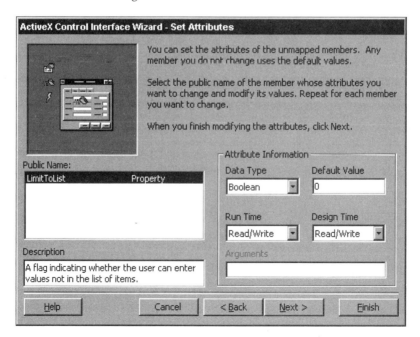

Wrapping up the Wizard

Clicking Next will bring us to the final panel of the wizard.

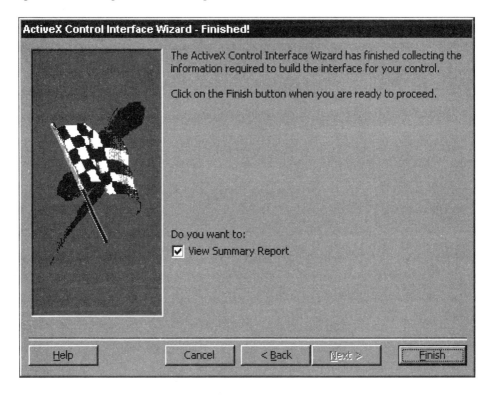

At this point, we are all done with the wizard and can move on. It will take a while when you click the Finish button, as the wizard will generate all the code to manage our control's interface and insert that code into our control's code window.

You may choose to view the summary report, which will give a list of activities you should perform at this time. We will walk through those activities in the remainder of this chapter. At this stage you should make sure to save your control.

Looking at the Code

If you open the control's code window, you'll see that it's full of wizard-generated code. The wizard has created code so that each property, method and event of our control's interface is automatically passed through to the **cboCombo** subcontrol to be processed.

It uses the **Event** keyword to declare the events that our control will support:

```
'Event Declarations:
Event KeyDown(KeyCode As Integer, Shift As Integer)
'MappingInfo=cboCombo,cboCombo,-1,KeyDown
Event KeyPress(KeyAscii As Integer) 'MappingInfo=cboCombo,cboCombo,-
1,KeyPress
Event KeyUp(KeyCode As Integer, Shift As Integer)
```

103

```
            'MappingInfo=cboCombo,cboCombo,-1,KeyUp
     Event Change() 'MappingInfo=cboCombo,cboCombo,-1,Change
     Event DropDown() 'MappingInfo=cboCombo,cboCombo,-1,DropDown
```

The wizard also creates code for each property that our control will support. The code for the **ForeColor** property is listed here as an example. Notice how the property is actually set, and retrieved, directly from the underlying **cboCombo** control. Each of our control's properties is actually handled by the **cboCombo** control with the exception of the **LimitToList** property, which we'll show next.

```
'WARNING! DO NOT REMOVE OR MODIFY THE FOLLOWING COMMENTED LINES!
'MappingInfo=cboCombo,cboCombo,-1,ForeColor
Public Property Get ForeColor() As OLE_COLOR
   ForeColor = cboCombo.ForeColor
End Property

Public Property Let ForeColor(ByVal New_ForeColor As OLE_COLOR)
   cboCombo.ForeColor() = New_ForeColor
   PropertyChanged "ForeColor"
End Property
```

Note the call to the **PropertyChanged** method in the **Property Let** routine. This method is important, as it notifies the environment (probably the Visual Basic IDE), that the property value has changed—so any displays, such as the Properties window, can be updated. This method is also very important when creating data bound controls, as discussed later in the book.

The **LimitToList** property is a custom property which isn't supported by the normal ComboBox control. As a result of this, **cboCombo** can't be used to manage this property, and so the code is somewhat different.

The wizard creates a local constant to hold the property's default value and it declares a module level variable to hold the current value of the property:

```
'Default Property Values:
Const m_def_LimitToList = 0
'Property Variables:
Dim m_LimitToList As Boolean
```

In the **UserControl_InitProperties** procedure, the wizard adds code to set the custom property's initial value to the default defined above:

```
'Initialize Properties for User Control
Private Sub UserControl_InitProperties()
   m_LimitToList = m_def_LimitToList
End Sub
```

The actual code to manage the property simply maintains the appropriate module level variable. We'll discuss, later, how to use the value within our code to implement the desired functionality.

```
Public Property Get LimitToList() As Boolean
   LimitToList = m_LimitToList
End Property

Public Property Let LimitToList(ByVal New_LimitToList As Boolean)
   m_LimitToList = New_LimitToList
```

104

```
        PropertyChanged "LimitToList"
    End Property
```

Like the properties, all the methods are implemented to pass any call to our control's method directly to **cboCombo** by calling the method of the same name. The **Refresh** method is shown here as an example:

```
'WARNING! DO NOT REMOVE OR MODIFY THE FOLLOWING COMMENTED LINES!
'MappingInfo=cboCombo,cboCombo,-1,Refresh
Public Sub Refresh()
    cboCombo.Refresh
End Sub
```

In a similar fashion, the wizard passes all the events raised by **cboCombo** up through our control for use by the programmer. This is done using the **RaiseEvent** method, as shown below:

```
Private Sub cboCombo_Change()
    RaiseEvent Change
End Sub
```

When programmers use controls, they typically set various properties of the controls at design time. If they save the project and bring it back up later, they will usually expect that those design-time properties will have the same values that they entered earlier.

The wizard creates two routines to support this functionality, **UserControl_ReadProperties** and **UserControl_WriteProperties**. An example of these routines is shown below. We'll need to make some changes to these routines as well, but that's covered later in the chapter.

```
'Load property values from storage
Private Sub UserControl_ReadProperties(PropBag As PropertyBag)

    cboCombo.ForeColor = PropBag.ReadProperty("ForeColor", &H80000008)
    cboCombo.Enabled = PropBag.ReadProperty("Enabled", True)
    Set Font = PropBag.ReadProperty("Font", Ambient.Font)
    m_LimitToList = PropBag.ReadProperty("LimitToList", m_def_LimitToList)
End Sub
```

```
'Write property values to storage
Private Sub UserControl_WriteProperties(PropBag As PropertyBag)

    Call PropBag.WriteProperty("ForeColor", cboCombo.ForeColor, &H80000008)
    Call PropBag.WriteProperty("Enabled", cboCombo.Enabled, True)
    Call PropBag.WriteProperty("Font", Font, Ambient.Font)
    Call PropBag.WriteProperty("LimitToList", m_LimitToList, m_def_LimitToList)
End Sub
```

Handling the TO DO Items

The wizard does a very good job, but it isn't perfect. We still need to go through and fix some of the code where it's incorrect. The wizard has left a few **TO DO** notes as comments in the code. If you search for 'TO DO:' you'll get right to them.

Properties Not Available at Design Time

When we mapped our properties to the **cboCombo** subcontrol, we included a number of properties which are available at run time but aren't supposed to be available at design time. Unfortunately, the wizard doesn't properly generate code to handle these properties. Worse still, there's no easy way to know which properties these are, and so you'll need to manually compare your control's properties to those of the regular ComboBox to identify the ones to change.

So the first thing we need to do is rewrite the code which handles the properties that should be unavailable at design time. We will use the **ListIndex** property as an example. The code generated by the wizard looks like this:

```
'WARNING! DO NOT REMOVE OR MODIFY THE FOLLOWING COMMENTED LINES!
'MappingInfo=cboCombo,cboCombo,-1,ListIndex
Public Property Get ListIndex() As Integer
  ListIndex = cboCombo.ListIndex
End Property

Public Property Let ListIndex(ByVal New_ListIndex As Integer)
  cboCombo.ListIndex() = New_ListIndex
  PropertyChanged "ListIndex"
End Property
```

The **Property Get** code is fine. It simply passes the **ListIndex** value from **cboCombo** out to the program that called our property. However, the **Property Let** code needs to be changed to reflect the design time status of this property. We'll check the **Ambient** object's **UserMode** property to find if the control is in run-time or design-time. If it returns **False**, we know we are in design time—and so we return an error.

```
If Ambient.UserMode = False Then Err.Raise 382
```

Error 382 is 'Set not supported at runtime'. This is the value the wizard uses if you create a custom property through the wizard and indicate that it is not available at design time.

Using this technique, we can change the **Property Let** to look like this:

```
Public Property Let ListIndex(ByVal New_ListIndex As Integer)
  If Ambient.UserMode = False Then Err.Raise 382
  cboCombo.ListIndex = New_ListIndex
End Property
```

This way, when the IDE tries to work with the property in design mode, the property will return an error, and the IDE will not display it in the list of properties.

Note that we also removed the line:

```
PropertyChanged "ListIndex"
```

Since this property is not available at design time, and since our control is not a data bound control, we don't need to notify our environment that the value has changed.

The following properties need to have these same changes made to their **Property Let** routines:

FontBold	FontItalic	FontName	FontSize
FontStrikethru	FontUnderline	SelLength	SelStart
SelText	ListIndex	TopIndex	

As we discussed earlier, the wizard has also added code so that our control will automatically save its design-time state and restore that state. Visual Basic stores this information in the FRX file associated with the form that's using our control. Other products which utilize ActiveX controls may store this information elsewhere.

This code is stored in two procedures, **UserControl_ReadProperties** and **UserControl_WriteProperties**. Properties which aren't available at design time shouldn't be saved or restored in this manner, since they can't be affected during the design process. However, the wizard puts the code in regardless. The following lines of code in the **UserControl_ReadProperties** routine retrieve the unneeded values, and can be removed:

```
cboCombo.FontBold = PropBag.ReadProperty("FontBold", 0)
cboCombo.FontItalic = PropBag.ReadProperty("FontItalic", 0)
cboCombo.FontName = PropBag.ReadProperty("FontName", "")
cboCombo.FontSize = PropBag.ReadProperty("FontSize", 0)
cboCombo.FontStrikethru = PropBag.ReadProperty("FontStrikethru", 0)
cboCombo.FontUnderline = PropBag.ReadProperty("FontUnderline", 0)
cboCombo.ListIndex = PropBag.ReadProperty("ListIndex", 0)
cboCombo.SelLength = PropBag.ReadProperty("SelLength", 0)
cboCombo.SelStart = PropBag.ReadProperty("SelStart", 0)
cboCombo.SelText = PropBag.ReadProperty("SelText", "")
cboCombo.TopIndex = PropBag.ReadProperty("TopIndex", 0)
```

And in the **UserControl_WriteProperties** routine there are matching lines of code to save the values. These, too, can be removed.

```
Call PropBag.WriteProperty("FontBold", cboCombo.FontBold, 0)
Call PropBag.WriteProperty("FontItalic", cboCombo.FontItalic, 0)
Call PropBag.WriteProperty("FontName", cboCombo.FontName, "")
Call PropBag.WriteProperty("FontSize", cboCombo.FontSize, 0)
Call PropBag.WriteProperty("FontStrikethru", cboCombo.FontStrikethru, 0)
Call PropBag.WriteProperty("FontUnderline", cboCombo.FontUnderline, 0)
Call PropBag.WriteProperty("ListIndex", cboCombo.ListIndex, 0)
Call PropBag.WriteProperty("SelLength", cboCombo.SelLength, 0)
Call PropBag.WriteProperty("SelStart", cboCombo.SelStart, 0)
Call PropBag.WriteProperty("SelText", cboCombo.SelText, "")
Call PropBag.WriteProperty("TopIndex", cboCombo.TopIndex, 0)
```

Property Arrays

The wizard doesn't know how to handle properties which are property arrays. In our case, this means the **ItemData** and **List** properties. The actual property code is generated, but the **UserControl_ReadProperties** and **UserControl_WriteProperties** routines are not fully created. Instead, the wizard puts some **TO DO** comments in these routines.

The **TO DO** code for the **UserControl_ReadProperties** routine is listed below.

```
'TO DO: The member you have mapped to contains an array of data.
'    You must supply the code to persist the array.  A prototype
'    line is shown next:
```

107

```
    cboCombo.ItemData(Index) = PropBag.ReadProperty("ItemData" & Index, 0)
'TO DO: The member you have mapped to contains an array of data.
'   You must supply the code to persist the array.  A prototype
'   line is shown next:
    cboCombo.List(Index) = PropBag.ReadProperty("List" & Index, "")
```

As you can see, there are **TO DO** comments above both the `ItemData` and `List` entries, with instructions about how to read in the values for these properties.

In our case, we don't need to worry about this. Neither the `ItemData` nor `List` properties can be altered at design time and so we don't need to save or restore them in these routines.

This means that we can remove the above code from the `UserControl_ReadProperties`, and we can remove the following code from the `UserControl_WriteProperties` routine:

```
'TO DO: The member you have mapped to contains an array of data.
'   You must supply the code to persist the array.  A prototype
'   line is shown next:
    Call PropBag.WriteProperty("ItemData" & Index, cboCombo.ItemData(Index), 0)
'TO DO: The member you have mapped to contains an array of data.
'   You must supply the code to persist the array.  A prototype
'   line is shown next:
    Call PropBag.WriteProperty("List" & Index, cboCombo.List(Index), "")
```

Adding Our Own Code

OK, we've put together the shell of our control. At this point, we have a user control which is essentially just a subset of the normal ComboBox control, with no extra functionality at all. In fact, we've given up some functionality, since our control won't allow a programmer to change any of the normal ComboBox properties which are read-only at run time: as we discussed earlier, they can't be changed within a custom control created using Visual Basic CCE.

Getting Things Right at Design Time

The wizard did almost all of our work for us in terms of setting up the control's interface and general behavior. However, there is one key piece of functionality that we need to add so that our control will resize properly at design time.

User controls are normally resized independently of any subcontrols they may contain. This means that changing the size of our custom control doesn't change any underlying subcontrols.

In our case, however, we want our WComboBox control to resize just like the regular ComboBox control. This is as simple as adding some code into the `UserControl_Resize` event routine.

```
Private Sub UserControl_Resize()
  If Height <> cboCombo.Height Then _
     Height = cboCombo.Height
  cboCombo.Move 0, 0, ScaleWidth
End Sub
```

This will keep our control's height the same as the ComboBox subcontrol (since that control has a fixed height). It will also make sure that the ComboBox control stretches to the same width as our user control. To the programmer, our control will appear to work just like a regular ComboBox.

Adding the Basic Features

Now let's add our own new features to make this control useful. First of all, we need to create a routine to search through the list of items in the control to find a match. While this can be done most efficiently with some API calls, we'll stick with regular VB code in this case for simplicity.

The following routine takes whatever text is currently in the control and uses it as search criteria against the items in the list. As soon as it finds a match, it sets the control's **ListIndex** property to the matching item and quits searching. We use the **StrComp** function to provide case-insensitive searching through the list.

As we'll discuss later, this routine will be called from **cboCombo**'s **Change** event so that a new match will be found each time the user presses a key.

```
Private Sub FindItem()
   Dim lIdx As Long
   Dim sText As String
   Dim lLen As Long

   sText = cboCombo.Text
   lLen = Len(sText)
   For lIdx = 0 To cboCombo.ListCount
      If StrComp(sText, Left$(cboCombo.List(lIdx), lLen), vbTextCompare) = 0 Then
         cboCombo.ListIndex = lIdx
         Exit For
      End If
   Next lIdx
End Sub
```

We'll use this simple routine as a base to build from. As we incorporate it into our actual control we'll have to add a few more features to the routine to make everything work the way we want. For now, let's add this code to our control's code window.

Selecting the Event

As the user enters text into the control, we'll want to invoke the **FindItem** routine. Since **FindItem** searches are based on the text in the control, we'll put our call into the **cboCombo_Change** event. This event fires after any text that the user has entered has been put into the control, and so it seems perfect.

```
Private Sub cboCombo_Change()
   FindItem
   RaiseEvent Change
End Sub
```

We'll leave the **RaiseEvent** call in the routine. This call passes the event up for use by the programmer, and so even though we've done some processing here, we are still enabling the programmer to react to the change event as well.

If you've worked with VB much, you'll notice right away that we've introduced a bug. Setting the **ListIndex** property in our **FindItem** routine will cause another **Change** event to fire in a recursive loop.

109

To overcome this problem, we'll add this code to the General Declarations section of the module:

```
'true if FindItem is running
Private bFinding As Boolean
```

We'll use this variable in both the **FindItem** and **Change** event code to avoid the recursive loop:

```
Private Sub FindItem()
  Dim lIdx As Long
  Dim sText As String
  Dim lLen As Long

  bFinding = True
  sText = cboCombo.Text
  lLen = Len(sText)
  For lIdx = 0 To cboCombo.ListCount
    If StrComp(sText, Left$(cboCombo.List(lIdx), lLen), vbTextCompare) = 0 Then
      cboCombo.ListIndex = lIdx
      Exit For
    End If
  Next lIdx
  bFinding = False
End Sub

Private Sub cboCombo_Change()
  If bFinding Then Exit Sub
  FindItem
  RaiseEvent Change
End Sub
```

Note that **FindItem** relies on the contents of the text in the control as criteria. At the same time, we want the user to be able to enter text just by normal typing. Unfortunately, **FindItem** selects items from the list, thus actually changing the content of the text that the user is typing.

We need to make sure the user's cursor location in the text is preserved. As well as that, we want to select all the text from the cursor to the end of the line—so that text is removed when the user presses another key. This will allow the user to enter a series of characters without needing any extra keystrokes, while our control does a match each time a character is entered.

All of this can be handled from our **FindItem** routine with the addition of a few lines of code. First, we will store the original cursor position within the text. We'll store this in a module level variable by adding the following code to the General Declarations section:

```
'current cursor position within the text
Private lPos As Long
```

We'll see why this needs to be a module level variable later in the chapter.

After we've done our match, we'll reset the cursor position back to that spot. Finally, we'll use the **SelLength** method to highlight all the text to the right of the cursor.

```
Private Sub FindItem()
  Dim lIdx As Long
  Dim sText As String
```

```
    Dim lLen As Long

    bFinding = True
    lPos = cboCombo.SelStart
    sText = cboCombo.Text
    lLen = Len(sText)
    For lIdx = 0 To cboCombo.ListCount
       If StrComp(sText, Left$(cboCombo.List(lIdx), lLen), vbTextCompare) = 0 Then
          cboCombo.ListIndex = lIdx
          Exit For
       End If
    Next lIdx
    cboCombo.SelStart = lPos
    cboCombo.SelLength = Len(cboCombo.Text)
    bFinding = False
End Sub
```

We also need to handle the special case where there is no text in the field at all. We'll add that code to the **Change** event. Note that here we are using the module level **lPos** variable declared earlier. We need to maintain the cursor position both in this routine and in the **FindItem** routine.

```
Private Sub cboCombo_Change()
    If bFinding Then Exit Sub
    If Len(cboCombo.Text) = 0 Then
       lPos = 0
    Else
       FindItem
    End If
    RaiseEvent Change
End Sub
```

If you try this code, you'll see that everything works except for one thing. When the *Backspace* key is pressed, it just removes the selected text, leaving **FindItem** to match the same exact entry and fill it in.

> *You can test this code by adding the control to a form and running it. See the end of this chapter for more details*

This behavior isn't surprising. Typically, when text is highlighted and the user presses *Backspace*, the highlighted text is removed without removing any other text. Unfortunately, in our case, this renders the *Backspace* key entirely useless. We actually want *Backspace* to not only remove the highlighted text, but also to remove the character immediately to the left of the cursor, so that **FindItem** repeats the search it did before the user typed the last character.

To solve this problem, we'll capture this key in the **cboCombo_KeyPress** event and remove the highlighted text ourselves. Then pressing *Backspace* will remove the character the user intended, and **FindItem** can make a more intelligent match.

```
Private Sub cboCombo_KeyPress(KeyAscii As Integer)
    If KeyAscii = 8 Then
       bFinding = True
       cboCombo.SelText = ""
       bFinding = False
    End If
    RaiseEvent KeyPress(KeyAscii)
End Sub
```

111

The final bit of code we need to add handles our **LimitToList** property. If this property is set to true, we need to prevent the user from entering any value that isn't found in the list of items in our control.

The first thing we need to do is track the **ListIndex** value of the last item we found. We'll add the following code to the General Declarations section to store this value.

```
'index value of the last item selected
Private lIndex As Long
```

This code will go into the **FindItem** routine, so if that routine doesn't find a match it can reset the value to the previous state.

```
Private Sub FindItem()
  Dim lIdx As Long
  Dim sText As String
  Dim lLen As Long
  Dim bFound As Boolean

  bFinding = True
  lPos = cboCombo.SelStart
  sText = cboCombo.Text
  lLen = Len(sText)
  bFound = False
  For lIdx = 0 To cboCombo.ListCount
    If StrComp(sText, Left$(cboCombo.List(lIdx), lLen), vbTextCompare) = 0 Then
      cboCombo.ListIndex = lIdx
      bFound = True
      Exit For
    End If
  Next lIdx
  If m_LimitToList And Not bFound Then
    cboCombo.ListIndex = lIndex
    If lIndex = -1 Then cboCombo.Text = ""
    cboCombo.SelStart = lPos - 1
  Else
    cboCombo.SelStart = lPos
    lIndex = cboCombo.ListIndex
  End If
  cboCombo.SelLength = Len(cboCombo.Text)
  bFinding = False
End Sub
```

Then, in the **Change** event, we'll add a line to set the **ListIndex** value to **-1** if there is no text in the field. A **ListIndex** of **-1** indicates that no item is selected from the list.

```
Private Sub cboCombo_Change()
  If bFinding Then Exit Sub
  If Len(cboCombo.Text) = 0 Then
    lPos = 0
    lIndex = -1
  Else
    FindItem
  End If
  RaiseEvent Change
End Sub
```

Also, we'll need to initialize the **lIndex** module level variable; so we'll put that code into the **UserControl_Initialize** routine. By setting the index to **-1**, we are indicating that no item is selected from the list.

```
Private Sub UserControl_Initialize()
   lIndex = -1
End Sub
```

UserControl_Initialize is always the first event fired in a control. It indicates that the client program has created an instance of our control and that they may continue to work with it. This is a good place to initialize internal variables and generally get the control ready for use.

At this point, between the wizard, our **FindItem** routine, and the changes to **cboCombo_Change** and **cboCombo_KeyPress**, we have implemented all the functionality for our new control.

Setting the Bitmap Shown in the Toolbox

To add some polish to our control, we'll want to set the toolbox bitmap so that developers who use our control can easily identify it. This is an easy process, as we saw in Chapter 2. All we need to do is set a property in the control's Properties window.

In the Project Explorer window click on the **WComboBox** control item. This will bring up the properties for our control. Scroll down in the Properties window until you can see the **ToolboxBitmap** property. The diagram below shows this property with a bitmap already loaded.

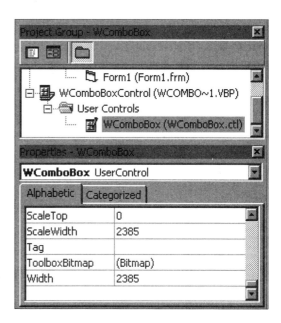

Double clicking on this property will bring up a standard File Open dialog window. Now we just need to choose a bitmap to for the toolbox.

You can choose any bitmap which is about the right size to fit on the toolbox. The size of a bitmap displayed on the toolbox is 16x15 pixels. If you choose a bitmap of another size it will automatically be scaled to fit into this size.

113

Compiling the Control

We are now ready to compile the control and move on to testing it. To make the control, just choose the File | Make WComboBox.ocx menu option. You will be presented with a standard dialog window where you can choose the directory and final file name for your control.

The file name you choose is important. The process of making the control will not only compile it, but will also make the necessary Windows registry entries so that other programs can use your control. To change the file name after the fact will require you to unregister the control, rename the file and then reregister the control.

> *Of course it is possible to just go change the file name and then register the control under the new name. This is a bad practice however, as it may leave invalid entries in your registry.*

You must compile the control before you can move on to test it or use it in any other programs.

Testing the Control

Basic testing of our control is very simple. We'll just add another project into the CCE environment, add a form, and use our control.

Adding a Project

Without closing the control project, choose the File | Add Project menu option. Choose the Standard EXE option and click Open.

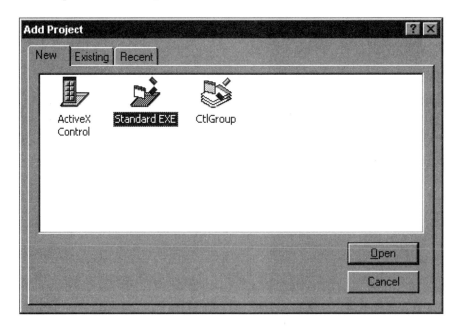

This will add a new project to our project group. As this is a new project, CCE will automatically add a form for us.

If you look in the Project Explorer window, you'll see that Project1 is now listed along with our control project. Also, the Project1 project is listed in bold to indicate that it's the startup project in this group. CCE did this automatically, since a control project can't be a startup project—whereas a Standard EXE project can.

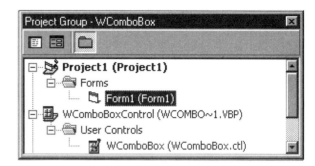

Adding a ComboBox Control

We'll put a regular ComboBox control on our test form just for comparison with our new control. Simply add a label and a ComboBox control as shown here:

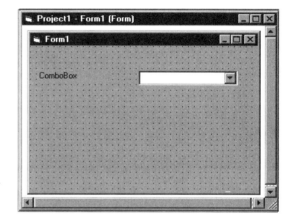

The ComboBox will be named **Combo1** by default and we'll just leave that alone. You should blank out the **Text** property on the control so that it starts out blank when we run the project.

Adding Two WComboBox Controls

Our control can be added in exactly the same way as a standard control. The bitmap you added should be visible on the toolbox—if it's grayed out, check that you've closed the control's design window. You need to do this before you can use the control.

115

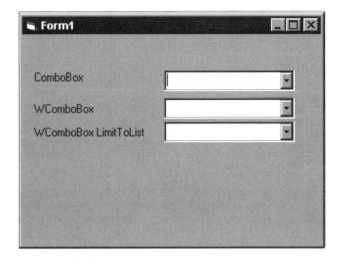

Add two WComboBox controls to the form. Then add a couple of labels to make your form look like this:

Our two new controls should be called **WComboBox1** and **WComboBox2** by default. These names are automatically derived from the **Name** property we used for our control. We'll leave these names for the moment.

Now click on the bottom one of the two new controls, and change its **LimitToList** property value to True in the Properties window. This will allow us to test whether the control does in fact prevent the user from entering values not in our list.

Our Test Code

Now that we have a simple test form set up, let's add some code to populate the three controls. To get a decent set of test data, while at the same time avoiding a lot of typing, we'll generate a few hundred random strings for each control by putting the following code in the **Form_Load** event:

```
Private Sub Form_Load()
  Dim Index As Long
  Dim LenIndex As Long
  Dim lLen As Long
  Dim sText As String

  For Index = 1 To 300
    lLen = Rnd * 10 + 1
    sText = ""
    For LenIndex = 1 To lLen
      sText = sText & Chr$(Rnd * 25 + 65)
    Next LenIndex
    Combo1.AddItem sText
    WComboBox1.AddItem sText
    WComboBox2.AddItem sText
  Next Index
End Sub
```

If you try to compile your project, you'll notice that the File-Make menu option is disabled, though you can still run your program within the Visual Basic CCE environment. This is because CCE is intended entirely for making controls. The ability to create other types of projects is only present so that you can test your controls.

We can now press *F5* to run the project, and from here, we can test our control.

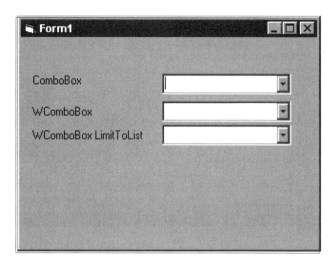

The program's form should come up looking like this:

First, let's try just entering a single character into each control. In the following example we just entered 'A'.

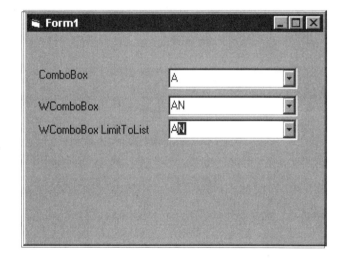

You can see how the normal ComboBox did nothing special, but our new control found a match and displayed it. Since the focus is still in the last control, you can see how the text to the right of the cursor is highlighted.

Now try entering a series of characters into each control. In the example shown below, we have just tried to enter four 'X' characters into each control. Of course, since the list items are random, your results may vary slightly.

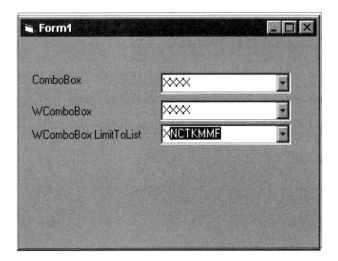

Notice how the last control limited our entry to the items in the list, while the first two controls just let us enter a value with no match.

Summary

In this chapter, we've seen how quickly and easily the combination of a single subclassed control, ActiveX Control Interface Wizard, and a little extra code of our own, can produce a useful working control. We won't be showing you this wizard again, but bear in mind that where we have existing controls included in our new controls, we would generally use it to create the shell for the control.

The important points to note about this chapter are:

- You can subclass existing controls and then add extra code to extend their functionality
- When designing new controls, decide on the requirements up front
- The ActiveX Control Interface Wizard can be used to quickly and easily create the shell for a new control.
- New controls can easily be tested by adding another project

This is the first of the three basic types of control that we outlined in Chapter 1. It wraps up a single control into a new ActiveX Control object that can be used just like any other control. In the next chapter, you'll see how we can aggregate more than one constituent control into a new ActiveX Control object, and arrange for all of them to work together within the single control.

An Aggregate Address Control

Building simple controls that encompass and expand on the features of a single control is a useful technique, and these types of controls are often the most flexible and reusable. Although only a relatively small programming effort is saved by using simple controls, these small savings add up over time, and so the use of such controls will always be popular. However, simple controls only provide small building blocks, and as such can be compared to writing small reusable generic routines.

In this chapter, we'll be talking about packaging several standard controls together to form a more complex aggregate control—a process generally referred to as **aggregation**. Larger and more complex controls have an inherently greater functionality to offer client applications. This means that more work is saved each time the control is used. However, as the control becomes more specialized in its task, it's more likely that it will only be applicable to applications with specific functionality requirements.

We'll create an Address control to illustrate the principles involved in aggregation. So, in this chapter we'll show you how to:

 Determine the features our aggregate component will provide

 Design and implement the appearance that the control will display

 Design the component interface—that is, the properties, methods, and events provided by the control

By the end of the chapter we'll have a nice simple control that we can reuse in any Visual Basic 4 or 5 project, as well as in an HTML document. However, before we get too wound up in the intricacies of the control, we'll talk about the process of control aggregation in general.

The Aggregation Process

Aggregation is the process of building complex controls out of simpler, standard controls. At the end of the process, we end up with a control that requires a moderate programming effort to implement in the first place, but can save a great deal of programming when the control is used in projects.

You can see that there's a relationship between the complexity and reusability of the control—the more work that is involved with creating the control in the first place, the more work that you're likely to save each time the control is used in another project. And, of course, there's nothing stopping us using other custom ActiveX controls that we've already created to make a more complex control.

So, what do we have to do in order to get multiple controls to belong to our Address control, and how do we specify what functionality will be provided?

We'll see that the process of creating controls using aggregation involves the following steps:

- Think about the functionality that's required by the control
- Plan the design-time and run-time appearance of the control
- Determine the design-time and run-time properties that will be exposed to the developer
- Determine the methods that will be exposed to the developer at run-time
- Manage any data persistence required as the control instance is destroyed and re-created
- Implement the control, including all the features of the design
- Define any property pages that will be used by your control

With the exception of the property pages, you'll see how we tackle all these tasks in this chapter. We'll move on to creating the custom property pages that will make using our control much easier for the developer in the next chapter.

Designing the Address Control

Many applications in use today need to store name and address details, such as a Personal Information Manager application (PIM), or perhaps a web page application which collects visitor's details. As a result, there are numerous applications that use similar form layouts to capture contact details. Imagine all the work that can be saved by using a standard Address control in all of these cases, and just tweaking it a little so that it appears and functions exactly as required. Furthermore, by using in-house created controls, we can ensure that all applications that use them have a similar and consistent look and feel. This is what we're going to achieve by creating our Address control.

As with all controls, we'll need to decide what functionality our control will need to provide to the hosting application. We'll design the control to make it as generic as possible so that it can be used in any application. Here's how the control will look in a client project design-time, once it's finished:

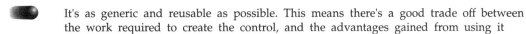

The Features Our Component Will Provide

There are many issues to think about when producing a control, but probably the most important of all is 'what constitutes a good control?' We want to limit the functionality of our control so that:

- It's as generic and reusable as possible. This means there's a good trade off between the work required to create the control, and the advantages gained from using it

- It's as user friendly and intuitive in operation as possible, and allows the programmer using it to concentrate on other aspects of their application

- In use, the control provides validation checks to make sure it's being used as intended. At the very least, this will ensure that the control will behave correctly, and may highlight errors in the client application.

In the case of our Address control, we'll cover the first point by providing text boxes to hold a name, address including city, state and zip code, country, telephone number and email address. We could include other details, such as fax number, company name, mobile number etc., but the fields given above will serve to illustrate the concepts. By not including too many specialized fields, we are retaining the generality of the control, and by allowing the developer to control which fields are displayed, we make it even more useful.

Designing User-configurable Controls

You may wonder if it's really necessary to display the Country and Email fields, as many applications don't use them. Indeed, many applications are only designed to operate in one particular country, but we want to make our Address control as generic as possible. To do this, we allow the developer to change the appearance of the control, depending on the locality. This will make the captions suitable for the American address format when the control is used on a computer which has been set up for the American locale, and British when it's used elsewhere.

The screen shot of our control in design-time doesn't show some of the dynamic aspects of the control that would be welcome. What we can actually do is make the Country and Email fields optional. Being optional doesn't mean that the end-user has a choice as to whether they enter in a value or not—that functionality constraint should be dealt with in the host application that uses the control. In our case, we mean making these two fields, and the general appearance of the Address control, change—depending on whether these fields are required in the application.

Making Controls Easy to Use

We can also help both developers and end-users by making the control intuitive to use. In other words, it shouldn't behave in an unexpected way. You may have noticed that when you place a control on to a form in Visual Basic, it generally has a caption or text which reflects the actual name of the control. Although it's possible to select the control by looking up the name in the list at the top of the Properties window, it's much easier for developers to select the control by clicking it on the form in design mode.

You may have also noticed that the text boxes used as part of our Address control have values in them already. These are representative of the names of the properties that will be used to access the text box values at run-time. Of course, we don't want to display these values when the control is in use at run-time, so we'll blank them out in this case.

Notice that this isn't the way many standard controls behave. They automatically set the text to the control name when placed on a form, and it remains set to this until you specifically change it at run-time.

Property Names and Control Captions

When in use, we'll allow developers to get at any of the values entered into the text boxes of our control by using the appropriate property names. So they could interrogate the **ContactName** property of a control called **Address1** at run-time using the usual syntax **Address1.ContactName**. What we don't want the user to do is access this property within the design-time environment of Visual Basic—we already know what the design-time values of the address properties would be because we'll be setting them to the names of the properties. Also, if we're intending our control to be suitable for use in both the US and UK, the names of the properties we'll expose will need to be appropriate to the locale mode it's running in.

Let's briefly summarize the properties we'll define for access:

Property name	Access type at run-time	Environment	Display Status	Locale	Availability
ContactName	Read only	Run-time	Mandatory	UK, US	Always
ContactStreet, or	Read only	Run-time	Mandatory	US	US mode only
ContactAddress	Read only	Run-time	Mandatory	UK	UK mode only
ContactCity, or	Read only	Run-time	Mandatory	US	US mode only
ContactTown	Read only	Run-time	Mandatory	UK	UK mode only
ContactState, or	Read only	Run-time	Mandatory	US	US mode only
ContactCounty	Read only	Run-time	Mandatory	UK	UK mode only
ContactCountry	Read only	Run-time	Optional	UK, US	Always

Table continued on following page

124

Property name	Access type at run-time	Environment	Display Status	Locale	Availability
ContactZip, or	Read only	Run-time	Mandatory	US	US mode only
ContactPostcode	Read only	Run-time	Mandatory	UK only	UK mode
ContactEmail	Read only	Run-time	Optional	UK, US	Always

We'll also allow the captions of the labels to be changed to suit the developer. This will allow access keys to be implemented, and changes made to the caption of the control itself:

Property name	Access type	Environment	Default value	Locale	Availability
Caption	Read/write	Run/design-time	Address Details	UK, US	Always
Caption_Name	Read only	Run-time	Name:	UK, US	Always
Caption_Street, or	Read only	Run-time	Street:	US	US mode only
Caption_Address	Read only	Run-time	Address:	UK	UK mode only
Caption_City, or	Read only	Run-time	City:	US	US mode only
Caption_Town	Read only	Run-time	Town:	UK	UK mode only
Caption_State, or	Read only	Run-time	State:	US	US mode only
Caption_County	Read only	Run-time	County:	UK	UK mode only
Caption_Country	Read only	Run-time	Country:	UK, US	Always
Caption_Zip, or	Read only	Run-time	Zip:	US	US mode only
Caption_Postcode	Read only	Run-time	Postcode:	UK	UK mode only
Caption_Email	Read only	Run-time	Email:	UK, US	Always

We'll also need to include properties that will switch the control's locality and determine whether the Country and Email fields will be shown. These will also be interrogated within the code to determine which of the properties shown above are valid for the currently selected locale. We'll introduce three more properties for this purpose:

Property name	Access type	Environment	Value 1	Value 2
Country	Read/Write	Run/Design-time	0 - US	1 - UK
View_Country	Read/Write	Run/Design-time	0 - Show country	1 - Hide country (default)
View_Email	Read/Write	Run/Design-time	0 - Show email (default)	1 - Hide email

125

These are just features that make the control easier for the developer to use. We'll now move on to designing the form layout for both design and run-time.

Specifying the UserControl Appearance

Since we are providing bilingual support for our control, we'll need to think about how it will appear at design-time and run-time for both supported locales. We'll first consider how the control will appear when **Country** is set to 0 - US.

The US Design-time Appearance

In design-mode, we'll want to show the name of the control, and the easiest way to do this is to set the caption of the frame that encompasses the other controls. In this case the control name is **Address1**. Frames act as good containers to hold together other controls, and they also differentiate the control easily from other elements that will exist alongside it on the form.

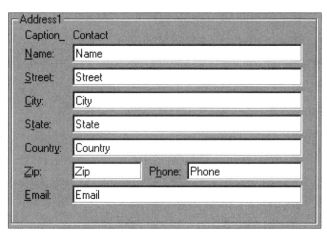

Notice how we've also specified the next part of the access property names for each of the text boxes, so that they're readily available at design-time when the control is used. Let's now have a look at the desired run-time appearance of the control.

The US Run-time Appearance

You can now see that the name of the control is no longer displayed, and has been replaced by 'Address Details'—the **Caption** of our control. In fact, this is the default caption, but we'll want to allow the developer to change it, so that our Address control is suited to the run/ design time context in which it'll be used. Also notice how the text boxes no longer display the name of their access property.

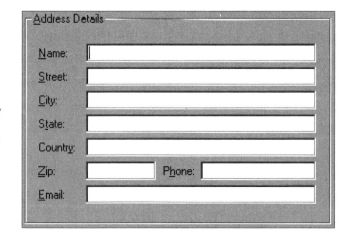

The UK Design-time Appearance

When the **Country** property is set to the value of 1 - UK, both views of the control change. The names of the access properties are also different. We also want to change the captions of the fields so that they'll be appropriate to the locality we choose.

We can see that the design-time appearance of the control is very similar in this case to that of US design-time. The notable differences are the changed address captions, and the names of the access properties which are displayed in the text boxes.

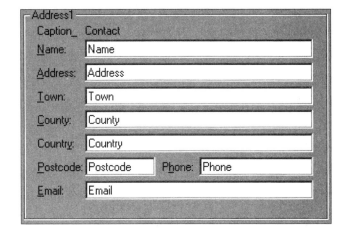

The UK Run-time Appearance

At run-time, the text box captions are changed to reflect the new locality of the control, and the text boxes themselves are empty.

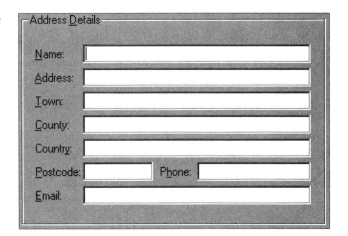

So we can see that the control can appear differently, depending on which locality is selected. We've seen how these views change between the design-time environment of VB, and the run-time environment of the project. We need to keep this in mind when we come to code our control.

Defining the Control Behavior

Once complete, our Address control will slot into a VB form, or be available in HTML pages, just like any other ActiveX control. The developer using our control will change the property values, and hence the appearance, so that it fits in to their application. We've allowed for changing the locality of the control and for specifying whether the Country and Email fields are displayed at run-time. This provides extra flexibility when the control is used in a form.

Imagine that an application used our control to collect both American and British residents' details. We want the end-user to be able to select an option which changes the display to allow either address format. We can display the appropriate view of the Address control by just setting one property of the Address control in code, based on the user's selection.

To do this, we're going to add code to the control, so that it includes the appropriate text boxes, and redraws itself properly, when changes to the appropriate property are made.

What is Delegation?

As you may recall from Chapter 2, the **Extender** collection contains a set of base properties for the control which you can access. This shouldn't be confused with **Ambient** properties (such as **Name** etc.) which fire the event **Ambient_Changed** on modification. We'll show you how to use the **Ambient_Changed** event later, but for now let's talk about **delegation**. Delegation is the process by which we effect the need to make the constituent parts of our control behave as we'd expect, based on a global change in the host application.

For instance, we'll need all of our control to be disabled when the **Enabled** property is set to **False**. Even though the **Enabled** property is an object provided by the **Extender** collection, it's only available to developers when we write the appropriate property procedures for its access, and set the procedure ID for this procedure. We discussed these concepts in previous chapters. To assign the procedure ID for the **Enabled** property, we:

- Select Procedure Attributes on the Tools menu to open the Procedure Attributes dialog.
- Select the Enabled procedure in the Name drop down list.
- Select Advanced to reveal the Procedure ID drop down list.
- Select Enabled from the Procedure ID box to give the property the correct identifier.

The reason we have to do this has to do with the way that VB deals with disabled containers. After all, that's what the **UserControl** object is—a special container for the controls that we've placed on it.

Defining the Control's Methods

Quite often, we'll want to let a developer make the control perform a certain complex operation, without having to retrieve and set lots of properties. When creating a control, we regularly come across sets of properties that fit right into this area, and become a real candidate for coding into a method. More often than not, it's the really common operations that we want to perform that are best suited to becoming methods that a user can invoke.

We define methods by writing public subroutines in our control's code, which perform the appropriate operations within our control. For example, in this simple, first version of the Address control, we're just going to provide a **ClearAll** method that clears all the text boxes. It's a useful method to include as we're not providing developers with **write** access directly to them, only **read** access. It also means that end-users of the control could easily be supplied with a button to reset all the values. In a control named **Address1**, the code for that button would be just **Address1.ClearAll**.

*Of course, we can also write routines that are only available for our own use, within the control. These must be defined as **Private** so they aren't directly available to users of the control.*

Defining the Control's Events

When writing a control, we'll often want to provide a way for the developer to know when something has happened to our control. They may want to include code in their application that will be executed when an event occurs. This is known as *providing events,* and is a simple way to extend the functionality of our control, using custom code authored by the developer.

In the context of our Address control, we want to provide events that will fire when any of the text fields are altered, when the viewing status of the Country and Email fields are changed, and when the locale mode is changed.

Determining Control Data Persistence

One more aspect of our control that we'll need to consider is that of **data persistence**. When we're using a control created by someone else, we usually set its name and size, and perhaps some custom properties, at design-time. We expect these values to be retained as our project flits between design-time and run-time modes.

Wearing our control creator's hat, we must provide code in the control that will save and retrieve these values at appropriate times. Usually though, values entered at run-time are not retained from one project run to another. We therefore have to filter out which values we want to keep—and by exclusion, which values we are not interested in storing. In the Address control, we're going to want to store any properties that will be accessible at design-time.

This is the general rule. As you saw in Chapter 1, we tend to store just the values of the properties that the user works with at design time. If they change the values at run-time, we would normally restore them to the last saved design-time setting when their application project returns to design mode.

Address Control Interface Diagram

Just as in previous chapters, we can provide an interface diagram that summarizes the structure of our control. Here's what the diagram looks like for the Address control:

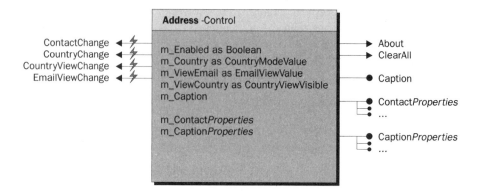

Implementing the Address Control

Now we've covered the basic design principles, we'll start to actually develop the Address control. We'll use this screen shot as the basis of the control appearance at *control* design-time:

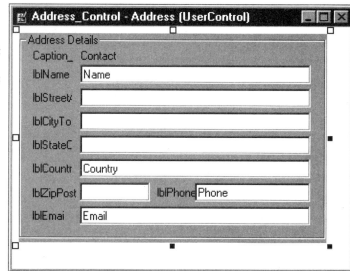

We're going to blank out the Caption_ and Contact text when the control is in use at run-time. They're just there to jog the memories of the developers, by showing the first part of the names of the properties; the second parts will be displayed in the text boxes in design-mode. Notice how we've already filled in **Name**, **Country**, **Phone** and **Email**. We know that the names of these properties are not dependent on the country mode—but the others are dependent. The captions besides the text boxes will be displayed at project design and run-time. The screen shot shows the defaults that are used. If the developer has modified them, their values will be shown here instead.

Using Enumerated Properties

When designing our Address control, we decided that it will be possible to switch on and off display of the Country and Email fields. We're also allowing the control to support the American address format as well as the British.

The neatest way to manage these on/off state properties is with enumerations, as we've seen used in earlier chapters. First we have to define the type name itself, and then the active members (also known as symbolic constants). Here's an arbitrary example to show what the code looks like just to define the enumeration:

```
Private Enum StyleType
   adStandard = 0
   adGraphical = 1
End Enum
```

This will set up the member values, and give us the type—named **StyleType**—that can be used in declaring variables. So, if we want to use this enumerated type for our own private use, we can do so by declaring variables of this type:

```
Private enMyStyle As StyleType
```

The variable **enMyStyle** can then be set to the required value using the symbolic constants:

```
enMyStyle = adStandard
```

or:

```
If enMyStyle = adStandard Then
   enMyStyle = adGraphical
End If
```

Of course, this won't make the variable (or the type) available for use outside the control, because they're declared as **Private**. We will still need to declare a **Property Get** to make the property available in the Properties window within VB:

```
Public Property Let Style(ByVal enNewStyle As StyleType)
   m_Style = enNewStyle
End Property
```

```
Public Property Get Style() As StyleType
   Style = m_Style
End Property
```

Here **m_Style** is of type **StyleType**, and has the value **adStandard** (**0**), or **adGraphical** (**1**). There is, however, one problem with this setup: if we want to return values that will be available in the Properties window, then we need to define the enumerated type as **Public** rather than **Private**.

```
Public Enum StyleType
   adStandard = 0
   adGraphical = 1
End Enum
```

131

This gives us the effect we want, and also gives the user of our control access to the members of the enumeration. Developers can then use the constants we've defined in their code. For example, in the client application's project they could use:

```
...
If ControlName.Style = adStandard Then
  MsgBox "Standard style set"
Else
  MsgBox "Graphical style set"
End If
...
```

Of course, we'll still need to define what should happen when a property value is retrieved and updated, and this is what we're going to show you in the next section.

It's worth remembering that all values supplied as a parameter to a property procedure should be passed by value, rather than reference. This way, if we were to change the value of the parameter (whether on purpose or accidentally) the new value wouldn't be propagated back to the user of the control.

Updating the Country View

Since our control is going to run in both US and UK modes, we will use a property to keep track of the mode of operation to which the control is currently set. We'll first define the enumeration and the members of the type:

```
Public Enum CountryModeValue
  US = 0
  UK = 1
End Enum
```

We'll use a variable rather than a constant to hold the default value. This will enable us to retrieve the client machine's locale setting, and arrange for the control to start in US or UK mode as appropriate. We couldn't do this using constants.

```
Private m_def_Country As CountryModeValue
```

*It's now possible to declare the **m_def_Country** variable before the type has been defined. This is a more flexible system allowing type use before declaration for enumerated types.*

When the control starts up, we'll assign the default locale setting. The setting will be dependent on the configuration of the machine which is being used to develop the client application.

```
Private Sub UserControl_AmbientChanged(PropertyName As String)
  Select Case PropertyName
  Case "DisplayName"    If Not Ambient.UserMode Then
      fraAddress.Caption = Extender.Name
    End If
  Case PropertyName = "LocalID"
      m_def_Country = IIf(Ambient.LocaleID = 1033, UK, US)
  End Select
End Sub
```

What we've done is make the default value of **m_def_Country** be UK, if the client application is being created on a UK configured machine. For any other configuration, we'll assign US as the default value. By doing this, we can often cut down the amount of work a developer would have to do to set the control up—it automatically sets itself to the appropriate country!

We need a variable to hold the current value of our property. We define it as **Private** so that it's only available within our control. Any references to this variable are made indirectly through the property procedures, and these can perform additional validation and functionality.

```
Private m_County As CountryModeValue
```

This has defined the property to hold the country value, but we still need to store and retrieve the value so we can re-instantiate the control to the same country mode every time it's created.

Using Constants for Easier Coding

We've covered the importance of using constants for default property values in Chapter 2, but there's another advantage they bring to coding the Address control. Property values are read and stored using **ReadProperty** and **WriteProperty** statements. One of the parameters required when calling these methods is the name of the property, in the form of a string. In order to avoid spelling mistakes, and possibly faulty control performance, we strongly recommend the use of a constant string defined at the start of the project. We'll be extending their use later in the chapter, but for now we'll just introduce a constant string in the declaration section of **UserControl**. We'll need it soon:

```
Const prpCountry = "Country"
```

We can then proceed to initialize the value based on the default:

```
Private Sub UserControl_InitProperties()
  'Assignment is of form:
  'm_Property = m_def_Property.
  ...
  m_Country = m_def_Country
...
  UpdateView prpCountry
  ...
End Sub
```

This has the effect of setting the **Country** property to the default value (**m_def_Country**), and updating the control so that it displays itself with the correct captions. You'll notice how we've passed the value of **prpCountry** to our **UpdateView** routine, so that the routine knows what needs to be updated. Don't worry about how **UpdateView** works at the moment, we'll cover it later on. All you need to know at present is that it updates the view of the control dependent on the property values.

We need to retrieve and store the design-time property values between creation and termination of the control, and this is done using **ReadProperty** and **WriteProperty** statements:

```
Private Sub UserControl_ReadProperties(PropBag As PropertyBag)
  ...
  m_Country = PropBag.ReadProperty(prpCountry, m_def_Country)
  ...
  UpdateView prpCountry
```

133

```
   ...
   End Sub

   Private Sub UserControl_WriteProperties(PropBag As PropertyBag)
      ...
      PropBag.WriteProperty prpCountry, m_Country, m_def_Country
      ...
   End Sub
```

We also need to have a look at the appropriate **Property Let** and **Property Get** procedures which set and retrieve the property value of **m_Country**:

```
   Public Property Let Country(ByVal enCountryValue As CountryModeValue)
      m_Country = enCountryValue
      PropertyChanged (prpCountry)
      UpdateView prpCountry
   End Property
```

First we've updated the value of the private variable **m_Country** so that it has the value of the new property setting. Notice how we don't need any validation for this as the only allowable choices are the members of the enumeration **CountryModeValue**. **m_Country** is also defined to be of this type.

As usual, we want to keep the new value of the **Country** property. We let VB know that we want to store the value. This is done using **PropertyChanged**, and VB will then store that property value when the control's **WriteProperty** event is fired.

Defining the **Property Get** procedure is really easy, because all we need to do is retrieve the current value. This also allows the **Country** property to be viewed and changed from the Properties window, within the IDE.

```
   Public Property Get Country() As CountryModeValue
      Country = m_Country
   End Property
```

Next, we'll introduce a property that will be used by the Address control to determine whether or not the Email field will be displayed and available.

Updating the Email View

We're going to let the developer decide whether the Email field is to be displayed. We'll define another property variable that will keep track of this, and start by defining another enumeration and the constituent members:

```
   Public Enum EmailViewValue
      Show_Email = 0
      Hide_Email = 1
   End Enum
```

We'll use a constant as the default value for the **View Email** option in our Address control, and make the control automatically show the Email field when first created:

```
   Const m_def_ViewEmail = Show_Email
```

Once again, we'll need a variable to hold the current value of our property:

```
Private m_ViewEmail As EmailViewValue
```

And just like the last time, we'll use a constant for the property name string:

```
Const prpViewEmail = "ViewEmail"
```

We can then proceed to initialize the value based on the default:

```
Private Sub UserControl_InitProperties()
   'Assignment is of form:
   'm_Property = m_def_Property.
   ...
   m_ViewEmail = m_def_ViewEmail
   ...
   UpdateView prpViewEmail
   ...
End Sub
```

When the control is created, the default property value for **m_ViewEmail** is set to the default, **Show_Email**. We also update the view of the control with our **UpdateView** routine, which includes setting it to the correct size. As before, we need to retrieve and store the values between creation and termination of the control. This is done within the **ReadProperty** and **WriteProperty** routines:

```
Private Sub UserControl_ReadProperties(PropBag As PropertyBag)
   ...
   m_ViewEmail = PropBag.ReadProperty(prpViewEmail, m_def_ViewEmail)
   ...
   UpdateView prpViewEmail
   ...
End Sub
```

```
Private Sub UserControl_WriteProperties(PropBag As PropertyBag)
   ...
   PropBag.WriteProperty prpCountry, m_Country, m_def_Country
   ...
End Sub
```

We'll also need to provide the appropriate **Property Let** and **Property Get** routines for the variable **m_ViewEmail**. And again, we update the value of **m_ViewEmail**, inform VB that the new value needs to be saved, and then call the **UpdateView** routine to update the view of the control:

```
Public Property Let View_Email(ByVal enViewEmail As EmailViewValue)
   m_ViewEmail = enViewEmail
   PropertyChanged (prpViewEmail)
   UpdateView prpViewEmail
End Property
```

```
Public Property Get View_Email() As EmailViewValue
   View_Email = m_ViewEmail
End Property
```

135

The property **m_ViewCountry**, which controls the display of the Country field, and the property procedures for setting it, are very similar to those already discussed.

Setting the Address Control's Caption

So far, we've covered three aspects of our control: the locale mode, and whether to show or hide the Email and Country fields. We're now going to discuss how we make the design-time caption of the control display the name of the control, and how we can update it when the name of the control changes.

When the control is used within the run-time environment of the project, we also want it to display the caption that's defined by the user. This is how other controls work.

Introducing the Caption Property

Instead of just hard coding a caption to something like Address Details, we're going to allow the developer to set the caption that's displayed at run-time. This allows the control to have a caption that fits in with the application in which it's going to be used, as well as allowing the setting of the underlined access key (hot key). As usual, we'll define a property name constant:

```
Const prpCaption = "Caption"
```

Like most properties, we want to define a default value that will be used until it's changed by the developer:

```
Const m_def_Caption = "Address Details"
```

Notice that we haven't included the '&' character for use as an access key. If we hard-code an access key like this, it restricts the access keys available to the developer for other controls on the same form. Of course, we'll allow the control caption to be changed anyway, so this isn't really an issue. Here's the property variable declaration that will hold the current caption string:

```
Private m_Caption As String
```

We can then proceed to initialize the value based on the default:

```
Private Sub UserControl_InitProperties()
  ...
  m_Caption = m_def_Caption
  ...
  UpdateView prpCaption
  ...
End Sub
```

We also deal with the retrieval and storing of the **Caption** value each time the control is destroyed and re-created:

```
Private Sub UserControl_ReadProperties(PropBag As PropertyBag)
  ...
  m_Caption = PropBag.ReadProperty(prpCaption, m_def_Caption)
  ...
  UpdateView prpCaption
  ...
End Sub
```

```
Private Sub UserControl_WriteProperties(PropBag As PropertyBag)
   ...
   PropBag.WriteProperty prpCaption, m_Caption, m_def_Caption
   ...
End Sub
```

We'll also need to have a look at the appropriate **Property Get** and **Property Let** procedures for the variable **m_Caption**. The **Property Get** routine is simple, as we just retrieve a string value:

```
Public Property Get Caption() As String
   Caption = m_Caption
End Property
```

However, the **Property Let** routine warrants extra explanation:

```
Public Property Let Caption(ByVal strNewCaption As String)
   m_Caption = strNewCaption
   If Ambient.UserMode Then    'Run-time
     UpdateView prpCaption
   Else
      'Design-mode so keep the change. No need to update the control view
      'now as it does it automatically next time the control is created.
      PropertyChanged (prpCaption)
   End If
End Property
```

After setting the caption variable **m_Caption**, we test to see whether the control is being re-created in a run-time environment. If this is the case, we update the view of the control to show the caption (this is actually done in the routine **UpdateView** which we'll discuss later). If the control is being used in design-mode, we keep the change, and the control view is automatically updated the next time its created. We don't need to update the view in this case, because we're using the name of the control as the caption.

Changing the Control Caption to the Control Name

Looking at the Address control in project design-mode, you can see that the name of the control is displayed as the caption of the frame. How do we go about changing this caption so that it's representative of the name of the control?

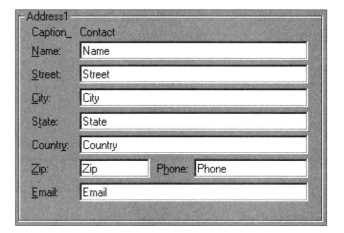

The way we've tackled this is to still keep the value of the **m_Caption** variable the same regardless of which mode the control is being used in. What we actually do is just let the caption of the frame be either the name of the control (in design-mode), or the value of the **m_Caption** variable (if used in a run-mode environment). We make use of the **AmbientChanged** event that's fired when any property of the **Ambient** collection is changed. This enables the caption appearance to be continuously updated on the control as the developer enters a new name for it.

```
Private Sub UserControl_AmbientChanged(PropertyName As String)
   Select Case PropertyName
      Case "DisplayName"
         If Not Ambient.UserMode Then
            fraAddress.Caption = Extender.Name
         End If
      ...
   End Select
End Sub
```

When such a property changes, the string name of the property is passed to the **AmbientChanged** event. Even though we're just looking for one value in this example, using a **Select Case** construct is good practice, since you can easily add code later for any other **Ambient** property changes. **Extender.Name** just gives us the actual name of the control. You may be wondering how the frame caption is set correctly if we don't change the control name. This is done by the **UpdateView** routine we've called in **InitProperties** and **ReadProperties**.

We'll now move on to looking at how we actually code the **Contact** property procedures and the associated properties. These will be used to retrieve the entered values from the Address control in run mode.

Implementing the Contact Properties

The way that developers will access the values in the Address control's text boxes is via the use of the **Contact** properties. Since we've got quite a few of these, we've written a generic routine that deals with the validation and return of the new value appropriately. Before we show you that, we'll look at a couple of property procedures that show how it's called.

Reading the Contact Properties

All of our **Contact** properties are read-only at design-time, and so we won't need to provide any **Property Let** procedures at all. In fact, because of this, the Properties window won't display the list of **Contact** properties. This is exactly what we want—it won't be possible to access the property in design-mode at all. Here's the **Property Get** routine which gets the value of the name entered in the Name textbox:

```
Public Property Get ContactName() As String
   ContactName = m_ContactGetValue(txtName.Text, Independentuse)
End Property
```

And similarly for the Street text box:

```
Public Property Get ContactStreet() As String
   ContactStreet = m_ContactGetValue(txtStreetAddress.Text, USuse)
End Property
```

Notice that the **ContactName** property is always available, no matter whether the control is set up for American or British locality, while **ContactStreet** is only to be accessed when the control is in the US mode. This is reflected by the use of the parameters passed to **m_ContactGetValue**. As well as passing the text value, we are also passing the values **Independentuse** in the first instance, and **USuse** in the second. These two values are members of another enumeration, which is very similar to the **Enum_CountryModeValue** enumeration, but includes another member, **Independentuse**:

```
Public Enum AttemptedCountryUsage
  USuse = 0
  UKuse = 1
  Independentuse
End Enum
```

We don't really care what the value of **Independentuse** is, so we'll let VB allocate us a value. We do, however, want the other values to match up with the appropriate values defined in **Enum_CountryModeValue**.

The **AttemptedCountryUsage** value informs our routine of the intended use of the property access. We've named all text boxes that are used in both the US and UK modes to be indicative of their use. Here's the definition of **m_ContactGetValue** which checks for this appropriate use:

```
Private Function m_ContactGetValue(strNewPropertyValue As String, _
               enAttemptedCountryUse As AttemptedCountryUsage) As String
   If (m_Country = enAttemptedCountryUse) _
   Or (enAttemptedCountryUse = Independentuse) Then
     m_ContactGetValue = strNewPropertyValue
   Else
     If Ambient.UserMode Then    'Can raise errors to alert improper use.
       Select Case enAttemptedCountryUse
         Case UKuse
           Err.Raise Number:=errUKUseOnly.Number, _
                     Description:=errUKUseOnly.Description
         Case USuse
           Err.Raise Number:=errUSUseOnly.Number, _
                     Description:=errUSUseOnly.Description
       End Select
     End If
   End If
End Function
```

Defining the Error Variables

In the code above, we've used some error variables. Their definition actually resides in another module, so that their scope exists globally in the control. Here's how they're defined:

```
Private Const errOffset = 512
Public errReadOnlyRun As AddressError
Public errPropDesignOnly As AddressError
Public errUKUseOnly As AddressError
Public errUSUseOnly As AddressError
Public errEmailNotAvailable As AddressError
Public errCountryNotAvailable As AddressError
```

The constant **errOffset** is just a extra 'error margin' we added in order to prevent conflicts with any defined error values in other controls and OLE objects. We've also created a new **AddressError** type which will make life easier when we come to access values from the error variables.

```
Type AddressError
  Number As Long
  Description As String
End Type
```

Any code in the **Sub Main()** section of our control executes first, since we've set this to be the startup procedure. This assigns the appropriate error value numbers and descriptions:

```
Sub Main()

  errReadOnlyRun.Number = vbObjectError + errOffset + 1
  errReadOnlyRun.Description = "Property is read-only at run time."

  errPropDesignOnly.Number = vbObjectError + errOffset + 2
  errPropDesignOnly.Description = "Property is not available at run time."

  errUKUseOnly.Number = vbObjectError + errOffset + 3
  errUKUseOnly.Description = "Property only available when Country is UK."

  errUSUseOnly.Number = vbObjectError + errOffset + 4
  errUSUseOnly.Description = "Property only available when Country is US."

  errEmailNotAvailable.Number = vbObjectError + errOffset + 5
  errEmailNotAvailable.Description = _
              "Property only available when View_Email is Show_Email."

  errCountryNotAvailable.Number = vbObjectError + errOffset + 6
  errCountryNotAvailable.Description = _
              "Property only available when View_Country is Show_Country."
End Sub
```

It's also worth mentioning that there are a couple of non-standard **Contact** property procedures that need some extra validation. Remember that we can show or hide the Country and Email fields. We'll only allow property access to these fields when they're displayed. Here's the code that does this:

```
Public Property Get ContactCountry()
  If Show_Country = View_Country Then  'Can get the value.
    ContactCountry = m_ContactGetValue(txtCountry.Text, Independentuse)
  Else
    If Ambient.UserMode Then
      Err.Raise Number:=errCountryNotAvailable.Number, _
              Description:=errCountryNotAvailable.Description
    End If
  End If
End Property
```

```
Public Property Get ContactEmail() As String
  If Show_Email = View_Email Then       'Can get the value.
    ContactEmail = m_ContactGetValue(txtEmail.Text, Independentuse)
  Else
```

```
        If Ambient.UserMode Then
            Err.Raise Number:=errEmailNotAvailable.Number, _
                      Description:=errEmailNotAvailable.Description
        End If
    End If
End Property
```

Implementing the Caption Properties

In our Address control, we allow the developer to set the captions for the various text boxes. This allows them to set unique access keys, as well as modifying the control's appearance. Since we'll want to keep the values set at design-time, we'll define constants that will be used in the **ReadProperty** and **WriteProperty** routines, as we did earlier. Here's the list of property string values for our **Caption** properties:

```
    Const prpCaptionName = "CaptionName"
    Const prpCaptionStreet = "CaptionStreetUS"
    Const prpCaptionAddress = "CaptionAddressUK"
    Const prpCaptionCity = "CaptionCityUS"
    Const prpCaptionTown = "CaptionTownUK"
    Const prpCaptionState = "CaptionStateUS"
    Const prpCaptionCounty = "CaptionCountyUK"
    Const prpCaptionCountry = "CaptionCountry"
    Const prpCaptionZip = "CaptionZipUS"
    Const prpCaptionPostcode = "CaptionPostcodeUK"
    Const prpCaptionPhone = "CaptionPhone"
    Const prpCaptionEmail = "CaptionEmail"
```

Earlier in the chapter, we introduced the idea of using constants for these string values. Here, we'll be extending their use; you may have noticed that in some of the string values shown end in 'US' or 'UK', while others don't include these characters at all. So why have we done this?

Detecting the Country Mode

We did this so that we can detect whether we're referring to a value that is designed for use when the control is set for US mode (**'US'** characters included), or UK mode (**'UK'** characters included), or, in fact, if the value is independent to the mode—in which case no such characters are included. We could do this by checking each of the string names within a **Select Case** statement, but then we'd need to update it whenever we modified our control by adding new values. Another advantage of using this approach is that we don't need to remember that State is an American concept, while County is British, etc. We make the coding easier for ourselves.

Setting the Default Captions

As usual, we'll use some default captions:

```
    Const m_def_CaptionName = "Name:"
    Const m_def_CaptionStreet = "Street:"
    Const m_def_CaptionAddress = "Address:"
    Const m_def_CaptionCity = "City:"
    Const m_def_CaptionTown = "Town:"
    Const m_def_CaptionState = "State:"
    Const m_def_CaptionCounty = "County:"
    Const m_def_CaptionCountry = "Country:"
```

141

```
Const m_def_CaptionZip = "Zip:"
Const m_def_CaptionPostcode = "Postcode:"
Const m_def_CaptionPhone = "Phone:"
Const m_def_CaptionEmail = "Email:"
```

And then initialize the default properties, updating the view of the control based on country mode:

```
Private Sub UserControl_InitProperties()
   ...
   m_CaptionName = m_def_CaptionName
   m_CaptionCountry = m_def_CaptionCountry
   m_CaptionPhone = m_def_CaptionPhone
   m_CaptionEmail = m_def_CaptionEmail
   m_CaptionStreet = m_def_CaptionStreet
   m_CaptionAddress = m_def_CaptionAddress
   m_CaptionCity = m_def_CaptionCity
   m_CaptionTown = m_def_CaptionTown
   m_CaptionState = m_def_CaptionState
   m_CaptionCounty = m_def_CaptionCounty
   m_CaptionZip = m_def_CaptionZip
   m_CaptionPhone = m_def_CaptionPhone
   m_CaptionPostcode = m_def_CaptionPostcode
   ...
   UpdateView prpCountry
   ...
End Sub
```

Updating the Captions

Any values stored from earlier **WriteProperty** calls are read in, as we want to maintain the values of the captions between control creation and termination:

```
Private Sub UserControl_ReadProperties(PropBag As PropertyBag)
   ...
   m_CaptionName = PropBag.ReadProperty(prpCaptionName, m_def_CaptionName)
   m_CaptionStreet = PropBag.ReadProperty(prpCaptionStreet, m_def_CaptionStreet)
   m_CaptionAddress = PropBag.ReadProperty(prpCaptionAddress, m_def_CaptionAddress)
   m_CaptionCity = PropBag.ReadProperty(prpCaptionCity, m_def_CaptionCity)
   m_CaptionTown = PropBag.ReadProperty(prpCaptionTown, m_def_CaptionTown)
   m_CaptionState = PropBag.ReadProperty(prpCaptionState, m_def_CaptionState)
   m_CaptionCounty = PropBag.ReadProperty(prpCaptionCounty, m_def_CaptionCounty)
   m_CaptionCountry = PropBag.ReadProperty(prpCaptionCountry, m_def_CaptionCountry)
   m_CaptionZip = PropBag.ReadProperty(prpCaptionZip, m_def_CaptionZip)
   m_CaptionPhone = PropBag.ReadProperty(prpCaptionPhone, m_def_CaptionPhone)
   m_CaptionPostcode = PropBag.ReadProperty(prpCaptionPostcode, _
                                       m_def_CaptionPostcode)
   m_CaptionEmail = PropBag.ReadProperty(prpCaptionEmail, m_def_CaptionEmail)
   ...
   UpdateView prpCountry
   UpdateView prpViewCountry
   UpdateView prpViewEmail
   ...
End Sub
```

142

We also need to store any changed values:

```
Private Sub UserControl_WriteProperties(PropBag As PropertyBag)
    ...
    PropBag.WriteProperty prpCaptionName, m_CaptionName, m_def_CaptionName
    PropBag.WriteProperty prpCaptionStreet, m_CaptionStreet, m_def_CaptionStreet
    PropBag.WriteProperty prpCaptionAddress, m_CaptionAddress, m_def_CaptionAddress
    PropBag.WriteProperty prpCaptionCity, m_CaptionCity, m_def_CaptionCity
    PropBag.WriteProperty prpCaptionTown, m_CaptionTown, m_def_CaptionTown
    PropBag.WriteProperty prpCaptionState, m_CaptionState, m_def_CaptionState
    PropBag.WriteProperty prpCaptionCounty, m_CaptionCounty, m_def_CaptionCounty
    PropBag.WriteProperty prpCaptionCountry, m_CaptionCountry, m_def_CaptionCountry
    PropBag.WriteProperty prpCaptionZip, m_CaptionZip, m_def_CaptionZip
    PropBag.WriteProperty prpCaptionPostcode, m_CaptionPostcode, _
                          m_def_CaptionPostcode
    PropBag.WriteProperty prpCaptionPhone, m_CaptionPhone, m_def_CaptionPhone
    PropBag.WriteProperty prpCaptionEmail, m_CaptionEmail, m_def_CaptionEmail
    ...
End Sub
```

The next stage is to provide the **Property Let** and **Property Get** procedures, so that we can set and view the captions. We're just going to cover a couple of them here, as they're all nearly identical:

```
Public Property Get Caption_Street() As String
    Caption_Street = m_CaptionGetValue(m_CaptionStreet, prpCaptionStreet)
End Property
```

```
Public Property Let Caption_Street(ByVal strNewCaptionStreet As String)
    m_CaptionLetValue m_CaptionStreet, strNewCaptionStreet, prpCaptionStreet
End Property
```

Validating the Captions

When we're retrieving values for the caption properties, we want to make sure that they're always being used in the right context. For example, the **Caption_Name** property can be retrieved when the control is in either US or UK mode, but **Caption_Street** should only be retrieved when the control is in US mode. We're not going to worry about this in every such **Property Get** routine. Instead we'll use the **m_CaptionGetValue** routine to sort this out for us.

If the attempted and actual country usage values match up, or if a text box contains a value which is independent of the country mode, we just return the required value as indicated by the parameter that's supplied:

```
Private Function m_CaptionGetValue(strCurrentPropValue As String, _
                                   prpCaptionProp As String) As String
   Dim enAttemptedCountryUse As AttemptedCountryUsage

   enAttemptedCountryUse = GetCountryUse(prpCaptionProp)
   If (m_Country = enAttemptedCountryUse) _
   Or (enAttemptedCountryUse = Independentuse) Then
      m_CaptionGetValue = strCurrentPropValue
```

If this isn't the case, then we check to see if the control is being used in the run-mode environment of the project. If this is the case, then we can warn the developer that the control is being used erroneously. Alternatively, if the value is being set at design-time, then we just return an empty string.

```
   Else
      If Ambient.UserMode Then     'Can raise errors to alert improper use.
         Select Case enAttemptedCountryUse
            Case UKuse
               Err.Raise Number:=errUSUseOnly.Number, _
                         Description:=errUKUseOnly.Description
            Case USuse
               Err.Raise Number:=errUKUseOnly.Number, _
                         Description:=errUSUseOnly.Description
         End Select
      Else
         m_CaptionGetValue = ""
      End If
   End If
End Function
```

Similarly, we want to enforce the conditions for changing the values of the caption properties, and we'll do this using routine called **m_CaptionLetValue**:

```
Private Sub m_CaptionLetValue(ByRef m_PropertyValue As String, _
            strNewCaptionValue As String, prpCaptionProp As String)
   Dim enAttemptedCountryUse As AttemptedCountryUsage
   enAttemptedCountryUse = GetCountryUse(prpCaptionProp)
   If (m_Country = enAttemptedCountryUse) _
   Or (enAttemptedCountryUse = Independentuse) Then
      m_PropertyValue = strNewCaptionValue
```

As long as the caption is being changed in the correct context, we can update the view. Then, as long as we're in design mode, we let VB know that we want to keep the new value that's been assigned by calling the **PropertyChanged** method.

Note that we need to update the view based on the *new* value of the property, and that's why we've passed it by reference. If we defined this routine to be a function, like the previous one, then it's only on the function return that the new value would be passed back to the property variable. By then it would be too late to update the view without carrying out extra tests. Here's the rest of the routine:

```
      UpdateView prpCaptionProp
      If Not Ambient.UserMode Then
         PropertyChanged (prpCaptionProp)
      End If
   Else
```

```
            If Ambient.UserMode Then      'Can raise errors to alert improper use.
                Select Case enAttemptedCountryUse
                    Case UKuse
                        Err.Raise Number:=errUSUseOnly.Number, _
                                  Description:=errUKUseOnly.Description
                    Case USuse
                        Err.Raise Number:=errUKUseOnly.Number, _
                                  Description:=errUSUseOnly.Description
                End Select
            End If
        End If
    End Sub
```

In both of these routines, we've used the separate function **GetCountryUse** which just returns the proper usage context of the property:

```
Public Function GetCountryUse(prpCaptionProp As String) _
                            As AttemptedCountryUsage

    If Right$(prpCaptionProp, 2) = "UK" Then      'Should be UK usage.
        GetCountryUse = UKuse
    ElseIf Right$(prpCaptionProp, 2) = "US" Then  'Should be US usage.
        GetCountryUse = USuse
    Else
        GetCountryUse = Independentuse
    End If
End Function
```

There are a couple of reasons why we've gone to the effort of using a handful of extra routines. For a start, it makes the **Contact** and **Caption** property procedures much simpler, and hence less prone to coding errors. We also don't have to worry about complex tests for each one, as we pass off the responsibility to other routines.

Run Time Properties and the Properties Window

By default, VB5 CCE shows properties that have **Property Get** and **Property Let** procedures in the Properties window, and we want this to occur if we are providing properties that will be set during design-time. But if we want properties to be read/write at run-time only, then they shouldn't be shown in the design-time Properties windows.

Coming back to our Address control, we ideally only want to show the **Caption** properties that are applicable to the locale mode currently selected. Unfortunately we can't achieve this functionality in VB5 CCE due to the dynamic property nature of our control; but we have made a compromise. With the routines as we've just described them, you'll notice that in using the control, only the caption properties applicable to the locale mode of our control have values that can be changed. On changing the mode, the other set of caption properties become available. A couple of screen shots will help to illustrate this:

Here, the Country mode is US, and so only US based captions show any values, or allow updates.

Here, the Country mode is UK, and so only UK based captions show any values, or allow updates.

All this is done in the routines you've just seen, **m_CaptionLetValue** and **m_CaptionGetValue**. In these, we check to see if the control is being used in design-mode (**Ambient.UserMode** is **False**). Only if this is the case do we change the captions:

```
...
If Not Ambient.UserMode Then
  PropertyChanged (prpCaptionProp)
End If
...
```

Updating the Control View

In this last section, we used a routine called **UpdateView**, which updates the appearance of the control. By using a separate subroutine to deal with the control redrawing, we only have to call that routine, letting it know which control we want updating. In this way, we can concentrate on getting our control to work as intended, and then get the redrawing to work afterwards.

We're not going to show you all of this routine, but just the important parts. The subroutine is called with the appropriate parameter indicating which control should be redrawn. It also deals with different cases depending on whether the control is being used within a run-time or a design-time environment:

```
Private Sub UpdateView(prpProp As String)
  Select Case prpProp
    Case prpCaption
      If Ambient.UserMode Then
        fraAddress.Caption = m_Caption
      Else
        fraAddress.Caption = Extender.Name
      End If
    Case prpCaptionName
```

```
            lblName.Caption = m_CaptionName
        Case prpCaptionStreet
            lblStreetAddress.Caption = m_CaptionStreet
        ...
        Case prpCaptionEmail
            lblEmail.Caption = m_CaptionEmail
        Case prpCountry
            UpdateView prpCaptionName
            UpdateView prpCaptionEmail
            UpdateView prpCaptionCountry
            UpdateView prpCaptionPhone
        ...
    End Select
```

Here, you'll have noticed that we've recursively called the **UpdateView** subroutine, and so it's easy to build in dependencies for controls that need to be updated as another one is updated. If you do this in your programs, make sure that you don't make control updates mutually dependent on each other, as your control will try to redraw itself indefinitely.

```
    Select Case m_Country
    Case US
        If Not Ambient.UserMode Then
            txtStreetAddress.Text = "Street"
            txtCityTown.Text = "City"
            txtStateCounty.Text = "State"
            txtZipPost.Text = "Zip"
        End If
        UpdateView prpCaptionStreet
        UpdateView prpCaptionCity
        UpdateView prpCaptionState
        UpdateView prpCaptionZip
```

If we're using the control in design-mode, then it's nice to display the contact properties so that it's easy for the user to know what they are without having to use the project browser.

```
    Case Else
        If Not Ambient.UserMode Then
            txtStreetAddress.Text = "Address"
            txtCityTown.Text = "Town"
            txtStateCounty.Text = "County"
            txtZipPost.Text = "Postcode"
        End If
        UpdateView prpCaptionAddress
        UpdateView prpCaptionTown
        UpdateView prpCaptionCounty
        UpdateView prpCaptionPostcode
    End Select

    Case prpViewCountry
        Dim intCountryTop As Integer
        intCountryTop = txtCountry.Top
        Select Case m_ViewCountry
        Case Show_Country
            lblCountry.Visible = True
            txtCountry.Visible = True
            lblZipPost.Top = intCountryTop + ControlGap + 40
```

147

```
         txtZipPost.Top = intCountryTop + ControlGap
         lblPhone.Top = intCountryTop + ControlGap + 40
         txtPhone.Top = intCountryTop + ControlGap
         lblEmail.Top = intCountryTop + ControlGap * 2 + 40
         txtEmail.Top = intCountryTop + ControlGap * 2

      Case Else
         lblCountry.Visible = False
         txtCountry.Visible = False
         lblZipPost.Top = intCountryTop + 40
         txtZipPost.Top = intCountryTop
         lblPhone.Top = intCountryTop + 40
         txtPhone.Top = intCountryTop
         lblEmail.Top = intCountryTop + ControlGap + 40
         txtEmail.Top = intCountryTop + ControlGap
      End Select
      UserControl_Resize

   Case prpViewEmail
      lblEmail.Visible = (m_ViewEmail = Show_Email)
      txtEmail.Visible = (m_ViewEmail = Show_Email)
      UserControl_Resize

   End Select
End Sub
```

We end the routine with a call to the control's **Resize** event code. This will redraw the control, and re-size it so that it displays the Country and Email fields if appropriate. We'll be looking at this routine later in the chapter.

Implementing the Control's Methods

So far in this chapter, we've talked exclusively about how we implement the **properties** of the control. As we've already discussed, **methods** can be used to perform multiple property settings in controls, which is particularly useful where there a lot of properties. Once coded into a method, developers can easily invoke these common operations. We're going to include the **ClearAll** method, which just clears all the text boxes of any user input. It only really makes sense to invoke methods during project run-time, although they are really available as soon as your control starts to execute.

The **ClearAll** method is really easy to write, and hopefully you can see that including methods with your controls is a really great way to make them even more useful than they otherwise would be. Any methods that we want to be used like this should be declared as **Public**, so they they'll be available for developers to use.

```
Public Sub ClearAll()
   'Don't need to test to see if country and email fields are displayed.
   'Just use direct access to the text boxes as no write properties defined
   'for Contact properties anyway.
   txtName.Text = ""
   txtCountry.Text = ""
   txtPhone.Text = ""
   txtEmail.Text = ""
   txtStreetAddress.Text = ""
   txtCityTown.Text = ""
```

148

```
      txtStateCounty.Text = ""
      txtZipPost.Text = ""
   End Sub
```

Notice how we haven't changed any property values here. We *can* do this, but in the context of our Address control we don't need to; the **Contact Property Get** routines only retrieve values from the text boxes. Of course, we could use parameters (or even optional parameters) to specify which fields should be cleared (**ClearAll(US)** for example), but this will serve as a simple example to demonstrate their use.

While methods are really useful in letting developers manipulate our controls in their code, we generally need to include a select set of **events** as well.

Implementing the Control's Events

Methods can be used to perform all kinds of operations within a control, but they don't actually inform the host application when certain conditions actually occur. It's possible for the application to continually test for a condition, but it's usually much better for the control to notify the application that's hosting it when it actually happens. In this way, the control can invoke code that's written by the developer. This is the basis for using **events**. We'll include four events in our control: **ContactChange**, **CountryChange**, **CountryViewChange**, and **EmailViewChange**.

Specifying the ContactChange Event

There isn't much work involved in specifying events. We just define them like this:

```
   Public Event ContactChange(ByVal ContactParam As String)
   Public Event CountryChange(ByVal CountryParam As CountryModeValue)
   Public Event CountryViewChange(ByVal CountryView As CountryViewValue)
   Public Event EmailViewChange(ByVal EmailView As EmailViewValue)
```

ContactChange is designed to notify the developer whenever one of the Contact fields values have changed. We could do this individually for Name, Street, Address etc., but we've decided to keep the control interface down to a minimum by passing a parameter that will have the string name of the field that's been changed. The developer will handle the event in their code with something like this:

```
   Sub Address1_ContactChange(FieldName As String)
```

What we need to do to make it work, inside the control itself, is specify conditions on which the method will be invoked by the control. We do this in the parts of the control code that themselves react to events of the constituent controls, and from there we can fire the event. For example, to fire the **ContactChange** event, we need to raise it using the **RaiseEvent** statement in the same module in which our control code's property procedures are defined.

The easiest place is in the **Change** event of our text boxes. We can inspect the locale mode to provide the appropriate string value as the event parameter. Here's how we've done it for the Street/Address field:

```
   Private Sub txtStreetAddress_Change()
     If m_Country = US Then
       RaiseEvent ContactChange("ContactStreet")
     ElseIf m_Country = UK Then
```

149

```
      RaiseEvent ContactChange("ContactAddress")
   End If
End Sub
```

Here's how you could use the parameter value in the host application's project:

```
Private Sub Address1_ContactChange(ByVal ContactParam As String)
   Select Case ContactParam
     Case "ContactName"
       MsgBox "You've changed your name!"
     Case "ContactStreet"
       MsgBox "You've moved somewhere else in America!"
     Case "ContactAddress"
       MsgBox "You've moved somewhere else in the UK!"
     Case Else
       MsgBox "The name of the Contact property to change is " & ContactParam & "."
   End Select
End Sub
```

Changing the value of any contact fields fires the event, and we trap the parameter using our code.

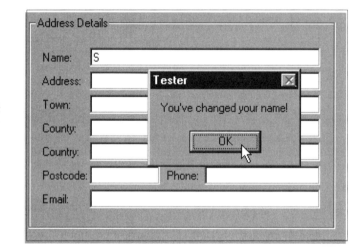

Implementing the Other Events

It's easy to raise the other events that we're supplying. This just involves adding a line to the **Property Let** routines we've already written. The **CountryChange** event occurs when the locale mode of the control is changed:

```
Public Property Let Country(ByVal enCountryValue As CountryModeValue)
   m_Country = enCountryValue
   PropertyChanged (prpCountry)
   UpdateView prpCountry
   RaiseEvent CountryChange(m_Country)
End Property
```

The **CountryViewChange** event occurs when the setting for the display of the Country field in the control is changed:

150

```
Public Property Let View_Country(ByVal enViewCountry As CountryViewValue)
  Dim intCountryTop As Integer
  m_ViewCountry = enViewCountry
  PropertyChanged (prpViewCountry)
  UpdateView prpViewCountry
  RaiseEvent CountryViewChange(m_ViewCountry)
End Property
```

A similar method is used to implement the **EMailViewChange** event.

Resizing the Address Control

We've now covered all the main stages in the design and implementation of our Address control bar one—what happens when the developer resizes it. To keep the control relatively simple, we're just going to make sure that the control resizes itself to a static size, based on whether the Country and Email fields are visible. We're not going to let the developer resize the control at this stage, but if you want to know how this is done, we'll be covering it in chapter 8 when we talk about the Card controls.

Using the Resize Event

To fix the size of any control, all we need to do is set the **Height** and **Width** properties to a constant value in the **UserControl_Resize** event. Our situation, however, is a little more complicated as we've got to determine the correct height because the Country and Email fields may or may not be visible. Here's the code that's executed when the **Resize** event is fired:

```
Private Sub UserControl_Resize()
  Dim intHeight As Integer
  Width = 4830
  intHeight = UserControlMinHeight
  If m_ViewEmail = Show_Email Then
    intHeight = intHeight + ControlGap
  End If
  If m_ViewCountry = Show_Country Then
    intHeight = intHeight + ControlGap
  End If
  fraAddress.Height = intHeight - FrameSpacing
  Height = intHeight
End Sub
```

The global constant **UserControlMinHeight** is just the height of the control when the Country and Email fields are not displayed. **ControlGap** is also a global constant, and is set to the height of a single text box plus the spacing between it and it's neighbor.

We're using a frame that acts as a container for our controls, to make it stand out from the other form elements. The global constant **FrameSpacing** specifies the distance between the bottom of the **UserControl** form, and the bottom of our frame. Resizing a control like this is a new aspect of control creation that must be considered when authoring your own controls.

Summary

In this chapter, we've created an aggregate control which acts as a single component, but actually includes several sub-controls. This is a useful way of cutting down the amount of work if you have several applications that require broadly similar functionality. And of course, it makes creating web pages much easier where you need to collect names and addresses. You only need place one control in the page, rather than trying to set up the layout of several.

We've worked through from design principles to a usable control, though we haven't talked about how you might compile and distribute it. These are common to all the controls we introduce in this book, and you'll see how it's done in other chapters. In fact this will be the way we tackle the rest of the controls in this book. In the next chapter, we'll be extending this control by adding property pages to it.

In this chapter, we have seen that we should:

- Recognize and think about the design- and run-time use of the control in a client application.

- Make the control have several *operating modes*—so that it only allows access to certain properties in one mode, or the other.

- Make your coding easier by using constants which have some internal meaning.

- Emulate familiar property selections by using enumerated types.

- Delegate the task of getting the control to update itself appropriately by using a separate subroutine. This also makes (sub)-control dependency easier to implement.

- Provide methods to allow developers to invoke commonly used processes within the control.

- Make events fire when certain conditions within the control are fulfilled. This allows developers additional flexibility by giving them a means to write custom code that's executed in particular circumstances.

Creating Property Pages

Property pages provide an alternative way of setting property values for controls. Often, a property provided from a control will have a structure that makes it difficult or inappropriate to set through the Properties window. It may be that the property type is an object with properties of its own (like the **Font** object), an array of values, or a collection of objects. In these cases, the only sensible way of providing a means to modify property values is through the use of property pages.

In the last chapter, we designed and built a generic Address control. In this chapter, we're going to cover property pages in some depth, and see how they can be created for complex controls like our Address control. The Property Page Wizard can't help us here, so we have to do almost all of the work ourselves.

Before we go too deeply into talking about the new General property page for the Address control, we'll give you an overview of property pages, and cover how they work internally. We're going to talk about the property page container and the Property Pages Dialog. Once we've done the groundwork, we'll show how we can build a property page for the Address control, using some of the principles given in the first half of the chapter.

You'll see:

> How we can make a developer's life easier by using property pages, rather than relying on the standard Properties Dialog.
>
> What we need to do to create these property pages, and how they work.
>
> How we create a new property page for our Address control.

So, we'll start this chapter with an overview of property pages.

The Property Pages Dialog

We're not limited to just one property page per control. The Property Pages Dialog, that you saw in the previous chapter, provides a means to select the property page we're after, and we can categorize different properties into different property pages. The screenshot shows what our Address control property pages look like in this dialog box.

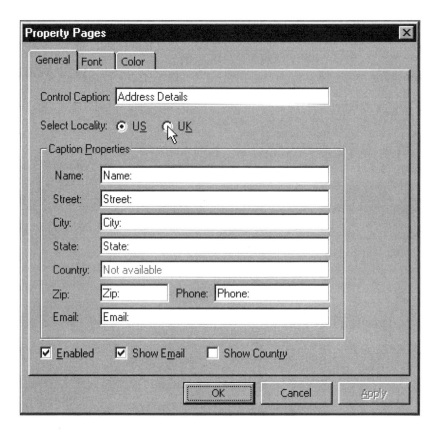

The Property Pages Dialog is provided automatically by VB5, and acts as a kind of container that holds our property pages together. When designing property pages, we don't need to add the OK, Cancel and Apply buttons as they are automatically defined in the dialog.

Each tab in the dialog represents one **PropertyPage** object. In our example, we've attached three property pages for our Address control—the General, StandardFont and StandardColor property pages. The tab texts for the dialog are taken directly from the **Caption** property values of the property page objects.

What we do need to do is define the property pages themselves, and attach them to our control. Our property pages work in conjunction with the dialog, by changing the property values and using the events defined by the **PropertyPage** object. We'll see how this is done shortly. It's critical to understanding how property pages work, and what we need to do to tailor our own property pages particular to a control.

The PropertyPage Container

A **PropertyPage** container can be inserted into a control project using the Project | Add Property Page menu item. When we do this, we are presented with what appears to be a blank form, but it's really the **PropertyPage** container. In a similar manner to VB Form containers, we can design the property page appearance by adding controls to it, and then write code to link them together.

However, the way in which **PropertyPage** containers work is quite different to a normal form. Each property page container provides access to all the controls within it, but also provides a **PropertyPage** object. This can be seen using the Object Browser. The object is also directly available in the Code window:

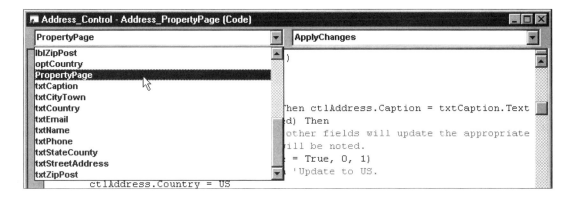

The **PropertyPage** object is different to the **PropertyPage** container. We can handle events for the property page container by using the members provided in the **PropertyPage** object, much like every **Form** container provides a **Form** object which is used to handle its events.

The **PropertyPage** object provides some of the normal members you'd expect, but it doesn't provide **Load** and **UnLoad** events. The Property Page Dialog creates instances of the property pages, and the **Initialize** event is the first event that the **PropertyPage** object receives. Extra members are defined that are specific to property pages. The key members are the **SelectionChanged** event, the **Changed** property, and the **ApplyChanges** event. These allow us to interact with the control and the Property Pages Dialog. Because each property page is distinct, each one will have these three members defined for it. For each property page we use, we must:

 Add code to the **SelectionChanged** event to obtain the property values to be edited.

 Update the **PropertyPage** object's **Changed** property value to **True** when a property value is edited by the developer.

Add code to the **ApplyChanges** event to copy the edited property values back to the selected control.

Coding the SelectionChanged Event

The **SelectionChanged** event is of primary importance for obtaining the property values to be edited. The event occurs under two situations. The first is when the property page is displayed, and the second when the list of currently selected controls changes.

Property pages should allow us to do at least what is possible by using the Properties window. However, there are some things we have to look out for. When the developer selects one text box control, the Properties window updates itself to show the properties supplied by that type of control along with the property values for the selected control instance. If they now extend that selection by selecting another control instance in addition to the currently selected one, the Properties window is updated again.

157

This time, however, it only shows the properties are defined for both the selected controls. Some of the properties of the individual ones won't appear, where they aren't available for all the selected of controls. And the actual values of the properties that are shown will only be available where they are the same for all the selected controls. For example, the **Name** property value has to be unique across all controls on a form (apart from the case of control arrays). It therefore wouldn't make much sense to be able to change the **Name** property to the same value across the list of selected controls.

In any case, whenever the list of controls changes in this manner, each property page receives a **SelectionChanged** event. Changing the selection of controls fundamentally changes the state of the property page. We need to code the **SelectionChanged** event as if the property page is being loaded for the first time.

When we used the Property Page Wizard in chapter 3, it created the code for the **SelectionChanged** event to bring in the properties that we selected. Dealing with multiple selected controls throws up more issues that we need to understand. We'll talk about these extra concerns a little later.

Enabling the Apply Button

Assuming that the property page is displayed with the control's property values, the developer can modify these values by interacting with the property page. The property page needs to be notified that new values have been set, otherwise it won't fire the **ApplyChanges** event. We notify the Property Page Dialog of this by setting the **Changed** property of that particular **PropertyPage** object to **True**. This also enables the Property Pages Dialog's Apply button.

But from where should we set the **Changed** property to **True**? The property page uses controls to represent the property values. So it's in these controls that the **Changed** property should be updated. In most cases, this just involves adding code in the **Change** event for these controls, or the **Click** event for a list box or set of option buttons. Here's a couple of simple examples:

For a textbox:

```
Private Sub Text1_Change()
  Changed = True
End Sub
```

For a listbox:

```
Private Sub List1_Click()
  'Assume that gintPrevListIndex is the default ListIndex
  'value when the property page was set up.
  If gintPrevListIndex <> List1.ListIndex Then
    Changed = True
  End If
End Sub
```

*Updating the **Changed** property in this manner has the same effect as specifying*
PropertyPage.Changed.

As long as **Changed = True,** the **ApplyChanges** event is fired when any of the following conditions apply:

- The Apply button is pressed
- A different property page is selected using the tabs
- The Property Pages Dialog box is dismissed

We now need to specify which values are copied back to the control, and this is done by adding code to the **ApplyChanges** event.

Coding the ApplyChanges Event

Assuming that only one control is selected, it's in the **ApplyChanges** event that we need to copy values back to the selected control. If we have only include a few properties in our property page, then we may want to copy all the values back to the control.

Imagine that **ctlControl** is an object variable that references our control, and that **Text1** and **List1** are controls defined within our property page. The simplest method is to copy all values back to the control, regardless of whether they've changed or not:

```
Private Sub PropertyPage_ApplyChanges()
   CtlControl.Property1 = Text1.Text
   CtlControl.Property2 = List1.List(List1.ListIndex)
End Sub
```

The problem with this code is that it updates all the property values of our control, even if they haven't changed. When we develop the General Address control property page later in this chapter, we'll show you how we get around this limitation.

Dealing with Errors in ApplyChanges

In all cases where a developer can provide free-form input (that is, not one of a small number of alternatives), there is always a possibility that the values provided may be rejected by the **Property Let**/**Set** routines in the control. Where this is possible, explicit error checking should be provided in the **ApplyChanges** event. Errors that aren't trapped eventually end up with the user of the control, which is clearly not a desirable outcome!

The simplest scheme is to use **On Error Resume Next**, and test **Err.Number** after each property assignment that may raise an error. When an error occurs we:

- Stop processing in the **ApplyChanges** event code.
- Display an error message to let the developer know what went wrong.
- Set the focus to the property that caused the error.
- Set the **Changed** property of the **PropertyPage** object to **True**.

You may wonder why we need to perform the last step. Setting **Changed = True** enables the Apply button on the dialog, much as you'd expect. It also prevents the dialog from being dismissed if the user has clicked OK. This is the only way to prevent the dialog from closing.

Providing the PropertyPage Appearance

So far, we've given you an overview of property pages, but we haven't considered the design as far as control layout is concerned. In addition to choosing where we should lay out our property page controls, there's another consideration—which controls should we use?

When we used the Property Page Wizard in chapter 3, the custom property page it created used text controls for representing strings and integer values, and checkboxes for boolean values. However, when crafting our own property pages by hand, we aren't restricted to using these controls. We can choose any editable representation that makes sense for a property.

Types of Controls

It's still best to use checkboxes to represent True/False Boolean values. However, if a property returns an enumerated type, there can be several fixed alternative values for the property. If there are only two or three possible values, option buttons are ideal. However, if there are more than, say, three values, a drop-down list might be provided instead. This results in the most efficient use of space within the property page. Ultimately, however, it's your decision.

Using Several Property Pages

Appropriate property page layout helps to limit the number of property pages required, which in turn limits the number of tabs displayed in the Property Pages Dialog. Despite this, complex controls with many properties will often still need several property pages to make the configuration of it more intuitive.

If we want to provide access to a complex control's properties through the Property Page Dialog, we might need to divide the properties over several different pages. This limits the complexity of each individual page, and we can organize which pages are responsible for which properties. We've seen this done in chapter 3, where we've used the General property page for our custom properties, with the wizard adding the StandardFont and StandardColor pages for the **Font** and **BackColor** properties. We'll extend this again in the next chapter by adding a DataBound property page to the Address control.

Using Standard Property Pages

VB5 automatically provides three types of standard property pages for use within your controls, namely StandardFont, StandardColor and StandardPicture. These standard property pages will automatically be associated with any properties of type **Font**, **OLE_COLOR**, and **Picture** respectively—even if there are several properties of each type. They won't, however, automatically be displayed in the Property Pages Dialog until they are explicitly included in the list of **active** property pages. We'll show you how to do this towards the end of the chapter, when we include these standard pages for use with our Address control. Note that whenever a standard property page displays multiple properties, the **ApplyChanges** event is raised each time a different property is selected.

Advanced Property Page Techniques

Up to this point, we've discussed the general background and techniques that can be applied to all property pages. In this section, we'll be extending on this to cover techniques that allow you to work with selections of multiple control instances, share property pages between controls, and associate property pages with individual properties.

Working with Multiple Selected Controls

So far, we've only talked about obtaining default values from, and updating property values to a single selected control. In this section, we'll see how this is done for multiple selected controls. First, we'll introduce you to the **SelectedControls** collection, as it's central to working with multiple controls.

The SelectedControls Collection

The **SelectedControls** collection contains all the controls that are selected, in the container the developer is working on. If a property page is shared by more than one type of control, then the collection may contain controls of different types. However, you don't need to worry that the collection might contain controls other than your own, such as labels. This is because the Property Pages Dialog only displays the pages that are used by all of the currently selected controls.

It's easy to find out if multiple controls have been selected. We just inspect the **Count** property of the **SelectedControls** collection:

```
If SelectedControls.Count > 1 Then
    'Multiple controls are selected
End If
```

We use this approach when writing the code for the **SelectionChanged** event.

Coding SelectionChanged for Multiple Controls

When working with multiple controls selections, it's often a good idea to categorize the properties into two main groups:

 Properties where it's sensible for multiple controls to have the same value, e.g. **BackColor** and **Font**.

 Properties where it doesn't make sense for multiple controls to have the same value, e.g. **Name**.

One method of handling the second case is to disable the edit fields for these properties whenever multiple controls are selected. This makes it obvious to a developer that the property value denoted by that field can't be edited, and it's impossible for the disabled control to set the **Changed** property to **True**. This is a better method than hiding controls that aren't applicable, as the property page will appear different. A developer would not be able to see where that property would be edited, and it makes working with the control confusing if the appearance of the property pages keeps changing.

161

It is up to you, the control author as to which properties can be sensibly shared between multiple control instances, and which can't.

Reading the Current Property Values

When we come to read the current property values from the selected controls, we may find that they are different for different instances of the same property name. The usual method of obtaining a default value to display in such a case is to inspect the first selected control.

We've defined **ctlControl** to be global to the property page. We've done this, because we feel that accessing the first control in the **SelectedControls** collection by using **ctlControl** is clearer than using **SelectedControls(0)** and we'll need to do this in at least the **SelectionChanged** and the **ApplyChanged** events.

In property pages declaration section:

```
'ControlName is defined in the control project.
Private ctlControl As ControlName
```

*In the **SelectionChanged** event:*

```
Set ctlControl = SelectedControls(0)
txtLeft.Text = ctlControl.Left
txtTop.Text = ctlControl.Top
'...etc...

If SelectedControls.Count > 0 Then
  txtName.Enabled = False
Else
  txtName.Text = ctlControl.Name
End If
```

Now that we've got a scheme for obtaining the default values where multiple control instances are selected, let's take a look at how these values are copied back to the controls.

Copying the Modified Property Values Back

For properties that can be sensibly shared amongst controls, we'll need to copy the changed values back to the appropriate controls. The way in which this is achieved is by iterating through each of the **SelectedControls** members in turn.

```
For Each ctlTemp in SelectedControls
  If txtName.Enabled Then
    ctlTemp.Name = txtName.Text
  End If
  ctlTemp.Left = txtLeft.Text
  ctlTemp.Top = txtTop.Text
Next
```

In the previous section we disabled the textbox for the **Name** property when there was more than one control selected. When it comes to copying property values that are only sensibly defined for single control selections, back to the control, we can examine that **Enabled** property of the appropriate property page controls. In this way, we only copy back property values when one control instance is selected, or when the property applies sensibly to all the controls selected.

*We don't need to test that more than one control is selected in the **ApplyChanges** event because the **For..Each** loop deals with this implicitly.*

Sharing Property Pages

Because property pages are just treated as files in a project, they can be added to other controls, and then linked in to become a member of the list of current property pages for that control. Often, such property pages are designed with generality in mind. They'll include most or all of the standard set of control properties, even if some of them won't be used for specific controls.

Where property pages are shared in this manner, we must provide error handling within the **SelectionChanged** and **ApplyChanges** events. If we attempt to read and write inappropriate property values from and to the selected control instances, we don't want any errors being shown to the users of our control!

In the **SelectionChanged** event, we can introduce simple error handling like this:

```
Private Sub PropertyPage_SelectionChanged()
  On Error Resume Next
  txtProp1.Text = ctlControl.Prop1
  If Err.Number > 0 Then 'No such property.
    txtProp1.Enabled = False
    Err.Clear 'Clear error status.
  End If
  '...etc...
End Sub
```

We now know which property values we can copy back to the selected controls by inspecting the **Enabled** properties of the controls in our property page:

```
Private Sub PropertyPage_ApplyChanges()
  Dim ctlControl As Control
  For Each ctlControl In SelectedControls
    If txtProp1.Enabled Then
      ctlControl.Prop1 = txtProp1.Text
    End If
    '...etc...
  Next
End Sub
```

Property page controls may be disabled for two reasons. First, it may be because multiple control instances have been selected, and the code in the **SelectionChanged** event has disabled its controls where the properties can't be sensibly applied to multiple controls. Second, it may be because the properties represented by those disabled controls are not applicable for the selected controls. When coding our **AppyChanges** event, we are not concerned with the reasons. All we need to do is check for disabled controls before we attempt to copy the property value back to the selected controls.

Associating PropertyPages with Properties

Often, a property is too complicated to set from the Properties window. This is one of the reasons for using property pages in the first place. In this case, it's convenient to associate a property page with an individual property, which will allow us to bring up the Property Pages Dialog by selecting the button with the ellipsis from the Properties window.

To set up this association, we have to perform a series of steps:

- Select the **UserControl** object using from the Project window

- Select Tools | Procedure Attributes to open the Procedure Attributes dialog box, and click on Advanced.

- Enter the property we wish to associate in the Name box.

- Select the required property page in the Use this Page in Property Browser list and then click on the Apply or OK button.

The EditProperty Event

We've seen how various elements of our property pages can be disabled when they are not appropriate to multiple controls selections, and we've talked about associating property pages to individual properties. We can take this a stage further, and associate multiple properties with the same property page. We may want to do this when we share property pages between controls, or if one property uses part of another property page's layout. In this case, we can use the **EditProperties** event to enable only those parts that we'll actually need within the property page.

When the ellipsis button for an associated property is clicked, each page in the Property Pages Dialog receives the **EditProperties** event as well as the events we've covered so far. By using the **PropertyName** argument supplied by the **EditProperties** event, we can identify which property was chosen from the Properties window.

Here, we have the opportunity to perform extra operations on the property page. For instance, we may decide to set the focus to the key control for the chosen property, or even disable inapplicable controls on the property page.

The Address Control Property Page

In chapter 3, we used the Property Page Wizard to quickly create property pages for our **Number Converter** control. Using this wizard is great for simple controls which use base property types, but it isn't so useful when our control becomes more complex.

When we used the ActiveX Control Interface Wizard, we had to complete the control by adding our own code. When it comes to creating property pages for our controls, we're faced with the same situation again—we'll need to add in extra functionality to make them really useful. In this section, we'll use the techniques we've discusses so far in this chapter to create our own property page for the Address control. We'll be showing you how to:

- Determine the properties to be included in your property page

- Design the appearance of the property page by adding controls to them

- Add code to the **SelectionChanged** event to obtain default values from the control

- Implement the functionality of the property page

- Add code to the **ApplyChanges** event that will propagate property value changes from the property page to the control

- Attach the property page to the control

Understanding Property Page Lifetime

Property pages are created and destroyed as a control is in use by the developer, in the same way as we saw with the controls themselves. Admittedly, the process is somewhat simpler, as we don't need to save and retrieve property values like we do for our controls.

As you've seen, it's quite possible for a control to have several property pages attached to it—just like a normal VB form may have many controls contained within it. Because each individual property page can exist in its own right, each has it's own set of code routines and events defined for it.

Setting Default Values

We need to set up the property page with default values, in a similar manner to how it was done for the **UserControl** object. The main difference here is that the default values we use will be obtained directly from the control, where available. Where this isn't possible, due to some properties only being available in certain circumstances (like in the Address control) then hard-coded defaults may be used.

When the property page has been created and displayed, the developer can proceed to change any or all of the property values. Here's what the finished General property page looks when it's displayed in the Property Pages Dialog box. We've included a shot of the Address control so you can see how the two match up.

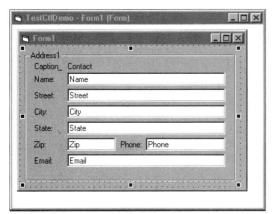

One thing that you'll notice is that the default values shown in the General property page on the right have taken on the values of the control shown on the left. Also, this instance of the Address control is not displaying the Country field, but we're still showing that field in the property page. While we don't want the Address control to take up more space than necessary, we've decided against making the property page resize itself when the Show Email and Show Country checkbox values have been changed. This ensures that our property page for the Address control always appears consistent to its users.

On the Property Page Dialog is a grayed out Apply button. it's only when one of the properties in *any* of the property pages has changed, that the control should be updated. Until a property has changed, the Apply button is inaccessible, and the OK button simply behaves the same as the Cancel button. As soon as one of the properties is changed in the property page, the Apply button becomes available, and the OK button also applies these new properties to the control. On selecting the OK or Cancel button, the Property Page Dialog is dismissed. We'll break down the process into more detail, and show you how we can make our property pages behave in this way.

Developing our General Property Page

One of the first things we have to decide is what name we're going to give to our property page. Generally, it's good style to separate out a large number of properties into different property pages. When running through the wizard in chapter 3, we saw how it picked up the **Font** and **BackColor** stock properties and allocated a special property page for each. We also added a property page for our custom properties, and named it General.

In most cases, where a relatively small number of custom properties are to be exposed, they can all be assigned to just one property page. By convention this becomes the General property page. The way in which we organise property page ordering ensures that the most frequently used property pages appear at the start of the list of available ones. Other property pages, such as those which deal with the control color, should appear towards the end of the list. In this section, we'll be creating the General property page and showing the parts that we need to be concerned with.

Determine the Properties to be Included

After we've decided which property pages we're going to use, our next job is to decide which properties from our control go into each property page. We may not want to include *all* of the properties that our control exposes, but only the most pertinent. This may be the case if we have properties that might only be set when the control is first placed on the form.

However, for the Address control, we're going to go the full hog, and provide every design-time property in the property pages. So, from our General property page, we'll be allowing developers to change the following property values:

`Caption`	`Country`
`Caption_Name`	`Caption_Street` or `Caption_Address`
`Caption_City` or `Caption_Town`	`Caption_State` or `Caption_County`
`Caption_Country`	`Caption_Zip` or `Caption_Post`
`Caption_Phone`	`Caption_Email`
`View_Email`	`View_Coutry`
`Enabled`	

> *We're not including the* `Contact` *properties in this list as they are read-only during project run-time, and so cannot be changed using a property page anyway.*

Designing and Implementing the Appearance

Now we've decided which properties are going to be included in the General property page, we can proceed to design the layout of the property page itself. In the same way that we need to design the **UserControl** appearance, so too is this necessary for property pages. Here's the layout that we've decided on:

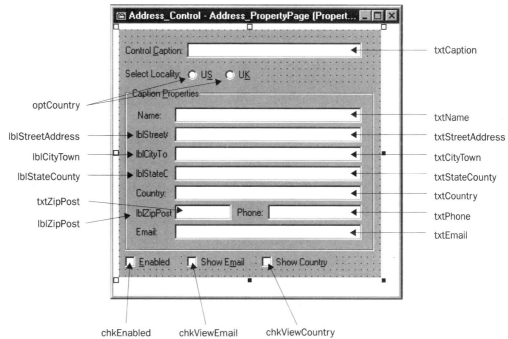

Since we're crafting this property page by hand, we can put the form elements where we feel most appropriate. In addition, we can now retrieve and change variables based on enumerated types so we've used option buttons for the Locality. We've also included check boxes which will be used to update the **View_Email** and **View_Country** property values, since their dual-state nature can be nicely represented this way.

You may have also noticed that within the Caption Properties frame, we've set the **Captions** of some labels to the name of the labels, while others have been set to Name;, Country;, Phone: and Email:. The reason is because some of the labels will need to have their **Caption** property altered when we switch between US to UK locality settings, but the others are standard for both localities. It's just a way of saving ourselves a bit of work later on.

Obtaining the Default Values from the Control

Now that our property page appearance is defined, we'll need to go about getting the property values from the control, where possible. Where this is not possible, providing suitable default values of our own is a very important stage in developing useful property pages.

Many developers take for granted when using property pages that they'll only need to change the required property values, just as if the Properties Window was being used. It wouldn't be an ideal situation if the developer had to go about resetting all the property page values to match those used in the control every time they opened the Property Pages Dialog.

The Address control has a few different modes of operation. For instance, it may be in **US** or **UK** mode, and be set so it either displays or hides the **Email** and **Country** fields individually. The way our Address control has been designed ensures that only the appropriate property values are available, depending on the operating modes of the control. Because of this, we'll get an empty string value back when attempting to retrieve the **Caption_Email** property when **Show_Email** is set to **0- HideEmail**.

To start with, let's define the variable **ctlAddress**, which we'll use to reference our Address control in the code. We've defined the variable of type **Address**, which is the project name we've given to our control. By using this variable, we can simplify references to the control later.

```
Option Explicit
Private ctlAddress As Address 'Needs to be the type of the control.
...
```

Coding the SelectionChanged Event

When we call up the property page, the event **SelectionChanged** is fired. It's in this event that we add code to get the default values for our property page.

We also have an **Initialize** event, that's fired when the property page is setting itself up before being displayed. When we talked about creating the Address control, we saw how we couldn't access the **Ambient** or **Extender** object in the **UserControl_Initialize** event, because they were only available after the control instance had initialised itself. We are faced with similar restrictions in the **PropertyPage_Initialize** event. In this case, however, we can't access the instance of the control that is selected, because the communication path that we need for obtaining the control instance's property values is only set up when the property page itself has initialized. This is why we use the **SelectionChanged** event to read in the property values from our control.

```
Private Sub PropertyPage_SelectionChanged()
  Set ctlAddress = SelectedControls(0)
  SetupDefaultValues
End Sub
```

Notice how we've used **SelectedControls** to access the selected control instance. When we have one or more control instances that we've selected, we don't know what the control names are going to be when we write code for our property pages. By using the **SelectedControls** property, we can access a collection that contains all currently selected controls on the form. In this way, we can access all the properties as though we were using the control in a design-time environment.

In the code above, we're accessing the zero'th control that's selected, which happens to be the first control selected on the form. We'll actually be taking the default values from this instance of the control. We've also called a subroutine that retrieves the default values, and sets up our property page so that these default values are used. We've used the **ctlAddress** object instead of **SelectedControl(0)** to make our code clearer.

First, we examine the current **Country** property value of the control, and set the appropriate option button to reflect this.

```
Private Sub SetupDefaultValues()
  Select Case ctlAddress.Country
  Case US
    optCountry(0).Value = 1
  Case UK
    optCountry(1).Value = 1
  End Select
```

Second, we'll need to get the property values (where appropriate) and update the property page display to show them.

```
With ctlAddress
  txtCaption.Text = .Caption
  txtName.Text = .Caption_Name
  If .View_Country = Show_Country Then
    chkViewCountry.Value = vbChecked
  End If
  UpdateCountryView
  txtPhone.Text = .Caption_Phone
  If .View_Email = Show_Email Then
    chkViewEmail.Value = vbChecked
  End If
  UpdateEmailView
  chkEnabled.Value = IIf(ctlAddress.Enabled, vbChecked, vbUnchecked)
End With

End Sub
```

We've used a couple of routines called **UpdateCountryView** and **UpdateEmailView** that update the property page views, depending on how the control is configured. It's in **UpdateCountryView** where we obtain the country specific property values. These two routines are very similar in nature, so we'll just talk you through the **UpdateCountryView** routine.

169

First, we've declared a **Static** variable that we'll use later in this routine. It will hold any intermediate modification that is made to the **Country** caption value, without changing that property value in the actual control. It also means that we are able to store any string value entered, and recall it if the developer decides to hide and then show the **Country** field.

```
Sub UpdateCountryView()
   Static strPrevValue As String 'Rely on default initialisation to ""
   If chkViewCountry.Value = vbChecked Then
      'Can enable country textbox
      txtCountry.Enabled = True
      txtCountry.ForeColor = vbMenuText
```

Now, if the variable **strPrevValue** contains the empty string (**""**), we haven't stored a value in it before. In this case, we can set **strPrevValue** to the value of the **Caption_Country** property from our control. If the **Country** field is currently not displayed in the control, then we can't get a default property value and so we just assign a default of our own. In the control, the default value for the **Caption_Country** property was Country: and so we'll use this value.

```
      If strPrevValue = "" Then        'Get value from UserControl
         strPrevValue = ctlAddress.Caption_Country
         If strPrevValue = "" Then
            'Just give default value as Country field was not displayed.
            strPrevValue = "Country:"
         End If
      End If
      txtCountry.Text = strPrevValue
   Else              'Disable the country textbox.
      'Save current value.
      strPrevValue = txtCountry.Text
      txtCountry.Text = "Not available"
      txtCountry.ForeColor = &H80000011   'vbDisabledText.
      txtCountry.Enabled = False
   End If
End Sub
```

Now we've determined the default values and updated our property page to show them, we need to make our property page 'react' so that it behaves correctly when any values are changed.

Making the Property Page Reactive

We've done quite a lot of work in setting up the property page to reflect the state of the control, and the good news is that we can re-use most of this again. Our real concern is what to do when we change the locality setting between **US** and **UK** modes. For a start, we need to change the labels in our property page to reflect the **Caption** properties that are applicable. Then there's the issue of getting the default values.

In the **SetupDefaultValues** subroutine discussed earlier, we set the appropriate **optCountry** option button's **Value** property to **True**. When this happens, or when the other option button is selected, we need to change the property page appearance to reflect the new mode of operation. Here's how we do it:

```
Private Sub optCountry_Click(Index As Integer)
   SetCountryMode (Index)
End Sub
```

We've introduced the **SetCountryMode** subroutine which does all the work for us. We retrieve the **Caption** property values for the country specific properties in this routine. If **Index = 0** we know that the option button for the US locality has been chosen. In this case, we can set the label captions' text to indicate the properties that they refer to.

```
Sub SetCountryMode(Index As Integer)
  Screen.MousePointer = vbHourglass
  Select Case Index
  Case 0 'US.
    'Get independent values
    lblStreetAddress.Caption = "Street:"
    lblCityTown.Caption = "City:"
    lblStateCounty.Caption = "State:"
    lblZipPost.Caption = "Zip:"
```

Next, we query the locality setting of the Address control itself. We need to do this so that we can determine whether we can access some meaningful Address control caption property values, or if we should just use some hard coded defaults instead. Incidentally, the hard coded defaults we've supplied are the same ones that we've used in the Address control.

```
    If ctlAddress.Country = US Then 'Can get the US field values.
      txtStreetAddress.Text = ctlAddress.Caption_Street
      txtCityTown.Text = ctlAddress.Caption_City
      txtStateCounty.Text = ctlAddress.Caption_State
      txtZipPost.Text = ctlAddress.Caption_Zip
    Else 'Stuff in some default values.
      txtStreetAddress.Text = "Street:"
      txtCityTown.Text = "City:"
      txtStateCounty.Text = "State:"
      txtZipPost.Text = "Zip:"
    End If
```

If the second option button was selected (**Index = 1**), then we perform the same steps, but this time specify UK based field values.

```
  Case 1 'UK.
    'Get independent values.
    lblStreetAddress.Caption = "Address:"
    lblCityTown.Caption = "Town:"
    lblStateCounty.Caption = "County:"
    lblZipPost.Caption = "Postcode:"
    If ctlAddress.Country = UK Then 'Can get the UK field values.
      txtStreetAddress.Text = ctlAddress.Caption_Address
      txtCityTown.Text = ctlAddress.Caption_Town
      txtStateCounty.Text = ctlAddress.Caption_County
      txtZipPost.Text = ctlAddress.Caption_Postcode
    Else  'Stuff in some default values.
      txtStreetAddress.Text = "Address:"
      txtCityTown.Text = "Town:"
      txtStateCounty.Text = "County:"
      txtZipPost.Text = "Postcode:"
    End If

  End Select
  Screen.MousePointer = vbNormal
End Sub
```

For every control defined in our property page, we've added code that will update the **Changed** property of the property page. However, we've done this through an auxiliary routine called **SetChanged**. The purpose of this routine is to update individual elements in an array, which indicate which property values have been modified in the property page. We'll explain how this is done in the next section. For now, have a quick glance at a few examples:

```
Private Sub txtName_Change()
   SetChanged (NameChanged)
End Sub
```

```
Private Sub chkEnabled_Click()
   SetChanged (EnabledChanged)
End Sub
```

```
Private Sub chkViewCountry_Click()
   SetChanged (ViewCountryChanged)
   UpdateCountryView
End Sub
```

Passing the New Property Values Back

Earlier in the chapter, we've talked about how, in the **ApplyChanges** event, the modified property values should be copied back to the control. We've also stated that for more complex controls, we should only copy back those values that have actually changed. Here, we're going to introduce a mechanism that will allow us to do just that. We'll also be making the framework as generic as possible, so it'll be easy for you to use the same approach in writing your custom property pages.

First off, we'll define an array of boolean values. We haven't specified the number of elements, because we'll re-dimension it later when we know how many values it should hold.

```
Private blnChangedArray() As Boolean
```

Next, we'll create an enumeration containing representations for all of our Address control's properties. We're using an enumeration because each member automatically has a unique integer value associated with it. Assuming that we're always going to provide an **Enabled** property for any control we create, and that we place it last in the list, we can use the integer value of this member in determining how many properties we'll be using. This provides us with a means to re-dimension our array later on.

```
Enum ControlSet
   CaptionChanged
   CountryModeChanged
   NameChanged
   StreetAddressChanged
   CityTownChanged
   StateCountyChanged
   CountryChanged
   ZipPostChanged
   PhoneChanged
   EmailChanged
   ViewEmailChanged
   ViewCountryChanged
   EnabledChanged
End Enum
```

Even though we can't get at the Address control in the **PropertyPage_Initialize** event, we can write code that will re-dimension and initialise our array of boolean values.

```
Private Sub PropertyPage_Initialize()
  Dim intIndex As Integer
  intChangedCount = 0
  ReDim blnChangedArray(EnabledChanged)
  For intIndex = 0 To UBound(blnChangedArray)
    blnChangedArray(intIndex) = False
  Next intIndex
End Sub
```

Recall how **SetChanged** is called:

```
Private Sub optCountry_Click(Index As Integer)
  SetCountryMode (Index)
  SetChanged (CountryModeChanged)
End Sub
```

Defining **SetChanged** is easy, since all we need to do is update the **Changed** property value, and the appropriate array element value, to **True.**

```
Private Sub SetChanged(ChangedControl As Integer)
  Changed = True
  blnChangedArray(ChangedControl) = True
End Sub
```

Copying the changed property values back to the Address control is now a fairly simple process. The properties that have been updated will be indicated by the appropriate element in the array being **True**. Here, we've given you the whole of the **ApplyChanges** listing, because we think it's important in demonstrating the checks that we perform, and the logic necessary to make sure our property page updates the property values according to the functionality of the Address control.

```
Private Sub PropertyPage_ApplyChanges()

  If blnChangedArray(CaptionChanged) Then ctlAddress.Caption = txtCaption.Text
  If blnChangedArray(CountryModeChanged) Then
    'Only need to update country, as other fields will update the
    'appropriate values since any change of text values will be noted
    If optCountry(0).Value = True Then    'Update to US
      ctlAddress.Country = US
    ElseIf optCountry(1).Value = True Then
      ctlAddress.Country = UK
    End If
  End If

  'Deal with independent changes first
  If blnChangedArray(NameChanged) Then ctlAddress.Caption_Name = txtName.Text
  If blnChangedArray(PhoneChanged) Then ctlAddress.Caption_Phone = txtPhone.Text

  'Update View_Country and View_Email values for control.
  If blnChangedArray(ViewEmailChanged) Then
    If chkViewEmail.Value = vbChecked Then
```

```
        ctlAddress.View_Email = Show_Email
      Else
        ctlAddress.View_Email = Hide_Email
      End If
    End If
    If blnChangedArray(ViewCountryChanged) Then
      If chkViewCountry.Value = vbChecked Then ctlAddress.View_Country _
                                       = Show_Country
      Else
        ctlAddress.View_Country = Hide_Country
      End If
    End If

    If optCountry(0).Value = True Then    'US properties may need updating
      If blnChangedArray(StreetAddressChanged) Then _
                  ctlAddress.Caption_Street = txtStreetAddress.Text
      If blnChangedArray(CityTownChanged) Then _
                  ctlAddress.Caption_City = txtCityTown.Text
      If blnChangedArray(StateCountyChanged) Then _
                  ctlAddress.Caption_State = txtStateCounty.Text
      If blnChangedArray(ZipPostChanged) Then _
                  ctlAddress.Caption_Zip = txtZipPost.Text
    Else 'UK properties may need updating
      If blnChangedArray(StreetAddressChanged) Then _
                  ctlAddress.Caption_Address = txtStreetAddress.Text
      If blnChangedArray(CityTownChanged) Then _
                  ctlAddress.Caption_Town = txtCityTown.Text
      If blnChangedArray(StateCountyChanged) Then _
                  ctlAddress.Caption_County = txtStateCounty.Text
      If blnChangedArray(ZipPostChanged) Then _
                  ctlAddress.Caption_Postcode = txtZipPost.Text
    End If

    'Now may need to update Country and Email caption properties
    If chkViewCountry.Value = vbChecked Then
      If blnChangedArray(CountryChanged) Then _
                  ctlAddress.Caption_Country = txtCountry.Text
    End If
    If chkViewEmail.Value = vbChecked Then
      If blnChangedArray(EmailChanged) Then _
                  ctlAddress.Caption_Email = txtEmail.Text
    End If
    If blnChangedArray(EnabledChanged) Then _
        ctlAddress.Enabled = IIf(chkEnabled.Value = vbChecked, True, False)

End Sub
```

Attaching Property Pages to a Control

Now that we've created our General property page, we need to attach it to the list of currently active property pages for our control. We do this through the **PropertyPages** property that's available on the Properties window.

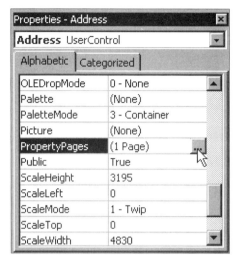

This brings up the Connect Property Pages Dialog, where we can add any property pages required.

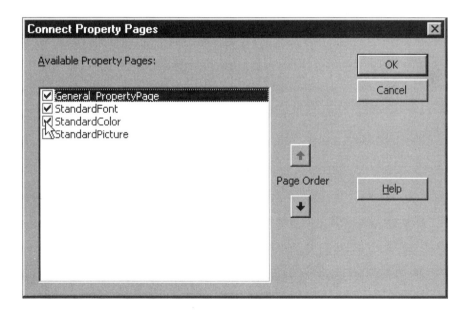

That's all there is to it. We'll leave you with a design guideline on creating property pages.

Property Page Design Guidelines

The following guidelines are intended to provide assistance in creating property pages that are professional-looking and easy to use.

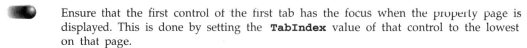

Ensure that the first control of the first tab has the focus when the property page is displayed. This is done by setting the **TabIndex** value of that control to the lowest on that page.

If several columns of controls are displayed on a page, the tab order should be go from top to bottom of the column, then move to the top of the next column.

You should provide access keys (keyboard shortcuts) for all the accessible fields in the property page.

The letter 'A' is not made available as an access key, because the Property Pages Dialog *box uses it for the* Apply *button.*

Place standard property pages for fonts, colors, and pictures at the end of the list of property pages for a control. They are often the least frequently used.

Group similar properties together where possible. When the control is sufficiently complex, all appearance related properties should reside on the same property page.

Use a uniform size for your property pages. When the Property Pages Dialog box displays several property pages, the dimensions of the largest page are used for all of them.

You may have noticed that the standard property pages are all the same size. If you're using any or all of these pages with your control, you should set the sizes of any other pages to this standard size. A quick way to do this is achieved by setting the **StandardSize** *property of the property page to* **Large** *at design time.*

For accessibility reasons, keep the number of tabs to a minimum. Using drop-down lists for enumeration types often provides the most efficient use of space.

Most controls have a General property page which contains items that are general to many controls.

Keep your pages concise and fast. Fancy property pages are often bigger, resulting in a bigger control to distribute. Such controls also use up more system resources, than simpler, light-weight controls.

It's possible to add a Help button to the Property Pages Dialog by adding a help file to your project via the Project Options General tab. You can make this help context-sensitive by setting the **HelpContextID** property for the property page, and their constituent controls.

Make sure you add labels to your property pages that include the name of the properties.

Create strings for named constants in an enumeration. The developer using your control will have to use these member names in the client project.

Avoid showing dialog boxes from your property page other than those displayed by using the common dialog control.

If a property dependency exists between several property values then put those properties on the same page.

summary
Summary

Summary

In this chapter, we've covered creating property pages by hand in some depth. We've talked about the Property Pages Dialog and its interaction with the property page containers. The most important points covered in this chapter are:

- Each property page is a container which provides a property page object.

- When the property page object is created, the **SelectionChanged** event fires. This is where we need to obtain the property values from the control.

- We must alert the Property Pages Dialog when any property value has been changed, by setting the **Changed** property of the **PropertyPage** object to **True**.

- We copy the changed property values back to the control in the **ApplyChanges** event.

- The standard property pages **StandardFont**, **StandardColor** and **StandardPicture** automatically provide an interface for changing any property values of type **Font**, **OLE_COLOR** and **Picture** respectively when those property pages are attached.

- We can access all selected control instances through the **SelectedControls** collection. Generally, we use the first selected control to obtain the property values for our property page.

- We can associate property pages with properties so that the property page is displayed whenever we attempt to alter that property through the Properties window.

177

Chapter

7

Data Bound Controls

So far, we have taken an in depth look at the new VB5 CCE and discovered the power and flexibility gained through the use and development of components. In this chapter, we will explore adding data access features to the components that you build.

We will cover:

- How we can populate the Address control from Chapter 5 with data from a database.
- Using the Jet Engine and DAO to access data.
- Accessing the ODBC API directly from your control.
- Navigating through recordsets.
- Modifying database records.

An Overview of Data Access

VB5 CCE does not include a built in data access layer. As such, in order to build a control that has data access capabilities, we will need to build in these capabilities ourselves. Fortunately, we don't have to start from scratch. In the following sections, we will take a look at two techniques that we can take advantage of in order to build data access capabilities into the controls we create with the VB5 CCE.

The first technique takes advantage of a flexible database engine called the Microsoft Jet Engine. The Jet Engine was originally developed as the underlying database for Microsoft Access. With the success of Access, Microsoft looked to the Jet Engine as a standard database engine that could be used across multiple product lines.

At that time, Visual Basic 1.0 was Microsoft's first real venture into the Windows development tool arena, outside of C. Although quite successful, Visual Basic 2.0 was much criticized for its lack of a built-in database or data access mechanism. The Jet Engine seemed a natural answer to this problem and was introduced as the default database engine for Visual Basic version 3.0.

Since that time, the Jet Engine has undergone a number of significant enhancements that have extended its ability to access ODBC (Open Data base Connectivity) data sources. It is now a powerful tool that, through the use of ODBC and other extensions, allows Visual Basic developers to interact through a common interface with any number of data sources, from simple flat files to enterprise-oriented relational database management systems such as Oracle and Sybase.

The second technique we will explore looks into accessing the ODBC API directly from VB5 CCE. The ODBC interface allows applications to access data in database management systems (DBMS) using Structured Query Language (SQL) as a standard for accessing data. It is one of the underlying technologies the Jet Engine uses to access relational data sources other then its native MDB format.

The ODBC interface permits maximum interoperability, allowing a single application to access many different database management systems. This flexibility allows an application developer to develop, compile, and ship an application without targeting a specific DBMS. Users can add modules, called database drivers, that link the application to their choice of database management systems.

When developing components, accessing the ODBC API directly gives us maximum interoperability in accessing data from a control. This approach is not dependent on the additional layers of software imposed by the Jet Engine and its Data Access Objects, that although can simplify the coding we are required to do, requires additional overhead and may be restricted by additional licensing issues and distribution concerns.

Data Access Objects

In response to marketing pressure from competitors such as Powersoft's PowerBuilder, in 1993 Microsoft announced the release of Visual Basic 3.0 with a built-in database engine called the Jet Engine.

> *Jet is not an acronym. Rumour has it that Jet stands for 'Joint Engine Technology', however most Microsoft folks dismiss this. Jet was the internal name of the development project and was never intended for outside use. However, it caught on and so we now have the Jet Engine.*

Jet was originally developed as the database engine for Microsoft Access version 1.0. Access was, basically, an easy to use interface to this powerful database tool and the initial release of Jet was limited in its ability to access data sources other then its native MDB format.

Jet version 1.1 was released with Access 1.1 in May of 1993 and included a number of improvements to provide greater connectivity between itself and Open Database Connectivity (ODBC) databases. An expanded ability to attach an MDB table to an ODBC data source was introduced, along with a number of improvements to the Data Access Objects (DAO) interface.

The DAO is an object library that provides the developer with access to Jet Engine resources through a series of objects. Introduced with Visual Basic 3.0, these objects allow a Visual Basic application to directly manipulate a database without needing to call external functions.

From its initial entry into the market, the DAO library has evolved from a limited set of simple objects to a robust tool that can access nearly all of the Jet Engine's functionality through a simple to use interface. The following table shows the evolution of DAO:

Interface	Host version	Major capabilities
DAO 1.0	Microsoft Access 1.0	Interface to table and query structures, objects to represent tables, dynasets, and snapshots with a limited number of properties.
Data Access Objects 1.0	Visual Basic 3.0	Added **TableDef**, **QueryDef**, and **Field** objects to programmatically expose structures.
Data Access Objects 2.0	Microsoft Access 2.0	First vestiges of OLE Automation, full programmatic access to almost all Microsoft Jet functionality. Full object model with robust set of objects and properties.
Data Access Objects 2.5	ODBC Desktop Database Drivers	Created for both 16- and 32-bit platforms. Designed for use with ODBC Desktop Database Drivers 2.0.
Data Access Objects 3.0	Microsoft Access for Windows 95, Visual Basic 4.0 (32-bit), Microsoft Excel 7.0, Visual C ++	Enhanced to support a stand-alone interface for any compatible host.

Using DAO with the VB5 CCE

VB5 CCE is not supplied with a data access mechanism or database engine, which means that the DAO object library and underlying Jet Engine are not included with the package. However, all is not lost. Visual Basic 4 (Professional and Enterprise Editions), MS Office 95 (Professional Edition) and various other Microsoft products come with the Jet Engine and version 3.0 of the DAO. If your are the legal owner of VB 4, you can take advantage of DAO 3.0 in the components you build with VB5 CCE.

To use the DAO version 3.0 with VB5 CCE, you must first install Visual Basic 4.0 or one of the other products mentioned, which include the Jet Engine and DAO. With one of these products installed, you then install VB5 CCE.

> Note that Visual Basic 4 and VB5 CCE may not run together under the same operating system. When you install VB 5.0 CCE, you may have problems using some of VB 4's features such as the Common Dialog control.

VB 4 may have some trouble running with VB5 CCE, however its data access libraries do not. We will take advantage of this to develop a control that has data access features.

Accessing the DAO from VB5 CCE

The DAO is implemented as an ActiveX Automation server that includes the various data objects made available to your program. ActiveX Automation is a service that allows applications to expose some or all of their functionality to other applications. Its primary focus is to allow the developer to take advantage of the features of an application package from within a program. The DAO exposes its data access capabilities to your application, allowing you to access the Jet Engine and thus various data sources.

The first step in using the DAO Automation server is to provide a reference to the DAO version 3.0 type library. This is a special file or library that contains ActiveX Automation standard descriptions of exposed objects, properties, and methods. To provide a reference to the library, select the References item on the Project menu. Then, on the References dialog box check the Microsoft DAO 3.0 Object Library.

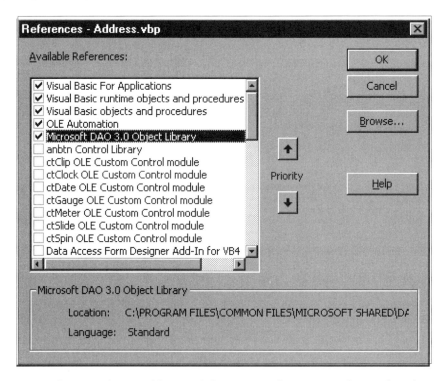

Visual Basic can then use the type library's definitions to allow your code to take advantage of **early binding**, as well as to perform basic syntax checking in your code.

Binding

Binding refers to the point in time when references to the exposed methods and properties of a server application are resolved. Early binding means that the references can be resolved at compile time, which significantly improves the performance of your application. If your application uses **late binding**, it means that it must make an extra call to the server in order to resolve the supplied name each time a reference is made to one of its properties or methods. This additional traffic reduces the overall performance of the application. The type library provided with the DAO allows us to take advantage of the performance benefits of early binding.

DAO Objects

The DAO is a hierarchy of objects, beginning with several high level structures that become much more detailed as we move down the hierarchy. Let's take a moment to briefly review the high level objects that we will be using. A more detailed review is beyond the scope of this book, but is available in the Visual Basic 4.0 Professional Edition Documentation or the Jet Database Engine Programmer's Guide from Microsoft Press.

Data Access Objects (DAO) Version 3.0

```
DBEngine
  └ Workspace
      ├ Database                                    User
      │   ├ TableDef        QueryDef       RecordSet   └ Group
      │   │   ├ Field          ├ Field         ├ Field     Group
      │   │   ├ Index          └ Parameter     ├ Relation     └ User
      │   │   │   └ Field                       │   └ Field
      │   └ Error                               ├ Container
      │                                         └ Document
```

Key:
- ▨ Object and Collection
- ▢ Object only

At the top of the hierarchy is the **DBEngine** object, which represents the Jet Engine itself. As the top-level object, it contains and controls all other objects in the hierarchy. Accessing an object in the DAO hierarchy will automatically load the **DBEngine** object into memory (this is usually referred to as instantiating the object).

The next level down the DAO hierarchy is the **Workspace** object. A **Workspace** object exists for each active session of the Jet Engine. A session begins when your application logs on to a data source and ends when it logs off. You can think of a workspace as a transaction area that is used by your application.

The Login ID and Password that you supply restrict the operations that are allowed within the defined workspace. The advantage of this is that your application can create several workspaces, each with its own independent transactions, user IDs and passwords. The **Workspaces** collection contains all **Workspace** objects defined by the currently running Jet Engine.

The **Database** object represents a currently open database. This can be a native Jet database file (MDB), an external ISAM database such as dBase or Foxpro, or an ODBC data source. You can have multiple databases open at a time, even databases of different types. The **Databases** collection contains all **Database** objects in a workspace.

The next object we will look at is the **Recordset** object. A **Recordset** object represents in memory, a set of records from one or more tables. **Recordset** objects are one of the most powerful constructs in the DAO because they allow you to programmatically access the data source specified in your code. This object can then be used to browse, update, and delete the data in a data source using a relatively simple set of methods.

Building a Control that Uses the DAO

Now that we have reviewed the DAO, let's take a look at using it in a control. We will expand upon the address control that we developed in an earlier chapter, providing it with the capability of accessing and displaying the address information stored in a database. In the following example, we will take a look at enabling our control to access and display data from the database while running as a part of an application, and when setting properties during design.

The Address Control Revisited

The address control, as we have seen, allows the developer to programmatically modify the caption information displayed to the end-user. Caption property information can be supplied both at design-time using a property page and at run-time by updating a number of **Public** caption properties. To add data access capabilities to the control, we will enhance the caption properties with a number of data properties and add a new property page that supports the selection of data access parameters.

Property Page Enhancements

To provide data access facilities, the user of the control must provide us with several pieces of information. These include the data source that we are going to work with, the table that contains the data we want to display, and the fields we will use for each of the address prompts.

In order to make providing this information as straightforward for the control's user as possible, a new property page has been added to the control. The property page, used at design-time, allows the user to enter the name of the data source, table and fields that will be accessed to present information by the control.

Let's start with the data source name. In our example, this can either be the name of an Access database (an MDB), or an ODBC connection string. The data source name is used by the DAO and Jet Engine to locate and attach to a selected data source. If an MDB file name is provided, then the DAO will look for the file at the location specified and attempt to connect to it. If an ODBC connection string is supplied, the DAO will access the ODBC API and attempt to connect to the source represented by the connection string.

You will notice in the screenshot on the next page, that the second prompt on the property page requests that the user enter a Table Name. The address control will use this table name along with the field names supplied to retrieve information for display at run-time. However, providing this information would be difficult if the user was not familiar with the data source being accessed. To make the task of supplying this information somewhat easier, a drop down list box is used to collect table and field names.

These list boxes display all of the table names associated with the given data source name and all of the field names associated with a supplied table name. Now supplying table and field information becomes a point and click affair.

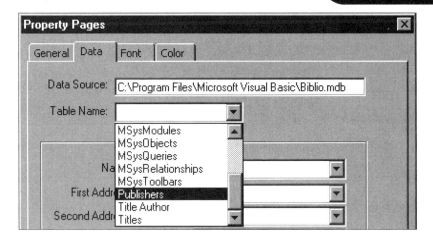

With the changes made, the values are stored as properties and will be used to display data on the address control within a program.

Building The Data Property Page

Now that we know what the property page does, let's take a look at how to build it. The first step is to create several object variables that will be used to reference the DAO. The first variable we need creates a reference to the DAO database object. This reference is used to interact with the data source name supplied by the user. A **wsWorkSpaces** object variable is included to reference the workspace object that the control will use when accessing a data source. Notice these variables are defined as **Private**, allowing only the procedures in the property page module to access them.

```
Private dbDatabase As Database          'Database
Private wsWorkspace As Workspace        'a workspace
```

In addition, two **Private** variables are defined that we will use to keep track of the control's data source connection as well as the data source name supplied by the user.

```
Private bConnected As Boolean           'are we connected
Private sConnectionName As String       'Connection name
```

With object variables defined, we can take a look at how to work with the data source name supplied. Before data from a data source can be retrieved, we must create a connection to the data source, supplying any security information it may require. To meet this need, we create a **Private** function called **fConnect**.

Making a Connection

The **fConnect** function is defined as **Private** so that it can be accessed from any point in the property page module, but cannot be accessed outside of it. This stops the developer using the control from inadvertently calling this internal function. A connection function that is designed to be called by the developer is addressed a little further on.

```
Private Function fConnect(sDataName) As Boolean
```

185

The **fConnect** function begins by setting the **dbDatabase** and **wsWorkspace** object variables to **Nothing**, thus releasing any current connections that may exist. When using the DAO, a disconnect method is not provided. The object library itself maintains responsibility for releasing connections as they are no longer used. However, this can become an issue if you need a connection released at a specific point, so that a new connection can be created. To force the DAO to release a connection to a data source, you set the associated object variables to **Nothing**.

```
bConnected = False
Set dbDatabase = Nothing
Set wsWorkspace = Nothing
```

In addition, we set our connection flag (**bConnected**) to **False**, indicating that we are no longer attached to a data source and a new connection can be made. The next step is then to connect to the supplied data source name and set our object variables to reference the new connection. This is done using the following code:

```
Set wsWorkspace = Workspaces(0)

If (InStr(sDataName, "ODBC") > 0) Then
    Set dbDatabase = wsWorkspace.OpenDatabase("", False, False, sDataName)
Else
    Set dbDatabase = wsWorkspace.OpenDatabase(sDataName)
End If

bConnected = True
fConnect = True
sConnectionName = sDataName
```

The first **Set** command assigns the **wsWorkspace** variable to the default **Workspace** object in the **Workspaces** collection. The next step scans the supplied data source name string for the **"ODBC"** string to determine whether or not the source name is an ODBC connection string or a file name. This simple example is a sufficient test for demonstration purposes, however in a production system, you may want to provide a more robust determination mechanism.

If an ODBC data source name is provided, the **dbDatabase** object variable is set to reference a database object created using the **OpenDatabase** function. The **OpenDatabase** function provides a database reference to a valid database or data source. Its syntax is as follows:

Set database = workspace.OpenDatabase(dbname[, exclusive[, read-only[, source]]])

*For a detailed break down of the **OpenDatabase** method's syntax see the VB 4.0 online help.*

In our case, if an ODBC data source name is supplied, we call the **OpenDataBase** method with an empty string for the database name and the value supplied by the user as our source name. This informs the method what type of data source to connect to. With a successful connection, we can set our private **bConected** flag to **True**, and private **sConnectionName** variable to the data source name supplied. Finally, the return value of the **fConnect** function is set to **True** and we exit the process.

186

The Table Drop-Down List Box

With a connection function in place, we are ready to look at how to supply a list of table names and fields to the user. Let's begin by looking at the table name list. When the developer clicks on the drop-down arrow of the Table Name drop-down list box, a connection is made to the specified data source and a list of tables is retrieved.

Our first step in the **DropDown** event of the Table Name drop-down list box (represented by **Private Sub ddlbTableName_DropDown**) is to define the variable that we need to access the required table information. This object variable will contain information concerning individual tables in the data source.

```
Dim tblLocal  As TableDef    'Table Object
```

With an object variable defined, our next processing step is to determine if we are already connected. This is done using:

```
If (fIsConnected = False) Then
    If (fConnect(txtDataSource.Text) = False) Then
        Exit Sub
    End If
End If
```

The **fIsConnected** function simply tests the value of the private **bConnected** flag, and uses the private **sConnectionName** variable to verify that the data source name has not changed since the last connection check.

```
Private Function fIsConnected() As Boolean
  If (bConnected = True And sConnectionName = txtDataSource.Text) Then
      fIsConnected = True
  Else
      fIsConnected = False
  End If
End Function
```

If we are not connected to a data source yet, the **fConnect** function is called to establish a new connection. If a failure occurs at any point, the function is exited and no data is supplied in the drop down list box.

Once a connection is either verified or established, we can clear any values that might already be in the list box:

```
ddlbTableName.Clear
```

After this, we loop through each table object in the **TableDefs** collection of the database object using the **For Each** construct:

```
For Each tblLocal In dbDatabase.TableDefs
    ddlbTableName.AddItem (tblLocal.Name)
Next
```

The DAO handles the retrieval of information concerning the tables and fields in a data source from the data source catalogs, and maintains it internally. From this information, we want the names of each of the tables in our data source. To retrieve the names of the tables, we loop

187

through each table object in the **TableDefs** collection, assign a reference to an individual table to the **tblLocal** variable, and then read the name using the **Name** method of the table object.

As each name is retrieved, it is added to the drop down list box using the **AddItem** method. A list of table names is now available in the list box for the control user to select from.

The Fields Drop Down List Boxes

To produce a list of field names, a similar procedure is evoked. However, this time we are looking for all the field names for a given data source and table name. Our first step in the **DropDown** event of each field drop-down list box (represented by **Private Sub ddlb{List box Name}_DropDown**) is to define a common function that will be used to display the requested information. As the processing for each field is basically the same, a single function can be used for all field name selection list boxes.

```
Private Sub FieldList()
```

The **FieldList** procedure handles querying the data source for the necessary field information. As in the **TableName** procedure, we start off by checking to see if a valid connection to the supplied data source name exists. Keep in mind that the data source name may have changed, or the user may not have selected a table name from a list and thus not have made a connection to the supplied data source name.

```
If (fIsConnected = False) Then
    If (fConnect(txtDataSource.Text) = False) Then
        Exit Function
    End If
End If

  If (ddlbTableName.Text = "") Then
      MsgBox "No Table Name Supplied", AttIcon, AppName
      fFieldList = False
      Exit Function
  End If
```

In this case, one additional test is made to verify that a table has been supplied. Without a table name, the application has no means of retrieving field information. As such, if a table name has not already been provided, a message is displayed and the function exited.

With a connection verified, we can begin the process of populating the currently selected drop-down list box. To do this, we must first know which list box to work with. This is dealt with by a private object variable labeled **objComboBox**. This variable is assigned a reference to the current drop-down list box when the **DropDown** event procedure for it is activated. For example, the following lists the **DropDown** procedure for the City/Town drop down list box:

```
Private Sub ddlbCityTown_DropDown()
  Set objComboBox = ddlbCityTown
  FieldList
  SetChanged (CityTownChanged)
End Sub
```

You will notice that the **objComboBox** variable is assigned to reference the current drop-down list box, using the **Set** command. With this reference in place, we can manipulate the current drop-down list box in the **FieldList** procedure. To do this, we assign the object variable to a local variable of type **ComboBox** (the same type as the control we are dealing with) and thus can access the properties and methods of the control as if we were using its name directly.

```
Dim cmbCombo    As ComboBox    'Type the object correctly
Set cmbCombo = objComboBox
```

*Note that this is a somewhat roundabout way of doing this. A bug in the beta of VB5 CCE prevents us from simply passing the control as a parameter to the **FieldList** procedure. This problem will likely be resolved before the release of VB5.*

To retrieve the field names, we begin by clearing the current drop-down list box, making sure that any previous values are removed.

```
cmbCombo.Clear
```

Then using the **For Each** construct, we loop through the **Fields** collection of the **TableDef** object, selected by the supplied table name.

```
cmbCombo.Clear
For Each fldLocal In dbDatabase.TableDefs(ddlbTableName.Text).Fields
    cmbCombo.AddItem (fldLocal.Name)
Next
```

The names are added to the drop-down list box's list and displayed to the user. In this manner, the user of your control is given ample assistance to determine what table to use to retrieve data and which fields to use when displaying this data in the Address control's prompts.

Applying the Changes

The only thing we have left to do on the property page now is update the Address control's **Private Sub PropertyPage_ApplyChanges()** procedure to include the new data source information we just supplied. Making the information supplied available to the address control is simply a matter of adding a few new property variables to the control and then updating them in the **ApplyChanges** event of the property page. For example:

```
If (blnChangedArray(NameChanged)) Then
    ctlAddress.ContactName = ddlbNameField.Text
End If
```

This code updates the **ContactName** property that had been added to the Address control to support data access.

Address Control Data Methods

Now that we have the data access properties defined in the Address control, we have to add a number of new methods in order to make data access available to the developer. Just as we did previously, we will create a number of private object variables that will be used to reference objects of the DAO. Here we will add one new variable to reference a **Recordset** object. The **Recordset** object is used to retrieve the requested data from the data source.

```
Private m_rcRecordSet As Recordset        'a default record set
```

With this, let's take a look at how our control will retrieve and present data.

Providing a Connection Method

The most logical place to begin then is with making a connection. Just as we did with the property page, we will add a function that will be used to connect to a specified data source. The difference here, however, is that the user of the control will call this connection function, as opposed to the internal procedures of the control.

```
Public Function pfConnect() As Boolean
```

To make the new method available to external users it is defined as a **Public** function. This means that once a developer has placed the Address control on their application's form and created a reference to it, they can invoke this procedure from within their application.

The **pfConnect** function begins by checking that the various parameters that are required have been supplied by the user. If they have not and these critical values are missing, the function returns **False** and stops processing. Here again these checks are sufficient for learning purposes, but for a real application you would likely make these far more robust.

```
If (m_DataSource = "") Then
    pfConnect = False
    Exit Function
End If

If (m_bConnected = True) Then
    pfConnect = False
    Exit Function
End If

If (m_TableName = "") Then
    pfConnect = False
    Exit Function
End If
```

If the parameters we need have been supplied, we can connect to the data source much the same as we did in the previous example. However, this method has one additional step that was not required on the property page. Here we need to define a **Recordset** object, that will be used to retrieve the data from the data source. The **Recordset** object is defined as follows:

For an ODBC data source:

```
Set m_rcRecordSet = m_dbDatabase.OpenRecordset(m_TableName, dbOpenDynaset)
```

(where **m_TableName** is the name of the table supplied by the control user).

Or, for an Access data source:

```
Set m_rcRecordSet = m_dbDatabase.OpenRecordset(m_TableName, dbOpenTable)
```

A recordset is a special object of the DAO that represents the records in a table or multiple tables. The recordset is used to manipulate the records of tables, as well as retrieve information on the data stored in these records.

A recordset built from an ODBC data source is treated somewhat differently to that of a native Jet database. In our example, we cannot create a **table type (dbOpenTable)** recordset for an ODBC data source. An ODBC recordset represents the result set of a query, which is then manipulated by the Jet Engine. In this case, a **Dynaset** (Dynamic Set) recordset is created by retrieving a unique key for each record into memory.

The actual data is only retrieved when individual fields are referenced. This unique key is then used internally by the Jet Engine to manage the retrieval of additional information as the user scrolls through the recordset.

When a native Jet Engine data source is used, a somewhat more flexible option is presented—in the form of a table type (**dbOpenTable**) recordset. A table type recordset takes advantage of a unique index on the data source to retrieve records of data. The tight coupling of the Jet Engine and the database allows for much less overhead and improved performance over the other recordset types. In our example, we take advantage of the table type recordset when it is available to us, and resort to a dynaset type recordset when an ODBC data source is specified.

With a recordset object available to our application, it becomes very straightforward to navigate the data source and present results in the text boxes of the user control. In our example, we have the ability to move through the selected table's records as well as to add, update and delete records.

Navigating the Database

In order to give the control the ability to move through the recordset we just created, we need to provide the developer with a number of methods. Let's take a look at a method that will allow the user to move to the first record of the recordset and display the resulting data, using the fields supplied, in the Address control's text boxes.

We begin by declaring a public function with a descriptive name.

```
Public Function pfMoveFirst()
```

This is the method name provided to the end user. The **pfMoveFirst** method first determines whether or not the user has connected to the data source, and then calls the **MoveFirst** method of the recordset created by the **pfConnect** method.

```
If (pfIsConnected()) Then
    m_rcRecordSet.MoveFirst
    UpdateDisplay
    pfMoveFirst = True
Else
    pfMoveFirst = False
End If
```

With the current position of the recordset at the first record, we can call an internal **UpdateDisplay** procedure to update the text boxes of the Address control interface. The **UpdateDisplay** procedure, very simply, calls a procedure (**fFieldInCollection**) to compare each field represented in the recordset with each field name provided as a property by the developer. When a match is found, the corresponding text box on the address control is updated with the data retrieved for the matching field. This is done using the following code, which is repeated for each field:

```
If (fFieldInCollection(m_NameField)) Then
    txtName.Text = IIf(IsNull(m_rcRecordSet.Fields(m_NameField)), "",
```

```
                        m_rcRecordSet.Fields(m_NameField))
     End If
```

The only caveat is that a check must be made for a **NULL** character. Visual Basic treats NULLs as a special case, and distinct from an empty string. As such, if you attempt to assign a field value which is NULL to the **Text** attribute of a text box, a run-time error will occur. To avoid this, a test is implemented to look for a NULL and replace it with an empty string when found.

And that is all there is to it. **MoveLast**, **MoveNext**, or **MovePrevious** are implemented by following almost identical steps. Simply updating the recordset method call with the desired navigational command provides your control with the ability to move about the recordset and present retrieved data on the control. For example, the following code allows us to move to the last record:

```
Public Function pfMoveLast() As Boolean

     If (pfIsConnected()) Then
         m_rcRecordSet.MoveLast
         UpdateDisplay
         pfMoveLast = True
     Else
         pfMoveLast = False
     End If

End Function
```

and this code allows us, with only a few minor changes to deal with the boundaries of the data set, to move to the next record:

```
Public Function pfMoveNext() As Boolean

     If (pfIsConnected()) Then

         On Error GoTo Error
         m_rcRecordSet.MoveNext
         UpdateDisplay

     End If

     pfMoveNext = True
     Exit Function

Error:
     MsgBox "No More Records", AttIcon, AppName
     pfMoveNext = False
End Function
```

Adding and deleting data are no more difficult to implement. Let's take a look at how we might go about adding a new record to our data source. To start, we will define a public method called **pfAddNew**.

```
Public Function pfAddNew() As Boolean
```

This new member will check to see if a connection exists, just as in our previous example:

```
If (pfIsConnected()) Then
    .
    .
End If
```

We then replace the text of the address control field text boxes with spaces, using **ClearList** which is defined as:

```
Private Sub ClearList()

    txtName.Text = ""
    txtStreetAddress.Text = ""
    txtStreetAddress2.Text = ""
    txtCityTown.Text = ""
    txtStateCounty.Text = ""
    txtCountry.Text = ""
    txtZipPost.Text = ""
    txtPhone.Text = ""
    txtEmail.Text = ""

End Sub
```

Following this, we simply invoke the **AddNew** method of the recordset. The **AddNew** method creates a new record into which the developer or end-user can add data. In our example, the Address control text boxes are used to add data, which is then saved using the **Update** method of the recordset. The **pfAddnew** method is built as follows:

```
Public Function pfAddNew() As Boolean

    If (pfIsConnected()) Then

        ClearList

        On Error GoTo Error
        m_rcRecordSet.AddNew
        m_rcRecordSet.Update 'Make sure a record is added

    End If

    pfAddNew = True
    Exit Function

Error:
    pfAddNew = False
    MsgBox "Error: " & Err.Description, AttIcon, AppName
End Function
```

Granted this is a simple example, but it is really quite easy to manipulate data using DAO objects and the Jet Engine. Adding data access features to your user control can be as straight forward as including a reference to the DAO library in your VB5 CCE project.

An Overview of ODBC

With a good understanding of how to provide data access features to a control using the DAO under our belts, let's take a look at the ODBC API. You might wonder why you would go to the trouble of accessing the ODBC API directly when it's easy just to use DAO. Well there are a couple of reasons.

The first has to do with what you will do with your control once it is complete. If the control will be used in other applications, perhaps sold to other users, or used on a web page, data access methods can become a serious consideration. In these situations we want the smallest, fastest code possible, while still offering the features and functionality that are demanded by today's users. A control based on the ODBC API can offer this flexibility by providing a series of standard database functions without imposing the overhead of the DAO option.

The second has to do with the DAO itself. The DAO and underlying Jet Engine are not freeware, they are Microsoft products and are subject to Microsoft licensing restrictions. In addition, the DAO is designed for use with native MDB databases. It has been enhanced to provide ODBC connectivity, but you pay a performance price by using the high level objects of the DAO.

These issues must be taken into consideration when determining the correct solution for your problem. In order to develop the smallest, fastest control possible, while still allowing for multiple data source access flexibility, the ODBC API is the answer.

What is ODBC

Open Database Connectivity is an API that allows an application to communicate with multiple data sources using a consistent series of properties and procedures, along with a standard implementation of SQL (Structured Query Language). In the traditional database world, a database application usually meant a program that performed a specific database task with a specific database in mind.

These types of application were typically written using embedded SQL and vendor specific database system syntax and constructs. They were compiled using a special pre-processor that would turn the embedded SQL into code that could be used by the predefined DBMS. The resulting executable program could then be used with the predefined database or database management system only. In order to move to a new DBMS, the application had to be recompiled and relinked.

ODBC offers a new approach to developing database programs by providing a middle layer of software that interacts with both your application and the Database Management System. No matter what data source or DBMS you are communicating with, the ODBC API provides your application with the same set of functions to use to manipulate the data source.

The ODBC API is not a Visual Basic specific tool, and you will find that often the syntax and examples found for accessing the ODBC API assume your application is developed in C or C++. However, a Visual Basic application can take full advantage of the ODBC API.

Using the ODBC API with VB5 CCE

As the ODBC API is a general-purpose API, there are no special considerations to using it from within Visual Basic. In fact, unlike the DAO and Jet Engine, which provide a special type library and set of ActiveX data access objects, the ODBC API was designed for straightforward access from general purpose languages like C and C++ as well as Visual Basic.

Utilizing the services of the ODBC API is equivalent to calling functions in any DLL. The Visual Basic programmer must:

- Learn about the functions which need to be used.
- Declare the external functions and constants to Visual Basic.
- Call the procedures, just like any other Visual Basic functions.
- Process the results from the functions.

Each ODBC function name starts with the prefix **SQL** and accepts one or more parameters as arguments. Arguments are defined as input (to the ODBC driver) or output (from the ODBC driver).

Before we can access any of the functions of the ODBC API, the functions defined by the API must be declared to Visual Basic. In the past, the ODBC SDK version 2.0 included a number of Visual Basic Module files that provided these references for the developer. However, release 2.5 no longer supplies these references. As such, you may have to do a little leg work to track down the correct declarations.

> You'll find an **ODBCAPI.BAS** file on the Wrox web site. This VB source code module is used by the sample application we will discuss and contains all the definitions required by VB5 CCE to access the 32bit release 2.5 of the ODBC API.

Once we have defined the ODBC calls to our Visual Basic program, we are ready to take advantage of the API in our code. However, before we can connect to an ODBC data source, we must first define a connection in the ODBC configuration that the API will use to reference the actual data source.

The ODBC API provides your application with the means to configure and define ODBC data sources directly. A detailed discussion of this, however, is beyond the scope of this book. So for the purposes of our example, we will use the ODBC Administrator utility to define an ODBC data source.

> The ODBC Administration utility is included with VB 4.0 Professional Edition, Microsoft Office 95 and other Microsoft products, including the ODBC SDK. Note that the ODBC SDK is not included with VB5 CCE. It can be downloaded from Microsoft's web site or purchased separately. You will need the SDK or the ODBC 2.5 or later driver pack in order to execute the samples described here.

The ODBC administration utility can be found in your Windows 95 or Windows NT 4.0 Control Panel.

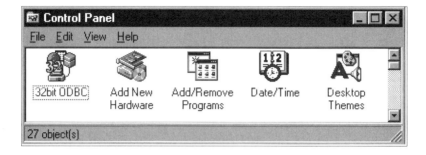

The 32bit ODBC Administration Utility is used to define ODBC data sources that will be accessed from 32bit applications, such as the ones you will create using VB5 CCE. The utility allows you to define three types of DSNs (Data Source Names).

A DSN is a name that is assigned to represent a data source. The three types of DSNs are **user**, **system** and **file**. A user DSN is only available to the user login in which it is defined. A system DSN is available to all users on the system, including remote users that have remote administrative authority on your system an the file type DSN allows users with the same drivers installed on the system to use the defined name. For a Windows 95 user, this means all users. However, for a Windows NT user, where distinct user environments are maintained, this could mean that some users will have access to the source and others will not.

For our example, we will define two system DSNs—one that is used to access an Access database data source and the other for a SQL Server 6.5 server database. To define a data source, click on the DSN type tag desired, in this case the System DSN tab. Then to create a new DSN, click on the Add button.

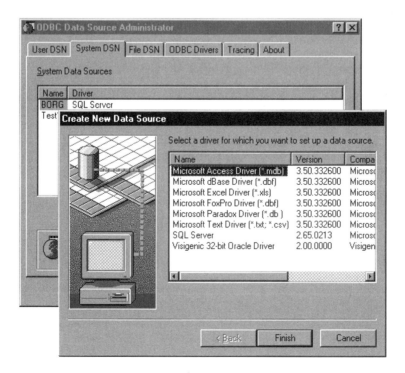

A DSN Creation Wizard will walk you through the process of creating a new Data Source Name and making it available to your applications. For more information on the ODBC Administration Utility see the ODBC API 2.5 SDK Documentation or the ODBC Administration Utility on-line Help.

With the two ODBC System DSN values created within the ODBC configuration, we can access these names from our program, thereby gaining access to the corresponding data source. With that, let's get started. As in our previous example, we'll be adding data access features to the Address control.

Calling External ODBC Functions

Now that we've seen how to define a DSN, let's take a brief look at how to go about calling the ODBC functions we will need to interact with a data source. Visual Basic and VB5 CCE are capable of calling functions that reside in external DLLs as long as they are declared to the Visual Basic environment before they are called.

Declaring an external function informs the VB environment where to find the requested DLL, what parameters to expect from it and send to it, and what data types these parameters are. After an external function is declared, the Visual Basic compiler can compare the type and parameter information you supply with the parameters actually passed to the function in a program when it compiles the code. If a mismatch is found, Visual Basic will produce an error. Search the on-line help for Declare to find out more information.

As you declare external functions, you must remember that the variable type the external function expects must map to a corresponding Visual Basic variable type. This can become an issue when working with external functions developed in C or C++. In our ODBC example, a number of the external functions that are called require parameter types that do not obviously correspond to a Visual Basic type. For example:

```
Declare Function SQLAllocEnv Lib "odbc32.dll" (env As Long) As Integer
```

This declaration, as defined in the SDK, requires an **env** variable to be of type **DOUBLE WORD**. Visual Basic does not have a **DOUBLE WORD** type. However, a **LONG** type variable type can be used to represent a **DOUBLE WORD**. A number of sources are available to help you determine the correct Visual Basic types to supply. I have found the most helpful resource for me has been the API Text Viewer supplied with Visual Basic 4.0. This viewer displays a list of 32bit Windows API calls as they should be declared in Visual Basic. Reviewing these declarations quickly gives you the information you will need when working with other external DLLs.

Property Page Enhancements

As with the DAO example, the ODBC version of the data enabled Address control provides the user with a simple means of supplying the name of a data source, the table to be accessed and the various fields to use when displaying data on the control. As such, just as in the previous example, we start out with a **Private** function to connect a data source using the information supplied by the control user.

Making a Connection

The ODBC version of the **fConnect** function requires a bit more work then its DAO counterpart. Keep in mind that we are working with a low level, general purpose API. As such, many of the things we could take for granted using the DAO (such as memory management) must now be dealt with in our application.

Let's take a look at how to go about making a connection to an ODBC data source. The **fConnect** function is defined as a **Private** function accepting a single string parameter labeled **sDataName**. The **sDataName** parameter supplies the function with a data source connection string that ODBC will use to make a connection to a data source.

Notice here that we refer to a DSN as a part of the ODBC connection string. When ODBC attempts to create a connection to a data source, it requires some additional information in addition to the DSN itself. This information includes the user ID and password to use when logging into the specified source, as well as a default database name and a number of other ODBC or data source specific parameters.

A ODBC connection string is made up of several keywords, followed by the parameters they require. The simplest connection string includes a DSN name, login ID and password. An example of this would be:

```
DSN=borg;UID=sa;PWD=admin
```

In this example, the DSN is represented by the **DSN** keyword. Keywords are separated from their parameters with an equals sign '=', and keyword parameter entries are delimited by a semicolon ';'. The parameters do not need to be supplied in any specific order. To specify the default database to use when attaching to a data source, the **DATABASE** key word is included:

```
DSN=borg;UID=sa;PWD=admin;DATABASE=pubs
```

Other parameters can specify information such as the amount of logging ODBC will perform, and whether ODBC will run synchronously or asynchronously. Not all parameters are available for all data sources. For a complete description of the parameters available, review the ODBC 2.5 SDK documentation.

The ODBC library has the ability to providing a detailed trace of the activity that occurs between the client application and the connected data source. The ODBC logging level, set in the connection string, determines how much information is included with this trace, if any.

The **fConnect** function is defined as:

```
Private Function fConnect(sDataName) As Boolean
```

The first thing the **fConnect** function must do is initialize the ODBC environment. Before an application can use any other ODBC function, it must initialize the ODBC interface and associate an environment handle with the environment memory pool created.

A handle refers to a variable that is used by the API to locate memory that has been allocated for a specific purpose. In this case, the environment handle is a variable that references the location of memory allocated for the ODBC API environment.

To initialize the interface, allocate environment memory and supply a handle, an application calls **SQLAllocEnv** and passes it the address of a variable that will reference the space allocated. The driver initializes the ODBC environment, allocates memory to store information about the environment, and returns a handle to this reserved memory in the supplied variable. This is done using the following code:

```
If (SQLAllocEnv(henv) <> SQL_SUCCESS) Then
    MsgBox "SQL Alloc Environment Failed", vbExclamation, AppName
    fConnect = False
    Exit Function
End If
```

The **henv** variable is defined as:

```
Public henv As Long
```

This environment handle variable is declared in a **MainEntryPoint.Bas** module, thus making it available to all modules of the control. The environment handle is used throughout the application.

With the ODBC environment initialized, we call **SQLAllocConnect** to allocate memory for ODBC to use to mange a connection to a data source. The **SQLAllocConnect** function returns a handle to this allocated space. This is done using:

```
if (SQLAllocConnect(henv, Connection.hdbc) <> SQL_SUCCESS) Then
    MsgBox "SQL Alloc Connection Failed", vbExclamation, AppName
    fConnect = False
    Exit Function
End If
```

The **Connection.hdbc** handle is used by the application to reference the memory pool allocated by invoking the **SQLAllocConnect** function. Notice here that the connection handle is a part of a Visual Basic type definition labeled **ConnectionInfo**, which is defined as:

```
Type ConnectionInfo
        hdbc As Long             ' Connection handle
        hstmt As Long            ' Statement handle
        Status As Integer        ' Active or Inactive
End Type

Public Connection As ConnectionInfo      ' Connection structure
```

The new type and corresponding **Public** declaration are also defined in a **MainEntryPoint.Bas** file, making them available to all Address control modules. So why is the connection handle part of the **ConnectionInfo** type, while the environment handle is not?

Although it is not obvious in this simple example, the ODBC API only has to be initialized once for each program that uses it. However, connection and statement handles must be initialized for each connection to a defined data source. The **ConnectionInfo** type is then defined as a simple means to package together the different handles required by our application. If the application supported multiple connections, this type would be used as the basis for an array of structures, each tracking a connection to the ODBC API.

With our ODBC environment initialized, and valid handles to environment space and connection space, we are ready to attempt a connection. The **SQLDriverConnect** function is called to establish a connection to a data source using the supplied connection string.

```
iRc = SQLDriverConnect(Connection.hdbc, 0&, sDataBuff, Len(sDataBuff), _
                       sBuff, MAXCHAR, iBuffLen, _
                       SQL_DRIVER_NOPROMPT)
```

The **SQLDriverConnect** function takes eight parameters and provides a number of flexible options for connecting to a data source. The first parameter is the handle we defined that references memory used for the connection. The second parameter is used to provide a handle to the current window. This is used if the ODBC API will produce a prompt for additional information when attempting to establish a connection.

The ODBC API can produce a prompt that allows a user to supply user ID, password, and connection string information, if this information is not supplied as parameters. In our case, we pass a special **0&**, representing a **NULL** to the API. When the API receives a **NULL** character for this parameter, it will not produce a dialog requesting further information from the user.

The next two parameters, **sDataBuff** and **Len(sDataBuff)** supply the function with a connection string entered on the property page by the control user. The length of the buffer is passed to allow the API to properly parse the string.

Following these input parameters, are a number of values that are used to return information to our application. The **sBuff** variable will hold the actual connection string used by the ODBC API to connect to a specific data source. The actual string and the string supplied by the user may differ in two situations. The first occurs when the user has supplied ODBC parameters when defining the data source using the ODBC Administration utility. The second occurs when a dialog is presented to the user by the API and additional connection information is provided. In both these situations the string returned will include the additional information entered by the user. This can be valuable to you should you have to disconnect at some point in your code and then reconnect.

The last parameter of interest to us is the **SQL_DRIVER_NOPROMPT** entry. This value instructs the driver not to prompt the user for additional information when a necessary value is missing. Notice this value is an all caps variable starting with the word SQL. This value is one of the constants defined by the ODBC API and used in our application. Constants, such as **SQL_DRIVER_NOPROMPT**, make much more sense than, say, a 0 would. For a complete list of the constants defined for the ODBC API, take a look at the sample application's **ODBCAPI.Bas** file on the Wrox web site.

The return value of this function call tells our application if an error occurred during the connection process. However, the return value does not provide us with enough information to know if the connection succeeded or failed and why. To determine what error occurred and how severe it was, we call the **SQLError** function.

The **SQLError** function provides an application with detailed information concerning the last error that occurred. It is used to determine if the error was something that caused the connection attempt to fail, or if it was simply a message returned by the data source.

```
iRc = SQLError(henv, Connection.hdbc, SQL_NULL_HSTMT, sErrBuff, Long,_
                     sErrExtBuff, MAXCHAR, iReturn)
If (InStr(sErrBuff, SQL_GENERAL_WARNING) > 0) Then
Else
    MsgBox "Connection Error: " & sErrExtBuff, AttIcon, AppName
    fDisConnect
    fConnect = False
```

```
          Exit Function
     End If
```

In this example, we supply a handle to the allocated environment memory, a handle to the allocated connection memory and a value indicating that no statement space has been allocated. The function returns a code to the **sErrorBuff** variable and a description of the problem to the **sErrExtBuff** variable. This information is then examined to determine the severity of the problem. In this example, if a general warning message is produced (**SQL_GENERAL_WARNING**), we know the connection succeeded, but a ODBC Driver message was produced.

If a more severe problem is detected, the warning is presented to the user. In this case, the program will call the **fDisConnect** function, thus releasing the environment and connection handles defined earlier, and exit the function. In a production application, you will likely want to further investigate these errors and provide appropriate responses.

Assuming that no severe error messages was detected, we are set to begin accessing the data source.

Using Catalog Functions to Retrieve Table and Field Names

In our previous DAO example, we were able to retrieve a list of table names and field names to provide our users with a much more intuitive property page. Using the ODBC API, we are able to accomplish the same level of functionality.

Let's take a look at how we might populate a list box with the names of all the tables available in the data source we just attached to. As in our previous DAO example, we'll create a private procedure named **ddlbTableName_DropDown** which is called by Visual Basic each time the user clicks on the drop-down button of the Table Name drop-down list box.

The first step is to check for an existing connection using a connection flag set in the **fConnect** function. If a connection does not exist, the **fConnect** function is called to create a new one. If it does, we can move on to retrieving table names.

The first step of this process is to allocate a **statement** handle. A statement handle is allocated using the **SQLAllocStmt** function, which will return a handle to memory allocated for the preparation and execution of SQL statements.

```
     iRc = SQLAllocStmt(Connection.hdbc, Connection.hstmt)
     If (iRc <> SQL_SUCCESS) Then
         MsgBox "SQL Allocate Statement Handle Failed", AttIcon, AppName
         Screen.MousePointer = Normal
         Exit Sub
     End If
```

The **SQLAllocStmt** function takes the current connection handle as its parameter and returns (by reference) a handle to memory allocated for use when preparing and executing SQL statements. As you may remember, the **hstmt** variable is a part of the connection type definition to help organize these variables.

Once a statement handle is allocated, we can interact with the data source. To retrieve a list of tables, we will call one of the ODBC catalog functions. A catalog function is a group of special procedures that allow you to programmatically determine information concerning the internal layout of the data source connected to. These catalog functions can also be used to retrieve the names and structures of the tables defined in a data source, as well as the specific fields defined in those tables. In addition, information such as access privileges, indexes and keys and object owners can be retrieved.

We will use the **SQLTables** catalog function to retrieve the table information needed.

```
iRc = SQLTables(Connection.hstmt, _
            0&, 0, _
            0&, 0, _
            0&, 0, _
            0&, 0)
```

The **SQLTables** function allows you to supply information that is used to filter what table information is returned. For example, we can supply a table name filter string that will restrict system table names from being retrieved. For our example, we will return all the table names found, and then filter the unwanted values in our program.

This illustrates one of the two filtering techniques available. The second filtering approach will be looked at when we address retrieving field information.

> *The ODBC API provides functionality that allows your application to test for specific levels of compliance, such as filtering. See the ODBC SDK for more information.*

When a query is made through the ODBC API to a data source and results are returned, the results are stored as a result set in memory. The result set is really a two dimensional array that represents the rows and columns that were produced as a result of a query.

To retrieve the data stored in this special memory area, we need to fetch the data into variables in our program. Fetching the data, simply means reading the data from the ODBC API memory area into variables we have defined in our program, typically row by row.

The ODBC API offers two techniques for retrieving data from a result set. The first approach requires that your application bind the result set to variables in your application. The **SQLBindCol** function is used for this purpose. Once each column in the result set is bound to a variable, you retrieve the actual data using the **SQLFetch** or **SQLExtendedFetch** functions.

This approach has the advantage of retrieving data of many different types into variables, one row at a time. A row of data can then be dealt with in your application as a single unit.

However, this approach can be limiting if the type of data and number of columns to be returned from the data source are not known. For example, if you attempt to bind a string variable to a integer data element, an error will occur. In addition, if a column is not bound to a variable, it may not be properly retrieved.

To avoid these issues, we can take advantage of the **SQLGetData** function. Used in conjunction with the **SQLFetch** function or **SQLExtendedFetch** function, **SQLGetData** is used to retrieve data from the result set field by field.

Here, we don't need to know how many columns will be retrieved beforehand. However, since we still don't know what type of data we are dealing with, this approach requires us to convert all results to a common data type. The risk of course, is that numeric data may need to be treated as numeric data by your application or a data type, such as a binary column, may not be able to be converted to a string. In our address example, however, we can safely treat all resulting data as string data.

To retrieve data from a result set, we will first determine how many columns are represented. To determine the number of columns represented in the result set, we call the **SQLNumResultCols** function.

```
iRc = SQLNumResultCols(Connection.hstmt, iNumCols)
```

This function takes a handle to the statement memory pool (allocated with a call to **SQLAllocStmt**), as an input parameter, and returns the number of columns in the **iNumCols** variable supplied. With this information, we can fetch a row of data using the **SQLFetch** function.

```
Do While (SQLFetch(Connection.hstmt) = SQL_SUCCESS)
```

We can then loop through each column to retrieve the data using the **SQLGetData** function.

```
ReDim sNames(iNumCols - 1)
For iCnt = 1 To iNumCols - 1
    sBuffer = Space(SQL_MAX_TABLE_NAME_LEN)
    iRc = SQLGetData(Connection.hstmt, iCnt, SQL_CHAR, sBuffer, _
                    SQL_MAX_TABLE_NAME_LEN, lOutLen)
    sNames(iCnt) = sBuffer
Next
```

The **SQLGetData** function accepts a handle to the statement memory area allocated earlier, a column count integer, a conversion value, a buffer variable to hold the data, the size of the buffer variable, and a variable that will store the resulting data length.

A buffer variable labeled **sBuffer** is used to store the resulting data and the **SQL_CHAR** constant is used to indicate we want the retrieved data represented as characters. An array labeled **sNames** is used to store the table information retrieved from the data source.

As you may remember, we indicated that we would filter the unwanted system tables from our list in the code. The **SQLTables** command returns a vast amount of information concerning the tables residing in a data source. This information includes their names, owners and types. Using this data, we will only process those tables of type **"TABLE"**, meaning that they are user tables and not system tables.

To do this, the fourth array element (representing the table type) is scanned for the correct text. If found, this name is processed, if not it is skipped.

```
If (InStr(sNames(4), "TABLE") > 0) Then
    sClean = sNames(2)
    If (sClean = "") Then
        sClean = Left(sNames(2), InStr(sNames(2), Chr(0)) - 1) & "." & _
                Left(sNames(3), InStr(sNames(3), Chr(0)) - 1)
    Else
        sClean = Left(sNames(3), InStr(sNames(3), Chr(0)) - 1)
    End If

    ddlbTableName.AddItem (sClean)
End If
```

As with the DAO sample, **NULL** characters must be dealt with specifically. The above snippet of code retrieves the table name from the second element of the **sNames** array, and scans the result for a **NULL** character to delimit the length of the string actually stored. If a **NULL** value is detected, a "" string will result as the value assigned. The procedure goes on to combine an owner with the table name, if an owner is assigned in the data source.

With that, we populate the list box making a list of valid tables available to the user.

With the table names provided, we can focus on providing the user with a list of field names defined in the selected table. Here, we use an ODBC API call with a very similar layout to the **SQLTables** function. The **SQLColumns** function is used to retrieve information on the individual columns that are defined in a given data source.

```
iRc = SQLColumns(Connection.hstmt, _
                 0&, 0, _
                 0&, 0, _
                 sTableName, SQL_MAX_COLUMN_NAME_LEN, _
                 0&, 0)
```

The one significant difference here is that we will take advantage of our second filtering option and supply a table name filter in this example. Although we could filter the field names in our code the same way we did table names, it would incur a great deal of unnecessary overhead. If we did not provide a table name filter, this call would retrieve every field name defined in the data source. If we are accessing a single Access MDB, that may not pose a problem. However, if we were accessing a SQL Server database, it could be a problem.

With that, we can present a list of fields to the user, providing the same ease of use facilities as those found in the DAO example.

Providing a Connection Method

As with the DAO example, we will provide the user of our ODBC data enabled address control with a number of functions and properties that they can use to interact with an underlying data source. To start with, the control will provide an ODBC version of the **pfConnect** function.

The **pfConnect** function in the ODBC version of the address control looks much the same as the **fConnect** function provided for the property page. To start, as the sample code illustrates, checks are made to assure that the user supplied a data source string, that we are not already connected and that a table name is provided.

```
pfConnect = 0
If (m_DataSource = "" or m_bConnected = True or m_TableName = "") Then
    pfConnect = -1
    Exit Function
End If

pfDisConnect
```

A call is made to the **pfDisConnect** function as the last validation step, to assure that a current connection does not already exist. Remember that in this example, we are using public handles to allocated connection and statement memory. If you point the handle for a connection memory area to a newly allocated one, the existing space will not be properly de-allocated.

The **pfDisConnect** function simply releases all connections for the defined handle and then releases the handles themselves. This frees the resources used for the connections, statements and the environment for use by the system.

```
SQLFreeStmt Connection.hstmt, SQL_CLOSE
SQLFreeStmt Connection.hstmt, SQL_DROP
SQLDisconnect Connection.hdbc
SQLFreeConnect Connection.hdbc
SQLFreeEnv henv
```

Once the parameters supplied to the control have been verified, we use **SQLAllocEnv** to reinitialize the ODBC API and **SQLAllocConnect** to allocate memory for our connection. Following this, the **SQLDriverConnect** function is called to attempt a connection using the provided data source connection string provided. If all goes well, we will have a valid connection to the required data source and will be ready to interact with the data.

> *Although a single environment handle can be used throughout an application, the example code*
> *de-allocates and creates a new reference each time a connection is made or ended. This is done to illustrate*
> *how the environment handle is allocated and de-allocated in a program.*

Before we can display address data on the Address control or navigate the database as we did in the DAO example, we need to tell the data source how to provide the data to our control and how to retrieve it. In the DAO example, we created a **RecordSet**, which was then used to navigate the database and display information. Under the covers, this process was submitting a query to the data source, creating a cursor, and scrolling through that cursor.

A cursor is a database process by which data is scrolled into a result set, row by row as it is requested by the client application. Advanced cursor capabilities include the ability to scroll forward or backward through a result set, save a specific position in the result set (also known as a bookmark), and to update or delete data at a given position within a result set.

Not all data sources have this capability. Fortunately, the ODBC API provides for cursor functionality even if the data source itself does not support it. This is done by bringing the results of a query into memory, and then manipulating those results as if they were a database oriented cursor. For our example, we will let the ODBC API determine if the data source supports cursors, and if it does not, provide the required behind-the-scenes processing required to simulate one.

Our first step is to build a SQL statement that requests the data we want to work with. For our example, we will take the field names supplied by the developer, along with the table name, and create a SQL statement that will return the corresponding data.

```
sDataBuff = "select " & IIf(m_NameField <> "", m_NameField & ", ", "") & _
    IIf(m_AddressField <> "", m_AddressField & ", ", "") & _
    IIf(m_SecondAddressField <> "", m_SecondAddressField & ", ", "") & _
    IIf(m_CityTownField <> "", m_CityTownField & ", ", "") & _
    IIf(m_StateCountyField <> "", m_StateCountyField & ", ", "") & _
    IIf(m_CountryField <> "", m_CountryField & ", ", "") & _
    IIf(m_ZipPostField <> "", m_ZipPostField & ", ", "") & _
    m_EmailField
```

```
sDataBuff = Left(sDataBuff, Len(Trim(sDataBuff)) - 1)
sDataBuff = sDataBuff & " from " & m_TableName
```

205

The resulting statement looks something like this:

```
select  fieldname, fieldname, fieldname from  owner.table
```

This SQL is then used to request data from the data source, and to build a result set that the user can browse using the address control.

However, before we submit this SQL to the server, we will set a few options that will tell the ODBC API how to deal with the data that will be returned by the query we just built. The syntax used here is a part of the ODBC 2.0 specification.

```
iRc = SQLSetStmtOption(Connection.hstmt, SQL_CONCURRENCY, _
                    SQL_CONCUR_READ_ONLY)
iRc = SQLSetStmtOption(Connection.hstmt, SQL_ROWSET_SIZE, _
                    SQL_ROWSET_VALUE)
iRc = SQLSetStmtOption(Connection.hstmt, SQL_CURSOR_TYPE, _
                    SQL_CURSOR_STATIC)
```

ODBC version 2.0 provides a single function call that is used to set options that relate to the current statement being executed. To set options that will affect all statements, the **SQLSetConnectOption** is the more appropriate function to use. The **SQLSetStmtOption** function accepts a handle to the statement memory pool and the setting options that are to be made.

In our example, the first setting specifies that the cursor that will be produced is read only, meaning that it cannot be used to make updates. The second call sets the number of rows that will be returned by a single fetch. The last call specifies that a static cursor will be built. A static cursor can be likened to a snapshot of the referenced table.

A static cursor normally has the associated risk that a different user might update the data source after we build our cursor. In this case, our cursor would not reflect the changes made. To alleviate this problem in a multi-user situation, you would want to build a dynamic cursor (**SQL_CURSOR_DYNAMIC**), that would reflect any changes made. However, for our simple example we will take the simplest approach and avoid the additional overhead required for a dynamic cursor.

Now we are ready to send the SQL statements created to the data source. This is done using the **SQLPrepare** and **SQLExecute** functions. The **SQLPrepare** function modifies the SQL supplied to conform with the connected data source, and then submits it to the source for preparation. This means that, in the case of a relational database server based data source, the SQL Server prepares an execution plan for the submitted SQL code. The **SQLExecute** function call then instructs the data source to execute the prepared SQL code.

```
iRc = SQLPrepare(Connection.hstmt, sBuff, MAXCHAR)
If (iRc <> SQL_SUCCESS) Then
        iRc = SQLError(henv, Connection.hdbc, Connection.hstmt, sErrBuff, _
                    lLong, sErrExtBuff, MAXCHAR, iReturn)
        MsgBox "SQLPrepare Call Failed:  " & sErrExtBuff, AttIcon, AppName
        Screen.MousePointer = Normal
        pfConnect = iReturn
        pfDisConnect
        Exit Function
End If
```

```
    iRc = SQLExecute(Connection.hstmt)
If (iRc <> SQL_SUCCESS) Then
    iRc = SQLError(henv, Connection.hdbc, Connection.hstmt, sErrBuff, _
                  lLong, sErrExtBuff, MAXCHAR, iReturn)
    MsgBox "SQLExecute Call Failed:  " & sErrExtBuff, AttIcon, AppName
    pfConnect = iReturn
    pfDisConnect
    Exit Function
End If
```

If an error occurs at any stage in the process, the **SQLError** function is called to retrieve error information, which is then presented to the user. If the process succeeds, the **Connection.hstmt** handle will reference a result set in memory that we can work with, much like we did with the **RecordSet** using the DAO.

Navigating the Database

Just as in the DAO example, we want to give the ODBC enabled control the ability to move through the result set we just created. Here again, we need to provide the control user with a number of methods. Let's take a look at the ODBC version of a method that will allow the user to move to the first record of the result set and display the stored data.

To begin, we will create a public method that the developer can call from their own code. We'll give it an intuitive name—in this case the same name provided in the DAO enabled control example. The resulting function is really simply a wrapper that calls an internal function which deals with the underlying complexities of moving about the result set.

```
Public Function pfMoveFirst()
  MovePosition (SQL_FETCH_FIRST)
End Function
```

The **pfMovePosition** procedure is where the real action is. This function accepts as its only parameter an indicator of which way in the result set we want to move. Here we call the function with **SQL_FETCH_FIRST**, meaning that we want to move to the top of the result set.

Notice that the term result set is used as opposed to cursor. The reason for this is that we do not know if the ODBC API was able to take advantage of the cursoring abilities of the data source and create a result set in the database, or if it is using a simulation of a cursor by bringing the resulting data into memory. As we mentioned earlier, a simulated cursor occurs when the driver retrieves all the data for a given query into memory, and then allows a user to navigate this result set row by row. Whichever occurred internally, the result to our application looks like we have a complete result set in memory through which we can move back and forth.

So let's look at the **MovePosition** function. Our first task is to make sure that we are connected to a data source. If we are not, there is not much use in going any further.

```
Private Sub MovePosition(iWhatPosition)
    If (pfIsConnected()) Then
    .
    .
    .
    End If
```

If we are connected to a data source, we call the **SQLNumResultCols** function to make sure that the result set we built in the connection function is still valid. This accounts for the case where a failure may have occurred, between the time we connected and built a result set and the time we want to browse those results.

```
iRc = SQLNumResultCols(Connection.hstmt, iNumCols)
If (iRc <> SQL_SUCCESS Or iNumCols < 1) Then
    MsgBox "Data Set Invalid", AttIcon, AppName
    pfDisConnect
    Exit Function
End If
```

After checking the result set is still available, we can bring the data into local memory variables using the fetch function. However, in this case we want to have the ability to move both forwards and backwards in a result set. As such, the **SQLExtendedFetch** function is invoked instead of **SQLFetch**, which only allows forward motion.

```
iRc = SQLExtendedFetch(Connection.hstmt, iWhatPosition, 1, lLong, _
        isResults)
If (iRc <> SQL_SUCCESS) Then
    If (iRc = SQL_NO_DATA_FOUND) Then
        MsgBox "No More Rows to Read", AttIcon, AppName
    Else
        iRc = SQLError(henv, Connection.hdbc, Connection.hstmt, sErrBuff, _
                    lLong, sErrExtBuff, MAXCHAR, iReturn)

        '
        ' check for general warnings and driver messages (some
        ' drivers don't support cursors
        '
        If (InStr(sErrBuff, SQL_GENERAL_WARNING) > 0) Then
            Else
                MsgBox "SQLExtendedFetch Call Failed:  " & sErrExtBuff, _
                        AttIcon, AppName
                pfDisConnect
                Exit Function
        End If
    End If
End If
```

In this example, **iWhatPosition** represents the direction we want to move within the result set.

As mentioned earlier, a result set is much like a table stored in memory. Using the **SQLExtendedFetch** function we can move up or down the table, just as you would move up or down a list. This enhanced fetch function gives us the ability to move to the top, to the bottom, or to a specific position relative to the top or bottom of a result set. In this example, we want to move to the first record, or the top of the result set.

Remember that this function is designed to handle any call that will move the current position in the result set. As such, a test is put in place that displays an error message if the user attempts to fetch the next record, and we are already at the bottom of the result set, or fetch the previous record when we are already at the top.

After the **SQLExtendedFetch** function is called, we test for any error conditions that may have occurred. This test must be somewhat forgiving as any number of messages may be produced that do not represent a fatal error. For example, if the data source does not support cursoring, a message will be displayed by the ODBC API indicating that cursor processing will be simulated. Although this does not affect processing from the client point of view, it produces an error and modifies the return code of the **SQLExtendedFetch** function.

The next step after we have adjusted our position in the result set is to read the data and update the control display. Just as we did in the DAO example, the **UpdateDisplay** procedure is called for this purpose.

```
Private Sub UpdateDisplay()
```

The **UpdateDisplay** procedure here again takes advantage of the flexible **SQLGetData** function to retrieve data from the result set into an array.

```
SQLNumResultCols Connection.hstmt, iNumCols
ReDim sNames(iNumCols)
For iCnt = 1 To iNumCols
        sBuffer = Space(MAXCHAR)
        iRc = SQLGetData(Connection.hstmt, iCnt, 1, sBuffer, MAXCHAR, lOutLen)
        sNames(iCnt) = Trim(sBuffer)
 Next
```

As the data control only displays a single record of data, we simply loop through each field of the record at the current location in the result set using multiple calls to the **SQLGetData** function. As the fields are retrieved, the **sNames** array is updated with the data returned. The end result is an array of character values, representing the data for the current record of the data source. In this example, the first record of the result set is represented.

All we have left to do now is to update the text fields of the address control. This is done through a simple process of comparing each field represented on the control with the fields actually retrieved from the data source. Matching fields are then updated.

```
iPos = 1
If (fFieldInCollection(m_NameField)) Then
    txtName.Text = sNames(iPos)
    iPos = iPos + 1
End If
```

This process is repeated for each text field on the control, until all the fields have had a chance to be updated. The end result is a control that allows the user to browse through a data source, displaying the data on the address control using the parameters supplied.

Summary

In this chapter, we've taken a fairly brief look at how you might build data access capabilities into your controls using VB5 Control Creation Edition. The most important points to remember in this chapter are:

- We have examined two techniques that you can employ to provide data access features to the controls you create. The first is by using the Jet Engine and the DAO. The second is by accessing the ODBC API directly from your control.

- The DAO provides a series of easy to use, high level objects that your control can use to access a wide variety of data sources, both Jet and ODBC.

- The ODBC API is a general purpose API that provides a series of functions that can be called by your control to provide data access facilities.

When deciding on how to provide data access features to a control you are designing, keep in mind that both the Jet Engine and DAO and ODBC API have merits in terms of ease of use, overhead, flexibility and licensing issues. However, these are not the only options available. For example, your control might bypass ODBC altogether and access a native database API directly. The examples reviewed here are intended to give you a glimpse into two of the many possible solutions.

User-Draw Card Game Controls

So far, we have limited the controls that we've developed to modified variants of the controls already present in the Visual Basic programmer's toolbox. This is all well and good, especially where you have some particular business rule that needs to be encapsulated, such as a text box which can validate its own input to specific business logic. Sometimes, however, you'll want to build something that is completely different to anything that's gone before. If this is the case, and you can't rely on other component controls to give you a visual presence, then you'll need to actually write the code to draw your control—as well as just exposing some methods, events and properties.

This type of control is usually referred to as a User-Draw or Owner-Draw control, because the 'owner' (that's you) has to do all the work of drawing both the design-time and run-time appearances. In this chapter we'll consider such a control. In fact, we'll be building an OCX control file that contains two individual control objects. One of these will have both a design-time and run-time appearance, but the other will be invisible at run-time. You'll see how we handle the latter situation in this chapter.

> *The term Owner-Draw is also often used in Windows programming circles to refer to controls, like list boxes, where the 'owner' is actually the window that is the parent of the control. We're using the more simplistic approach to the terminology here.*

So we'll be covering:

- The problems involved in creating User-Draw controls
- How we can use a Windows DLL to provide the appearance
- Thinking about the needs of the application developer
- How we build the two card game controls
- How the controls can be used in a card game application

Firstly, as in all successful projects, we need to look at the requirements for the controls. To do this, we have to consider what a card game actually consists of.

Drawing Controls and Cards

Almost every Windows computer has some simple card games installed that use the **Cards.dll** to provide playing card drawing functions. This DLL provides the graphics for the standard Windows card games such as Solitaire and Freecell, and can be found on all Windows installations from version 3.0. There are a few things to bear in mind with the different versions of this, but we'll come back to that later in the chapter.

Magazine articles have often described how to use **Cards.dll**, but they have tended to be for the 'C' community. We are going to encapsulate this DLL into an ActiveX control, to provide quick and easy access for developers to create their own favorite card game. Before we get down to the nitty-gritty of how to start drawing cards, however, we should first consider just what we want to give the developer in the way of an interface.

Cards, Hands and Decks: A Design Overview

The DLL only allows you to draw cards into a Windows **device context**. It's up to the developer to ensure that the device context is of adequate size to do all the necessary drawing. Our prime motive in creating the cards OCX is to remove this particular task from the developer, encapsulate all the control sizing into the control's code, and to abstract a few common features of most card games into the control's code.

> *A device context represents a drawing area for API functions to use. It is well beyond the scope of this book to go into full detail about this, but it's sufficient to know that any controls that allow drawing methods to be applied to them will expose a handle to their device context (hDC). Such controls are picture boxes, UserControls and a Visual Basic form itself.*

Common Features of a Card Game

The most basic unit of a card game is, of course, a card. A card has a value of pips, a suit, and a state (such as face up or face down). It also has a location in the game—for example, the ace of hearts may be in the deck, or it may be in one of the various player's hands. We'll come back to the card's location shortly. All these features of a card will be encapsulated into an object for the control. To allow the developer to build a card game, we'll provide them with two controls in our OCX:

 A **CardHand** control, which will display a hand of cards. They can use more than one instance of this control in games that require more than one hand.

 A **CardDeck** control, which will provide a home for all the cards when the game starts, and which acts as a draw and discard pile.

First, let's look at the way we can define the individual cards.

The wxCard Object

The following diagram illustrates the essence of a **wxCard** object.

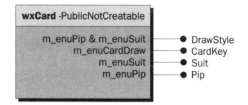

As you can see, this is a very simple object. It has **properties** but no **methods**. The card object doesn't know how to draw itself and it isn't itself, a user control. This is for efficiency—imagine a large card game with 52 controls on the form, just to represent all the cards. It would be unreasonable to expect a developer to produce code for the positioning of every card in the game. Instead, the card object encapsulates the basic attributes of a single playing card, and we'll be using a collection of them within another object to represent the whole pack. The controls that we'll build will revolve around the manipulation of **wxCard** objects.

The **wxCard** object is just a convenient data object we'll create within our controls to represent a single card. It's similar, in this way, to a **Node** object that you use with a **TreeView** control. Notice, in the diagram above, that we've specified the **DrawStyle** property for the **wxCard** object; this represents the state of the card. It can take on three values that cause the card to be displayed face up, face down or face up and inverted.

Since a **wxCard** is an object, it will be convenient for us to store it in Visual Basic collection objects. A card's location should always be in such a collection, and it's for this reason that the **CardKey** property has been provided. Whenever we need to add a card object to a collection, we can use this procedure to get a unique string key to reference the card in a collection, such as **Ace Spades**. It also helps in preventing errors from creeping into our code by prohibiting more than one card of the same value, to be added to a particular collection with the same **key**. Any attempt to do this causes a trappable run time error. So, any secreting of cards in a virtual sleeve would be caught pretty quickly!

> *There's actually a severe limitation with this particular approach—any games that require more than one deck of cards will start causing errors, since you then have at least two cards of any one type. For our control, however, we will live with this limitation.*

The values that are used for the **Pip** and **Suit** properties can be supplied as enumerated types. We've placed some public enumeration declarations in one of the control modules that we'll be using. It really doesn't matter which one, since declaring them public from such a module actually has the effect of entering them into the **type library** that will be produced for the control group. We'll discuss the type library later in this chapter. The enumerations will therefore be available to the entire project group, and also any developer who sets a reference to the OCX in their design environments. The complete enumerations follow. Don't worry about the actual values, since they are chosen for the convenience of the **Cards32.dll**, and all will become clear when we discuss the drawing of cards a little later.

```
Public Enum Pip
    Ace = 0
    Two = 4
    Three = 8
    Four = 12
    Five = 16
```

```
    Six = 20
    Seven = 24
    Eight = 28
    Nine = 32
    Ten = 36
    Jack = 40
    Queen = 44
    King = 48
End Enum
```

```
Public Enum CardStyle
    Crosshatch = 53
    Plaid = 54
    Weave = 55
    Robot = 56
    Roses = 57
    IvyBlack = 58
    IvyBlue = 59
    FishCyan = 60
    FishBlue = 61
    Shell = 62
    Castle = 63
    Beach = 64
    CardHand = 65
    Unused = 66
    X = 67
    o = 68
End Enum
```

Now we've determined that the basic object is the card, we have to consider where we'll be storing them. When starting a card game, cards are dealt from a deck. We therefore need to develop an object to represent the deck of cards.

The CardDeck Control

The deck of cards in our implementation needs to provide us with a number of services. These are shown as the members in the following diagram:

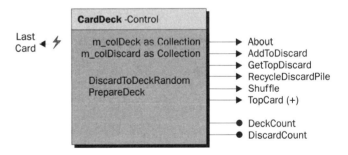

The first thing that should be obvious from the diagram above is that the deck object actually is a control, since it has an **event**. It could have been created as a simple Automation Server object, where after a card was taken from the deck the programmer could check the number of cards left in the deck through the **DeckCount** property, and then decide how the game should continue based on that value. By using an event, however, we allow the developer to concentrate on the game itself, and just react to the situation of the cards running out by writing event handling code for the **LastCard** event. This will fire when the last card object is taken from the **m_colDeck** collection.

216

You'll notice that there are no properties for the **appearance** of the deck control. This is because it will have no appearance at run time. The **CardDeck** control will only appear as an icon on the design-time form of a development environment. The actual screen drawing of a card will be handled in the second control, which we'll use in the project to represent a hand of cards. We'll come to this shortly.

Our **CardDeck** control handles the cards with two collections: one, to represent the unknown cards yet to be dealt; and another, to represent cards that have been discarded for whatever reason. There are five methods which manipulate these piles of cards.

Method	Usage
TopCard (default)	Returns a **wxCard** object from the randomly arranged deck collection (**m_colDeck**) of card objects.
AddToDiscard	Places a card object on the discard pile (**m_colDiscard**)
GetTopDiscard	Takes the last card added to the discard pile.
RecycleDiscardPile **(Shuffle as Boolean)**	Takes the discard pile, turns it over and uses it as the deck. If the shuffle argument is true, then it also shuffles the new deck.
Shuffle	Randomly moves the contents of the discard pile to the deck pile.

The deck control has to do with the movement of card objects between various collections. There is one other important facet of the **CardDeck** control, though. The deck is the origin of all cards and the **Initialize** event of the control contains the code to create all the cards necessary to make a complete deck.

```
Private Sub UserControl_Initialize()
    Call PrepareDeck
    Call DiscardToDeckRandom
End Sub
```

The **PrepareDeck** routine handles this creation.

```
Private Sub PrepareDeck()
    Dim intSuit As Integer
    Dim intValue As Integer
    Dim objCard As wxCard
    For intSuit = 0 To 3
      For intValue = 0 To 12
        Set objCard = New wxCard
        With objCard
            .Suit = intSuit
            .Value = intValue * 4
            m_colDiscard.Add objCard, objCard.CardKey
        End With
      Next intValue
    Next intSuit
End Sub
```

Cards are repeatedly created with the **Set ... New** statement, which will be executed 52 times. We set the **Suit** and **Pip** values of the card objects with an integer value from the loop counter. These are, in fact, enumerated types, and we have to multiply the value by 4 in order to draw the

217

correct card later, when using the API functions of **Cards.dll**. This is because the ordering of the card pictures is such that all the aces will be drawn first, followed by deuces, and through to kings. The suit number is just an offset from the pip value. So, the ace of clubs is card 0 and the king of spades is 48 + 3 or 51.

Each of the new cards is added to the discard collection. This is because the private **DiscardToDeckRandom** routine moves cards from the discard collection into the deck collection in a random manner. This routine is also used by the **Shuffle** method, although there is a little extra work done there.

```
Private Sub DiscardToDeckRandom()
   #If DebugMode = 1 Then
      Debug.Assert (m_colDiscard.Count + m_colDeck.Count < 53)
   #End If
   On Error Resume Next
      Randomize
      Dim intCount As Integer, intCurIdx As Integer
      Dim objTempCard As wxCard

      For intCount = 1 To m_colDiscard.Count
         intCurIdx = Int(Rnd * m_colDiscard.Count) + 1
         Set objTempCard = m_colDiscard.Item(intCurIdx)
         m_colDeck.Add objTempCard, objTempCard.CardKey
         m_colDiscard.Remove intCurIdx
      Next intCount

      If Err Then 'an error has occurred
         Select Case Err.Number
            Case 457: 'Key already exists
               Err.Raise vbObjectError + 1016, "wxCards.Deck",_
                     "Card exists in Deck"
            Case Else:
         End Select
      End If
End Sub
```

The first lines of this routine were added while the control was in development. This is just a quick check to make sure that we don't ever have more than 52 cards in the complete deck. If we do, then this statement will evaluate to **False**, and will halt execution of the code.

The basic mechanism to shuffle the cards is looping through the number of cards in the discard pile (which is currently sorted), removing them by a random index, and then placing these randomly selected cards into the deck collection. When adding cards to the deck, we use the **CardKey** property of the card object to assign it a unique string to reference the card in the deck collection. This isn't actually necessary, since we've provided no interface for accessing the collection items with a specific key. All that it will produce is a run time error if an attempt is made to add another card with the same properties, and we trap this error with our own object error code.

That's really all there is to the deck control. You add and remove card objects via its methods, and it fires an event when there are no more cards left. All we have to do now, before we can develop some great card games, is to decide where to use the card objects supplied by the deck, and then draw them on the screen. We leave this to our second control within the OCX, the **CardHand**.

The CardHand Control

The card hand control will be what the final user of a card game will interact with. It will be responsible for displaying a card, and giving out appropriate events for the game developer to use. The figure below describes the control.

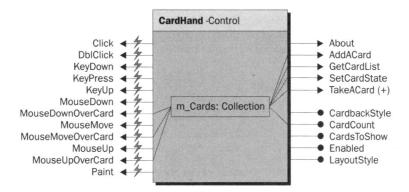

As you can see from the diagram, most of the control interface deals with the **m_Cards** collection. We have exposed the majority of the normal events that you would expect from a control, in order to give the intrepid developer a fully featured control.

You may have noticed the preponderance of mouse events. We could have just modified the **UserControl** mouse events to raise a single combined set of events, where the expected coordinate and our own card information were passed as one set of parameters to the event handler. Instead, we've left the items as separate events so that anyone can modify the drawing of our control in their own code, using such techniques as provided by the Windows API and the exposed **hWnd** property we give them. If a developer is simply interested in calculating which card is being moved over, then our own events return usable information as parameters, which can be used with the control's methods that we've defined.

With these two basic components of a card game, a developer should be able to quickly build some interesting games. We've created a test BlackJack 21 project to demonstrate the use of these controls. The final project looks like this:

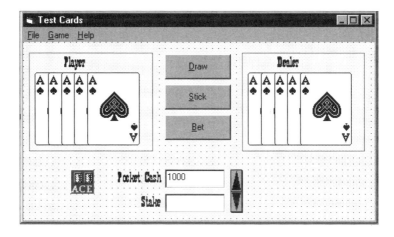

In this design time environment, you can see both our controls. In the bottom left of the form is the iconic representation of the deck control. This will be invisible at run time, and so we've coded its **Resize** and **Paint** events to keep it to the same size at all times, just like a **Timer** control. The two sets of five aces demonstrate the dimensions required to show five cards. The control will size itself automatically, based on the **CardsToShow** property of the **CardHand**.

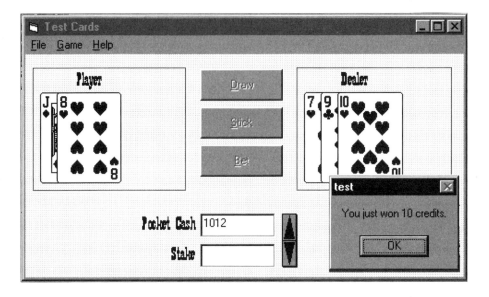

At run-time, the **CardHand** controls only display cards that exist in the member **m_cards** collection, although the control still occupies the same area of the form as depicted in the design time environment—unless you dynamically changed the **CardsToShow** property, but that would be wasteful here. The hand can hold more cards than it will show, because some games may require this facet. Notice that the deck control is not visible at run time.

Sizing and Painting the Controls

Now that you have a feel for what we're trying to achieve, it's time to look at the implementation details of the controls. We'll start with the **CardDeck** control, as it is the simplest to handle.

Displaying CardDeck Controls

Starting with the **UserControl** form visible in design mode, we've set its **Picture** property to a bitmap. This is just the image that the application developer will see in their development environment at application design time. There will be no run-time drawing of the control, because we have set the **InvisibleAtRunTime** property to **True**. We do, however, still have some code in the **UserControl Resize** event, so that the control always maintains a reasonable size within the design environment.

```
Private Sub UserControl_Resize()
   Size 32 * Screen.TwipsPerPixelX, 32 * Screen.TwipsPerPixelY
End Sub
```

This code will ensure that the control is always 32 pixels square when visible in the hosting application's design environment. No prizes for guessing that this also happens to be the size of the bitmap we produced for it. There's no **Paint** code for the control, since there is no run time representation.

You may feel that you need some form of visual representation of the cards in the deck control. For now, this can be achieved by using an extra **CardHand** control for display services. The card hand is where all the cards are painted on the screen.

Displaying CardHand Controls

The **CardHand** control is the most important part of our ActiveX control package. It's what the developer and user interact with most in card games that are produced with the **.OCX** file. The **wxCard** objects and the **CardDeck** control are really only used to keep track of data you need in a card game. Actually turning this data into something meaningful to an end user is the responsibility of the **CardHand** control.

Unlike the control in the previous chapter, we don't have any intrinsic text boxes that know how to draw themselves. We have to do all the drawing of the control ourselves, both in design-time and run-time modes. For this, we make use of some of the features of the **Cards.dll**. The version we're using is the 32 bit version supplied with Windows NT. Windows has had such a DLL since version 3.0, called simply **Cards.dll**. This was a 16 bit DLL and is still supplied with Windows 95. Windows NT also has a **Cards.dll**, but this one is a 32 bit DLL. As you can imagine this could cause some real problems with name clashes. You may need to modify the source code if you only have the 16 bit version. There are comments to guide you in the code.

The DLL itself exports just five functions. The Visual Basic declarations we are using for these are:

```
Private Declare Function cdtInit Lib "Cards.dll" (_
    dx As Long, dy As Long) As Long

Private Declare Function cdtDrawExt Lib "Cards.dll" (ByVal hdc As Long, _
    ByVal X As Long, ByVal Y As Long, ByVal dx As Long, _
    ByVal dy As Long, ByVal ordCard As Long, ByVal iDraw As Long, _
    ByVal clr As Long) As Long

Private Declare Function cdtDraw Lib "Cards.dll" (ByVal hdc As Long, _
    ByVal X As Long, ByVal Y As Long, _
    ByVal iCard As Long, ByVal iDraw As Long, ByVal clr As Long) As Long

Private Declare Function cdtAnimate Lib "Cards.dll" (ByVal hdc As Long, _
    ByVal iCardBack As Long, ByVal X As Long, ByVal Y As Long, _
    ByVal iState As Long) As Long

Private Declare Function cdtTerm Lib "Cards.dll" () As Long
```

We'll actually be making use of only three of these functions, **cdtInit**, **cdtDraw** and **cdtTerm**. As their names suggest, the **cdtInit** and **cdtTerm** functions involve initializing and cleaning up using **Cards.dll**. The parameters passed to the initializing function are passed by reference, and the function passes back the size in pixels needed to display one card in its standard size.

The control initialization routine is used to actually get these values, and we keep them in two of the control's module level variables:

```
Private mdx As Long
Private mdy As Long
'Pixel width and height of a card for the standard cdtDraw funtion
....
Private Sub UserControl_Initialize()
  Dim lngRet As Long
  'Prepare Cards32.dll
  lngRet = cdtInit(mdx, mdy)
End Sub
```

The reason that we need this function is because the graphic output from the **cdtDraw** function will be the same size across different screen resolutions. We'll use the values to scale the control at both run time and design time, so as to display the required number of cards. Of course, before we attempt to start drawing and sizing, we need to know just how many cards need to be displayed. This is the purpose of the **CardsToShow** property:

```
Public Property Get CardsToShow() As Integer
  CardsToShow = m_CardsToShow
End Property

Public Property Let CardsToShow(ByVal New_CardsToShow As Integer)
  m_CardsToShow = New_CardsToShow
  PropertyChanged "CardsToShow"
  Call UserControl_Resize
  ' call resize event & update display to new size
End Property
```

This property is essentially a simple integer. However, we've introduced some extra code in the **Property Let** procedure, to ensure that our control paints correctly. Since we are creating the code to actually paint and size the control ourselves, we need to ensure that a change in the value of this property triggers the **Resize** event, so that our code will execute. We achieve this by calling the **Resize** method of the **UserControl** object.

How Big is a Hand?

Before we launch into the code to resize a **CardHand** control, we need to consider how we intend to display the cards in a game. There are two properties which define how we should size the control. **CardsToShow** is obvious, and the other is the **LayoutStyle** property. This can take just two values, zero or one. To make life easier for the developer, we've defined a public enumeration for use with this property:

```
Public Enum LayStyle
  Left2RightOverlapped = 0
  Top2BottomOverlapped = 1
End Enum
```

The two styles are used to display cards in the following ways:

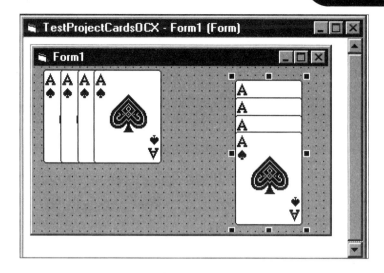

```
Public Property Get LayoutStyle() As LayStyle
  LayoutStyle = m_LayoutStyle
End Property

Public Property Let LayoutStyle(ByVal enuLayStyle As LayStyle)
  m_LayoutStyle = enuLayStyle
  PropertyChanged "LayoutStyle"
  Call UserControl_Resize
End Property
```

As with the **CardsToShow** property above, we've had to force a re-sizing of the control to run the **Resize** code:

```
Private Sub UserControl_Resize()
  Dim dx As Long, dy As Long
  dx = (mdx * Screen.TwipsPerPixelX)
  dy = (mdy * Screen.TwipsPerPixelY)
  'Scale to pixels, dx and dy are the dimensions of 1 card in TWIPS
  Select Case m_LayoutStyle
    Case Left2RightOverlapped:
    'allow mdx *((No. Cards)/4 + (3/4))
    dx = dx * (m_CardsToShow + 3) / 4
    Case Top2BottomOverlapped:
    'allow a quarter of WIDTH height drop between cards
    dy = dy + (m_CardsToShow - 1) * dx / 4
  End Select
  Size dx, dy
  Refresh
End Sub
```

The first thing we need to do in the **Resize** event is calculate what the size of a standard card is. The **cdtInit** function we used earlier gave us the pixel dimensions of a card. However, the **Size** method of the **UserControl** object always works in **Twips**, regardless of the current setting of **ScaleMode** for the form containing it. Therefore we use the **dx** and **dy** variables, which are just the values taken from **cdtInit** multiplied by the **TwipsPerPixel** factors of the **Screen** object.

The actual height and width of the final control depends, of course, on the layout style and the number of cards that will be shown by the hand. To calculate just how big an area we require, we've assumed that you will want to display just one whole card face. The others will be shown as a quarter of a card's width to the right, or below, the previous one. This equates to a quarter of the number of cards, plus three quarters. Notice that we are still using the width, even where we are sizing for a **LayoutStyle** of top to bottom. The last two lines of the code just size the control appropriately and call the **Refresh** method to ensure that it's repainted.

> *A quarter of a card is just enough to clearly see the number of the pip value. Actually there's some potential confusion when displaying aces top to bottom, since it isn't always obvious which suit the card belongs to.*

Painting a Card

Actually painting the card on the screen is where things get interesting, and the **cdtDraw** function of the **Cards.dll** now requires some explanation. Its definition is:

```
Return = cdtDraw(ByVal hdc As Long, _
    ByVal X As Long, ByVal Y As Long, _
    ByVal iCard As Long, ByVal iDraw As Long, ByVal clr As Long)
```

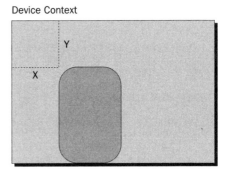

Device Context

The **hDC** parameter is easy—we just use the **hDC** property of the **UserControl** object. The **X** and **Y** values are the offset in pixels from the top left corner of the device context where the card is to be drawn.

The last three parameters are a little more complicated. The **clr** parameter is the color to be used when painting the back of a card, when the style is set to Cross Hatch. This will only be drawn if the value of **iCard** is **53** and **iDraw** is **1**. This value of **53** is a bit of a 'magic number', and using this explicitly in the code is generally bad news when the time comes to debug it. For that reason, we've introduced the **Crosshatch** member of the **DrawStyle** enumeration, which is equal to **53**.

Finally, there is the **iDraw** parameter. It can take three values, for which we've produced an enumerated type:

```
Public Enum CardDraw
    Face = 0
    Back = 1
    Invert = 2
End Enum
```

This particular parameter will be set in the card object that is to be drawn. In fact, this is the **DrawStyle** property of a **wxCard** object. If it's **Face**, then we will ensure that the **iDraw** parameter is set to zero, and **iCard** is the sum of the card's **Suit** and **Pip** properties. If the card

back is to be displayed, then **iDraw** will be one, and **iCard** will be the value of the
CardBackStyle property of the **CardHand** control. The **DrawStyle** setting of **Invert** is the
same as **Face**, but with **iDraw** set to two.

The **CardHand** control will use appropriate values for these parameters, based on its own and the
card object's properties. This insulates the developer from some of the complexities of the DLL,
which can cause a program to crash with some combinations of otherwise valid parameters.

The **Paint** code itself is split into two distinct halves—for the control running at design-time, and
at run-time. Since these two modes of operation require handling in quite different ways, we'll
look at the code in two chunks. First the design time painting of the control:

```
Private Sub UserControl_Paint()
  Dim intNoCards As Integer 'No Cards in hand
  Dim intCount As Integer   'Loop counter
  Dim lngRet As Long        'General purpose return value
  Dim dx As Integer, dy As Integer
  If Ambient.UserMode Then 'Run time
    '... Stuff removed for clarity
  Else 'Design mode
    intNoCards = m_CardsToShow - 1
    For intCount = 0 To intNoCards
      lngRet = cdtDraw(UserControl.hdc, CLng((mdx * intCount) / 4) * _
              (1 - m_LayoutStyle), CLng((mdx * intCount) / 4) * _
              m_LayoutStyle, 3, 0, RGB(255, 0, 255))
    Next intCount
  End If
End Sub
```

At design-time, all we want to do is draw an ace of spades as a place holder—to show the
developer what the run-time layout of the cards will look like. We know that there will be enough
space for all of our drawing, because the code we placed in the **Resize** event ensures this. The
way that we draw the cards is not the most efficient method in the world. Each card is drawn in
full, and the next card is then drawn over three quarters of it. However, this is a small price to
pay for the convenience of the code. For this design time appearance, we've hard coded the
parameter in the function call to draw an ace of spades.

What's interesting is the calculation of the **X** and **Y** offsets from the origins of the device context.
The first thing that becomes apparent is that one of these parameters must be zero, since the cards
should be drawn either all along the top edge of the control, or all down the left edge. We could
have just used a **Select Case** construct, but instead we have the convenient **LayoutStyle**
property to help us.

If the **LayoutStyle** is set to **Left2RightOverlapped**, then its numeric value is zero. Otherwise
it is one. So, multiplying the **Y** parameter by the **LayoutStyle** value will give zero or some
positive value as needed. By a similar argument, the **X** parameter needs to be multiplied by the
factor of one minus the **LayoutStyle** value. The actual distance from the origin of the device
context is calculated as a quarter of a standard card width, multiplied by **(n-1)** times the card
we're drawing. The value of **n** is just taken from the loop counter.

When it comes to run-time painting of the cards, the calculation for positioning (which was used
above) is almost identical. The only difference, this time, is that we need to work out the necessary
iCard and **iDraw** parameters.

```
      ... Stuff removed for clarity
      If Ambient.UserMode Then 'Run time
        intNoCards = m_Cards.Count
        Dim objCard As wxCard
        Dim intCardVal As Integer, intStyleVal As Integer
        For Each objCard In m_Cards
          'The next line takes care of the possibility of CardsToDisplay
          'being less than the number of cards in the hand.
          If intCount = m_CardsToShow Then
            Exit Sub 'Only display the first X cards
          End If

          Select Case objCard.DrawStyle
            Case 0:
              intStyleVal = 0
              intCardVal = CInt(objCard.Suit + objCard.Value)
            Case 1:
              intStyleVal = 1
              intCardVal = m_CardBackStyle
            Case 2:
              intStyleVal = 2
              intCardVal = CInt(objCard.Suit + objCard.Value)
          End Select
          'Important design issue:
          'An individual card object does not dictate
          'what its back style is. This is taken from the CardHand.
          lngRet = cdtDraw(UserControl.hdc, CLng((mdx * intCount) / 4) * _
                  (1 - m_LayoutStyle), CLng((mdx * intCount) / 4) * _
                    m_LayoutStyle, intCardVal, intStyleVal, RGB(255, 0, 255))
          'The intCardStyle is taken from the Card property.
          'This means that the above use of a select case block is
          'not strictly the best, but I prefer the readability of it.
          'Need I say more!
          intCount = intCount + 1
        Next 'Card object
        RaiseEvent Paint
      Else
      ... Stuff removed for clarity
```

This run-time painting of the hand has a great deal of interaction with the internal collection of card objects, **m_Cards**. Since we have an object collection to work with, the natural code construct to use is a **For..Each** loop. However, you should be aware that the hand can hold more cards than it will display. We have not limited the number of objects that can be stored in the **m_Cards** collection, so we leave it up to the developer to make sure that the **CardsToShow** property is set to an appropriate value. Of course, the game that the developer is producing may require that more cards are in a hand than will be shown on screen.

> *There is no type checking in this routine. We are trusting that the collection only contains valid card objects since that is all that the hand's **AddACard** method will allow.*

Generally, you would expect that the hand should be big enough to display the entire contents of the **m_Cards** collection. However, since we can't possibly know what the intrepid developer may do with the control, we check the value of the number of cards to be shown against our counter variable **intCount**, before we go ahead and paint them.

The decision about how to actually paint the card is taken from the **DrawStyle** property of the particular card object in the **Select Case** construct. The **iDraw** argument to the **cdtDraw** function is just the value of this property. The only decision really needed is what value to use for the **iCard** parameter. This will be the sum of the card's **Pip** and **Suit** values, if the face of the card is to be drawn (inverted or otherwise), or the value of the **CardBackStyle** property when the card is to be drawn face down.

Finally, at the end of our paint routine, we raise the **Paint** event back to the user, with the statement:

```
RaiseEvent Paint
```

Even though we've handled all the painting ourselves, it's quite polite to give the developer the event as well, so that they can code additional functionality for it in their own applications if required.

Card Game Services—Methods and Events

Now that we have a control that can be displayed, we need to take a look at some of the aspects of the interface that are needed to create a game. The following table summarizes the services that we provide through the **CardHand** control:

Service	Type	Description
AddACard	Method	Takes a **wxCard** object and places it in the internal collection of the hand
GetCardList	Method	Returns a variant containing an array of strings with the names of the constituent cards e.g. Three Hearts, Jack Diamonds.
MouseDownOvercard	Event	Similar to a mouse down, but the user friendly name of the card under the cursor is passed, along with its index from the internal collection.
MouseMoveOverCard	Event	Similar to **MouseDownOverCard**.
MouseUpOverCard	Event	Similar to **MouseDownOverCard**.
SetCardState	Method	Used to change the **DrawStyle** property of a card in the internal collection. e.g. **blnRet = SetCardState("Two Clubs", Invert)**
TakeACard	Method	Used to retrieve a card from a hand, presumably to add it to another hand control or the discard pile of a **CardDeck** control.

To understand these services better, we will use the BlackJack card game example. But first, let's take a look at some of the code.

Transferring Cards To and From a Hand

The **AddACard** and **TakeACard** methods are the two most important ones of the control. Without them, little could be achieved. The code for adding a card takes a single parameter—an object reference to a **wxCard** object.

```
Public Function AddACard(objCard As wxCard) As Boolean
    On Error GoTo err_AddACard
    m_Cards.Add objCard, objCard.CardKey
    AddACard = True
    UserControl.Refresh
    Exit Function
err_AddACard:
    Select Case Err.Number
      Case 457: 'Attempted to add object to collection with a key
                'that already exists
          'This card aready exist in the collection
          'Someone has been keeping hold of references
          'to a card and is trying to cheat!
          AddACard = False
          Err.Raise vbObjectError + 1015, "wxCards.CardHand",_
                  "Card already exists in hand"
                  'This is an error code of our own
      Case Else:
          AddACard = False
          Err.Raise Err.Number
    End Select
End Function
```

Since the function expects a **wxCard** object, then there should be little trouble with the routine. The only likely error is that the user may get a reference to a card, and then try to add it to the same collection more than once—paramount to virtual cheating! Since we use the card object to generate its own (hopefully) unique key in the collection, this sort of error will be trapped, and we can raise our own error code back to the developer.

Now that you know how cards are added to a hand, you need to be able to take them out again. Here's the code for this:

```
Public Function TakeACard(strKey As Variant) As wxCard
    'Take a card out of the hand and play it!
    On Error GoTo err_TakeACard

    Dim objCard As wxCard
    Set objCard = m_Cards.Item(strKey) 'Will cause an error if not there
    m_Cards.Remove (strKey) .
    Set TakeACard = objCard
    Exit Function
err_TakeACard:
    Set TakeACard = Nothing
    Select Case Err.Number
      Case Else:
          Err.Raise Err.Number
    End Select
End Function
```

The argument to the **TakeACard** function is really expected to be the string key of a card, but it's actually a **Variant**, since we allow the developer to grab the cards by their index values as well. This is particularly convenient when it comes to ending a game, and sending all the cards in play to the discard pile of the associated **CardDeck** control. You just call this method in a loop, equivalent to the number of cards in the hand. This is the **CardCount** property of the **CardHand** object.

Collection's automatically re-index their members in Visual Basic as you add or remove them, and the most likely error to occur is if the wrong string key is requested. In this case, we return **Nothing** to the calling function. It would be good practice to check this return value in the actual game code.

Flipping and Selecting a Card

By default, all card objects start face down, with their back showing. In fact, the **TopCard** method of the deck ensures that this is the case, by setting the **DrawStyle** property of the object to **Back** before the object is passed back to the developer.

```
objCard.DrawStyle = Back 'from the TopCard method of the CardDeck control
```

It's up to the developer to change this state if required. They can do this either when they first obtain the card from the deck (or another hand) and are setting its properties before it's once again added to a hand, or they can use a method of the **CardHand** object named **SetCardState**:

```
Public Function SetCardState(strCardKey As Variant, ByVal enuDrawState As
CardStyle) As Boolean
  On Error GoTo err_SetCardState
  m_Cards(strCardKey).DrawStyle = enuDrawState
  UserControl.Refresh
  SetCardState = True
  Exit Function
err_SetCardState:
  SetCardState = False
  Select Case Err.Number
    Case 457:
    Err.Raise vbObjectError + 1018, "wxCards.CardHand",_
    "Card not in hand."
    Case Else:
    Err.Raise Err.Number
  End Select
End Function
```

To make things simple, this method also takes the card key as a variant, to allow indexed updates to the cards collection. The reason for this is that it's faster than making the developer take the card from the hand, change its properties, and then add it back once more. We use the same generic error handling as above.

Getting References to Cards

All of the above has assumed one very important thing: that you know a reference to the card you want. There are several ways that you might come by this. You could have kept track of the cards going into the hand in your game, although this would require some extra overhead on the part of the developer—especially when the **CardHand** object provides a method for just this purpose! The **GetCardList** method returns a variant that contains an array of strings. The strings are just the keys of the cards found in that hand:

```
Public Function GetCardList() As Variant
    'return a variant containing an array of string keys
    Dim varList As Variant, intCount As Integer, intNoCards As Integer
    varList = Array("No Cards", "No Cards")
        'This will help prevent a wrong subscript error
        'when people check against the 0 or 1 element for a card.
    intNoCards = m_Cards.Count
    If intNoCards Then
      ReDim varList(0 To intNoCards) As String
      For intCount = 1 To intNoCards
        varList(intCount) = m_Cards(intCount).CardKey
      Next intCount
      varList(0) = CStr(intNoCards)
    End If
    GetCardList = varList
End Function
```

This method makes use of Visual Basic's **Array** function. It packages a list of arguments into an array contained within a variant. We create our variant array, initially, with two entries containing the string **"No Cards"**. Why two entries? This just gives protection against confusion about which is the first element. We expect that an array will generally start with an element at index zero, but collections always start at one. In the case of an empty hand of cards, the returned array can be accessed at either the zero or one index, and will still give the developer the return value of **No Cards**.

If the internal card collection is not empty, we first re-dimension the newly created array to contain the correct number of strings. Then we fill it by looping through the collection, retrieving the names of the keys with the **CardKey** property of the **wxCard** objects it contains. The user then has a complete list of the contents of the hand, in index order.

Another way that the developer can get a reference to a card is through a mouse event. In fact, for the more interactive games, this will be how they will allow users to grab cards. We've provided three such events in the **CardHand** control. These events are fired at the same time as the corresponding mouse events that you'll already be familiar with. They're handled like this:

```
Private Sub hndPlayer_MouseDownOverCard(strCardName As String, _
                                        intHandIndex As Integer)
  hndPlayer.SetCardState strCardName, Invert
End Sub
```

```
Private Sub hndPlayer_MouseUpOverCard(strCardName As String, _
                                      intHandIndex As Integer)
  hndPlayer.SetCardState strCardName, Face
End Sub
```

This code has the effect of highlighting the card covered by the mouse. The developer would use code like this to give the end user a visible indication of what they have just clicked. We expose this event through the normal mouse event of the **UserControl** object. At the same time, we raise a set of the more familiar mouse events to the developer. The **MouseUp** event of the **UserControl** has been coded as follows:

```
Private Sub UserControl_MouseUp(Button As Integer, Shift As Integer, _
                                X As Single, Y As Single)
  On Error Resume Next
  Dim intSelectedCardIdx As Integer
```

```
      intSelectedCardIdx = CalculateMouseOverCard(X, Y)
   Dim objCard As wxCard
   Set objCard = m_Cards.Item(intSelectedCardIdx)
   RaiseEvent MouseUp(Button, Shift, X, Y)
   RaiseEvent MouseUpOverCard(objCard.CardKey, intSelectedCardIdx)
End Sub
```

We've produced a function to calculate where in the user control the mouse is, and what card it's over, if any. We have similar code for all three mouse events of the **UserControl**. The function **CalculateMouseOvercard** takes the coordinates of the mouse, and scales them appropriately, to work out which card is under the mouse.

This function has several task to accomplish. It must first scale the **X** value passed to it in terms of quarter cards, since that is how much of a card we will normally display. It also needs to distinguish between the last card which is displayed in full, and also guard against the possibility that the hand may be displaying less cards than it is sized to. The following diagram focuses on the important issues.

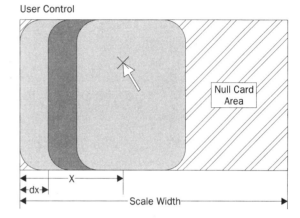

User Control

Null Card Area

```
   Private Function CalculateMouseOverCard(X As Single, Y As Single)
      'Number of cards shown is used to set scaling in the Resize event
      Dim intCards As Integer, intSelectedCardIdx As Integer
      intCards = m_CardsToShow
      Dim sngScaleSize As Single, sngSegmentSize As Single
      'Interpret the position based on the layout style
      If m_LayoutStyle = Left2RightOverlapped Then
         'X indicates c_Cards index
         'check which quarter card segment the mouse pointer is in
         sngScaleSize = UserControl.ScaleWidth
         'segment size = ScaleSize / No. of card quarters shown
         sngSegmentSize = sngScaleSize / (intCards + 3)
         intSelectedCardIdx = CInt(X \ sngSegmentSize) + 1 'integer division
      Else
         'Y indicates c_Cards index
         'This code is almost identical to above
         sngScaleSize = UserControl.ScaleHeight
         sngSegmentSize = sngScaleSize / (intCards + 3)
         intSelectedCardIdx = Int(Y \ sngSegmentSize) + 1 'integer division
      End If
      'since the last card is shown in full 4 quarters we need to prevent
      'an error occurring where too high an index number is generated
      If intSelectedCardIdx > (m_Cards.Count + 3) Then
         'The control is bigger than required to display
         'all the cards in the hand and mouse is over empty control
      ElseIf intSelectedCardIdx > m_Cards.Count Then
         intSelectedCardIdx = m_Cards.Count   'last card shown
```

```
      End If
      CalculateMouseOverCard = intSelectedCardIdx
   End Function
```

We're not interested in what the coordinates of the mouse are in this procedure, only which card is at that point. The coordinate that we choose to base our calculation on is determined by the **LayoutStyle** property. In the diagram, we're assuming **Left2RightOverlapped**, and hence it's based on the **X** value. We know that the control has been sized specifically for a number of cards designated by the value of **m_cardsToShow**, and so the **dx** value shown in the diagram is the scale size of the control, divided by the number of cards it can show. In the case of a left to right layout this comes down to the code:

```
      sngScaleSize = UserControl.ScaleWidth
      'segment size = ScaleSize / No. of card quarters shown
      sngSegmentSize = sngScaleSize / (intCards + 3)
```

The **+3** 'magic number' is the number of extra quarters of cards that could be shown in the given sized control. Working out which quarter card segment the mouse lies in is a relatively easy task. All that we need do is use integer division on the **X** value, with our segment size just calculated. One must be added to give us a usable card collection index, because the integer division will always round down.

```
   intSelectedCardIdx = CInt(X \ sngSegmentSize) + 1 'integer division
```

Of course, this number is just the card quarter segment that the mouse happens to be in, and so there is still some decision making to be done about which card you are really over. Up to the last but one card in the internal collection, this number is a usable index. For the last card (if there are less cards than the control can display) a value in the next four quarters will do since we have a whole card displayed. If there is blank space after the last card then we need to set the index to zero. The last **If** block of code is used to sort out the real index for us.

A value of zero will have an interesting effect in the actual mouse event handler. Look again at the code which raises our card event:

```
   Set objCard = m_Cards.Item(intSelectedCardIdx)
   RaiseEvent MouseMove(Button, Shift, X, Y)
   RaiseEvent MouseMoveOverCard(objCard.CardKey, intSelectedCardIdx)
```

In the case of a zero index, the assignment will fail because zero is never a valid index to a collection object. Fortunately, we have an **On Error Resume Next** statement at the top of the event handler, so execution will continue and the mouse event is still raised up to the developer. Following that, of course, will be another error when we attempt to raise the control event with **objCard** not set because of the previous error. This is exactly what we want. The developer will always get a **MouseDown** event, but only a **MouseDownOverCard** if the cursor is indeed over a card.

> *You may have been warned, previously, that you should always put error handling code in the* **UserControl** *event procedures. Now we will repeat that warning.* **Always handle errors in UserControl events!** *An unhandled error will crash not only your component, but also your user's application.*

Auxiliary CardControl Services

We've now just about covered all of the main services provided by our pair of controls. There are a couple of extra points that complete the controls, and make them easier for the developer to use. First, there is the obligatory self publicizing **About** method, and we'll also provide a **Default** member.

Adding the About Box

Where would the world be if you didn't have an About dialog? To minimize on the resources used by our control pair, we have made a single form do for both their **About** methods.

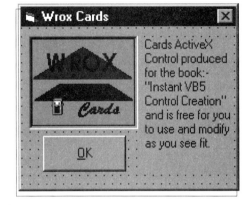

The code for the **About** method of each of the controls is very similar, they just use a different caption:

```
Public Sub About()
    Dim X As New frmAbout
    X.Caption = "wxCard Hand"
    X.Show vbModal
    Set X = Nothing
End Sub
```

*For controls that need to display a dialog, it should always be with the **vbModal** style. Attempting to display modeless forms will give you problems. If your control is intended for use with Internet Explorer, then displaying modeless forms can cause a crash.*

To make this work as expected, all we need to do is make sure that the procedure ID (**DISPID**) for our procedure is set to **AboutBox**. This is the method that will be called by the host application's code. Naming the routine **About** is not enough to get the result we want.

*Since ActiveX controls are COM objects, they support **interfaces** (one for each public class module or control) and each such interface has a set of methods which is automatically allocated a unique identifier— called a Procedure ID or **DISPID**. Some identifiers are standard, and one of those being the **About** method of a control. If this method exists in the interface, it will appear in the Properties window for the control when used in the Visual Basic design environment. Clicking the ellipses button for this property will then call the method with the **DISPID** of **AboutBox**.*

In the VB IDE, you need to use the Tools | Procedure Attributes ... dialog to set your method to the correct Procedure ID:

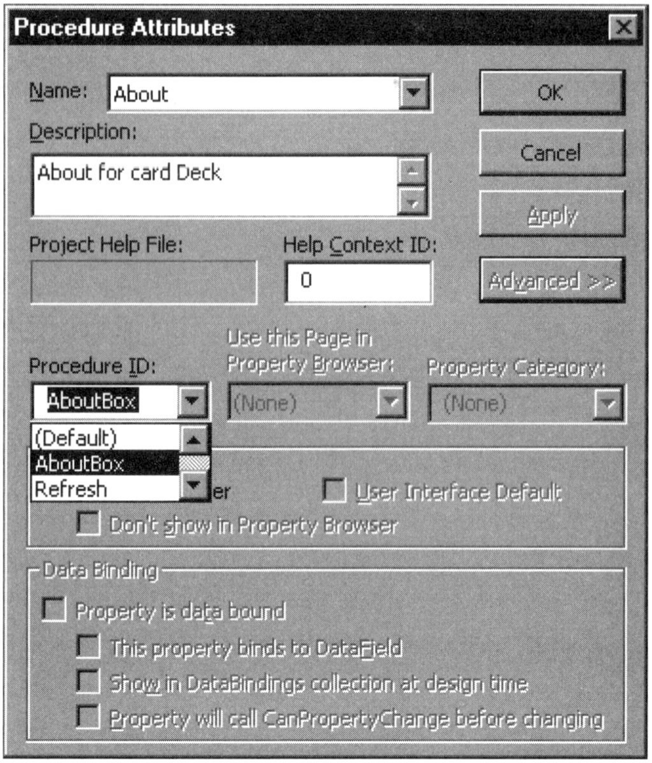

You should get comfortable with this dialog. It will help turn your control into more than just an object server that can draw itself. It will allow your control to really interact with the environment when used in other applications.

Visit this dialog as you create each of you methods, events, and properties, to set the Procedure ID field. You can, of course, add some descriptive text to the Description box. This text is displayed in the label at the bottom of the Properties window, and also in the Object Browser window. It gives the user of your control a little help in figuring out what these members actually do.

Setting the Default Event

A **default event** is the one which the code editor creates a handler for when the developer first enters code for a control event. For example, the default event of a form object is the **Load** event. Without defining this default, the programming environment will take the first event alphabetically. This sort of modification may not be necessary, but it is the kind of bells and whistles feature that makes the control more acceptable to the developer.

We will make the **MouseDownOverCard** event the default event handler in the developer's environment by selecting it in the top window of the Procedure Attributes dialog, and checking the User Interface Default box. A few other procedures that you should connect up with the outside world are the **Enabled** properties of both controls and the **BackColor** property of the hand control.

234

While you are tidying up the rough edges of your control, you should also think about the toolbox icons. These are bitmaps that are 15 pixels high and 16 pixels wide. We've seen how this is done in earlier chapters, and it can be a real challenge drawing something useful and descriptive in that amount of space!

Using the Cards Controls

Now that we've created the controls, we really should test them for usability. Although the Control Creation Edition of Visual Basic will not allow us to actually compile an application, we can build one to run within the IDE. From the File menu, we select Add Project and choose Standard EXE. We set the project options, give it a useful name, and we are then ready to start typing code. Our test project will be a simple game of BlackJack. You saw a glimpse of the finished program earlier.

The Game Requirements

For our sample we will need one **CardDeck** control, and two **CardHand** controls. We also need various buttons and labels for the basic game mechanics—as well as for aesthetic purposes. The game logic can be summarized quite simply:

Game State	Action to be taken
Betting and Start Up	Place bets. Once betting is completed, deal two cards to the player and one to the dealer (all face up).
Player Turn	Player draws cards (Draw) until either the hand score is more than 21 (player lose) or they are satisfied with their score (Stick).
Dealer Turn	Dealer draws cards until the hand score is greater than 16, at which point, the game result is calculated, or the dealer score is more than 21 and the dealer has lost.
End of Play	Calculate win or lose and points gain or loss. Reset the hands ready for the next game. Ensure the deck has enough cards for a new game

This format lends itself to **state programming**, where one variable takes on values representing the state of the game, and that variable is used to synchronize the user interface, enabling and disabling various aspects. We use an enumeration to set the value of our state variable to intuitively named values:

```
Private Enum GameState
    EndOfPlay = 0
    PlayerTurn = 1 'Bet has been committed and cards are drawn etc.
    DealerTurn = 2 'player has finished and score <22
    Betting = 3
End Enum
```

235

Thinking Carefully About Enumerations

Unlike the enumeration that we used with the controls, these **GameState** values are not valid outside the module in which they are declared. Even if we declare this enumeration as **Public**, and place it in a **.bas** module, it would still only be valid inside that particular application's project, and *not* inside the code of the control or outside the application. This is an essential difference between enumerations used in components, and those in normal applications.

Public Enumerations in an Application

When a control (or **Public** object server) is created, a **type library** is also produced. This contains the **interface** for all the **Public** components, including the enumerations and constants they contain. Hence, the hosting application can access these values. In an application, the **Public** enumerations can never be accessed from outside the application, or inside the various components it uses. In our test application's project, we can access such enumerated values as **Hearts** and **King**—but the control itself can never use **EndOfPlay**.

Public Enumerations in a Control

Because enumerations *in controls* are **Public**, you should also put some thought into deciding what names you give to their values. As an example, all Visual Basic intrinsic constants are prefixed with **vb**, such as **vbCrLf**, and the VBA data access objects have **db** for parameters like **dbOpenDynaset**. As more and more components enter the market, there will be greater possibility of getting name clashes, so be careful out there. If you are the victim of a name clash with someone else's component, then VB will resolve the matter by using the value from the library that appears first in the references dialog. This could cause some interesting logic errors in your code, or worse still, some really big crashes.

Consider the situation where you have a combination project that has card games and also domino games. If the **Domino.ocx** control (or whatever) has a **Public** enumeration called **Pip**, like our **Cards** control does, it may well have a different value for the member **Two**. In this case, either the card game or the domino game would start to behave really strangely. So, give yourself a good prefix for your exported enumerations and you should be OK.

Assuming that there isn't a domino control like this on your system, you can get on with creating some BlackJack! Here's the application again, in design mode:

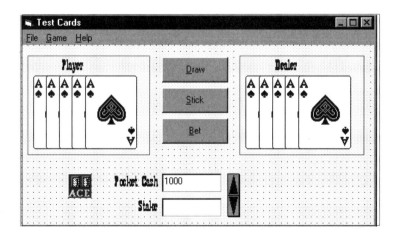

We're not going to look in depth at all the code for this—there are plenty of comments to guide you if you want to take a look at it. However, we will take a quick look at how we've used the card controls' interfaces.

Starting The Game

Once a bet has been placed (credit transferred to the stake and Bet clicked), we need to deal out some cards. For this we have the **DealCards** routine:

```
Private Sub DealCards()
  Dim objCard As wxCard, blnRet As Boolean
  Dim intCount As Integer
  On Error GoTo err_dealcards
  'dealer gets one card face up initially
  Set objCard = Deck.TopCard
  objCard.DrawStyle = Face
  blnRet = hndDealer.AddACard(objCard)
  'player gets two cards
  For intCount = 0 To 1
    Set objCard = Deck.TopCard
    objCard.DrawStyle = Face
    blnRet = hndPlayer.AddACard(objCard)
  Next intCount
  Exit Sub
err_dealcards:
  Err.Raise Err.Number
End Sub
```

We simply use an object reference variable bound to the **wxCard** type to pick up cards from the **Deck** control, and add them to the dealer's and players' hands, respectively. While we have the reference to the card, we change its **DrawStyle** to be face up, since all cards that come from the deck are face down by default.

When the user clicks the Draw button, we use the same technique to add a new card to the hand. At each point where a card is added to a hand, it's important that we check the overall score of the game. To do this we have made use of the **GetCardList** function of the hand control:

```
Private Function CheckScore(hndCards As Control) As Integer
  'need to be careful about handling ace's
  Dim arrCardList As Variant
  Dim strCardName As String, strPip As String
  Dim intSpPos As Integer, intCurValue As Integer, intCount As Integer
  Dim blnAces As Boolean
    'with one or more aces you may want to add 10, but never 20 or more!
  arrCardList = hndCards.GetCardList
  intCurValue = 0
  'loop through strCardName In arrCardList
  For intCount = LBound(arrCardList) To UBound(arrCardList)
    intSpPos = InStr(arrCardList(intCount), " ")
    If intSpPos Then
      'ignore the first numeric string, as it's just a member count
      strPip = Left(arrCardList(intCount), intSpPos - 1) 'lose the space!
      Select Case UCase(strPip)
      Case "ACE":
        blnAces = True
        intCurValue = intCurValue + 1
```

```
      Case "TWO":
        intCurValue = intCurValue + 2
      Case "THREE":
        intCurValue = intCurValue + 3
      Case "FOUR":
        intCurValue = intCurValue + 4
      Case "FIVE":
        intCurValue = intCurValue + 5
      Case "SIX":
        intCurValue = intCurValue + 6
      Case "SEVEN":
        intCurValue = intCurValue + 7
      Case "EIGHT":
        intCurValue = intCurValue + 8
      Case "NINE":
        intCurValue = intCurValue + 9
      Case "TEN":
        intCurValue = intCurValue + 10
      Case "JACK":
        intCurValue = intCurValue + 10
      Case "QUEEN":
        intCurValue = intCurValue + 10
      Case "KING":
        intCurValue = intCurValue + 10
      End Select
    End If
  Next intCount
  If intCurValue < 12 And blnAces Then
    intCurValue = intCurValue + 10 'Treat an ace as 11
  End If
  CheckScore = intCurValue
End Function
```

We have a variant which we call **arrCardList**. We've used this particular convention because, after the **GetCardList** method has been invoked, the variant will be an array as far as our code is concerned. This allows us to loop through the complete list adding up the score as we go. Notice the Boolean that we set to **True** when an ace is encountered. In BlackJack, an ace may be treated as either 1 or 11. This means that we may want to add 10 to the score, but only if the overall score is less than 12—after all, you shouldn't voluntarily go bust! Since two aces would never both be counted as value 11, it's only the existence of any aces in the hand that is needed, not how many are actually in the hand. Once you have the hand's score, the rest of the game is pretty easy to handle. The only thing that you have to worry about is cleaning up at the end of a game.

One of the few responsibilities of the programmer is not to lose the cards. When it comes to clean up time, you must ensure that cards are removed from the hands and placed back on the discard pile. To do this we have a small generic routine, **DiscardHand**:

```
Private Sub DiscardHand(Hand As Control)
  Dim intCount As Integer, objCard As wxCard
  Dim blnRet As Boolean
  For intCount = 1 To Hand.CardCount
    Set objCard = Hand.TakeACard(1)
    If IsNull(objCard) Then
      'do some error handling here!
    End If
```

```
      blnRet = Deck.AddToDiscard(objCard)
    Next intCount
  End Sub
```

Its only purpose is to remove cards from the hand, and use **AddToDiscard** method of the **CardDeck** to put them back there. We make use of the fact that **TakeACard** will take either an integer index or a string key. While there are cards in the hand, we can always get the first one of them out and dump it to the discard collection.

The last piece of logic that we have to worry about is the number of cards left in the deck. With BlackJack, we just keep on recycling the cards until the deck is almost empty, and then we just start again. So, at the end of any one particular game, we need to check the total number of cards left.

```
  Private Sub CheckDeck()
    Dim intCardsLeft As Integer
    intCardsLeft = Deck.DeckCount
    If intCardsLeft < 14 Then
      Deck.Shuffle
    End If
  End Sub
```

That is just about all there is to the BlackJack sample that demonstrates our controls. We have, however, added a couple of features on the menu for the application. There is a Help item which displays our About dialog. Notice the use of the tooltip—some things just have to be done!

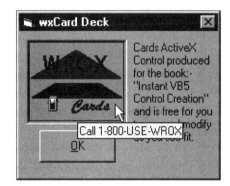

Summary

This chapter has introduced you to the idea of building your own controls from scratch. Without relying on contained components to build your control display, you find that quite a lot of your effort will be taken up by the painting and sizing of the control.

By using the functions from **Cards.dll** with this control, we've saved ourselves a lot of work. Of course, there's nothing to stop you making some really impressive graphical controls, by directly accessing the Windows API. In fact, you'll see this technique used in the next chapter. It's all a question of how much effort you are willing to put into the control. However, at the end of the day, the really important feature of a control is the interface that it exposes. The most attractive control in the world will be useless if you don't supply the right services to the application developer who is using your control.

The card controls that we have developed to demonstrate a user drawn control leave a few things to be desired. For instance, it's possible for a developer to change the **Pip** and **Suit** of a card.

The **Property Let** procedure should, really, have been protected against this possibility by declaring them as **Friend** rather than **Public**. Also, a lot of trust has been placed on the developer using the control not to lose references to card objects. It would be much better if the cards has some fail-safe method for preventing such losses. You may want to improve the control to do just this sort of thing. If you do, then here's a hint: all cards originate from a **CardDeck** object, and a **wxCard** object has a **Terminate** event!

In this chapter, you've seen four main points to bear in mind when creating your own user-drawn controls:

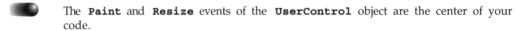 The **Paint** and **Resize** events of the **UserControl** object are the center of your code.

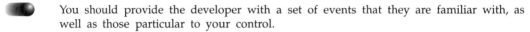 You should provide the developer with a set of events that they are familiar with, as well as those particular to your control.

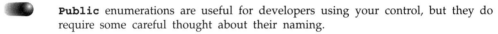 **Public** enumerations are useful for developers using your control, but they do require some careful thought about their naming.

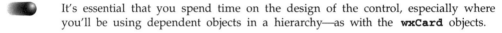 It's essential that you spend time on the design of the control, especially where you'll be using dependent objects in a hierarchy—as with the **wxCard** objects.

Beyond Visual Basic

Back in Chapter 4 we showed you how to enhance the functionality of an existing ComboBox control, making it appear as an entirely new component from the programmer's point of view. In a similar fashion, Chapter 5 took a number of standard controls (edit boxes and labels) and wrapped them up into a single, aggregated address control. You will find the same emphasis on the Microsoft samples included with VB5 CCE—in many cases, a complex control is built up from one or more pre-existing components.

While we've used sub-classing methods previously, there are times when this just isn't good enough. As an example, we'll develop a better Windows slider control. In this chapter, we'll show you how you can create a new control, which is designed to work in a similar way to existing ones. This is a similar technique to the way we created the cards controls in the previous chapter.

So you'll see how we:

 Find ways to improve on the functionality of an existing control

 Create a new control from scratch, without sub-classing an existing one

 Use the Windows Application Programming Interface to carry out tasks not possible, or poorly implemented, in Visual Basic

 Take into account extra requirements, like control orientation and responding to the keyboard.

Why You Need to Take Control

There will be times when the previous approaches to sub-classing existing controls are not adequate. For example, consider the Windows slider control. Slider controls (also called Trackbars) consist of a 'thumb' indicator which can be dragged along a track. Sliders provide a convenient way for a user to select from a number of possible consecutive values. You'll find sliders in many third-party applications and extensively used by Windows 95 itself. Look at the Settings page of the Display Properties dialog box (right-click on your desktop and select Properties from the pop-up menu). In this case, a slider is used to select the wanted size of the Windows desktop.

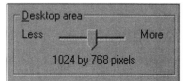

The slider is one of a number of 32-bit controls that are implemented within the **COMCTL32.DLL** library. Other controls implemented by this library include progress bars, property pages, list views, tree views, image lists and pretty well all the new Windows 95 control goodies. The fancy 'Coolbar' button style used by Internet Explorer 3.0 is also a recent addition to this library.

The **COMCTL32** library code implements the slider controls (and others) by making direct calls on the Windows API. It makes available the functionality of the slider control by providing a new window class called **msctls_trackbar**. Assuming that the **COMCTL32** library has been loaded and initialized, an application can create a slider control simply by specifying this class name when it creates a child window. The application can then control the appearance and behaviour of the slider by sending special messages to the child window. In the same way, it receives notification messages from the control to tell it that the user has moved the position of the 'thumb'.

From the perspective of a Visual Basic programmer, most of the Windows 95 controls are implemented as ActiveX components using the **COMCTL32.OCX** file. By doing things this way, rather than building a knowledge of the new controls into Visual Basic itself, Microsoft was able to kill two birds with one stone—not only do Visual Basic developers get access to the new controls, but so does every other development environment that can make use of OCX components.

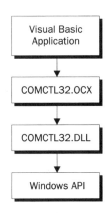

With the above in mind, you'll understand that when a Visual Basic program uses a slider control, it's actually communicating with an ActiveX component built into **COMCTL32.OCX**. This file, in turn, communicates with the underlying **COMCTL32.DLL** library and (finally) the DLL talks to the Windows API itself.

This might not sound like a terribly efficient way of doing things and, to be honest, it probably isn't. But it enabled Microsoft to support Windows 95 controls for many development systems at a stroke.

There is, however, one major problem with this layered approach. For maximum flexibility it's important that each layer should pass on the full range of capabilities to the layer above. In other words, if **COMCTL32.DLL** will let you have a slider control with a chrome thumb, green polka-dots and go-faster stripes (it won't, incidentally), then **COMCTL32.OCX** should expose this functionality to Visual Basic.

In the case of the slider control, the problems go deeper. Even with access to the full range of slider capabilities at the API level, we find that there's no control over the appearance of the thumb. Wouldn't it be great if we could somehow 'hook into' the control and add our own custom drawing effects?

In order to get this sort of flexibility, the only sensible approach is to dispense with the slider control and start from scratch. There's obviously some extra effort involved in going down this route but consider: one of the reason's Microsoft's own applications are so successful is because they consistently break with tradition and introduce new user-interface elements into their own products at an early stage! Very quickly, anyone else's software looks dated by comparison.

The Changing Face of Fashion

If you believe we're overstating the case here, think back over the last few years: Microsoft introduced the **CTL3D** library which added 3D effects to check-boxes, radio buttons and so on. But before making this technology available to developers in general, they'd *already* pioneered it in Microsoft Excel and Microsoft Word. Through an updated **COMCTL32.DLL** library, they've recently made available the Coolbar technology—but not before they'd *already* made good use of it in Internet Explorer. Take a look at the VB5 CCE development environment you're using. Notice those cute new menu bitmaps and the way menu bar items automatically 'pop-up' as you move the mouse over them? The same interface is used in Microsoft's Office 97 suite. For sure, Microsoft will make this technology available to other developers—when they're ready to do so.

The bottom line is this: Microsoft are well aware that first impressions *do* count. If you want your application to stand out from the crowd, you could do a lot worse than add some eye-catching custom controls to your application.

Just in case you're not convinced yet, here's a partial list of limitations associated with Microsoft's existing ActiveX implementation of the slider control. Understand that we're not knocking the slider control itself, nor the OCX wrapper around it. We're simply stressing that for maximum programming versatility, you've got to get into the driving seat yourself!

- No control over background color at design-time. When you first place a slider control on to a form, it takes the **BackColor** property of the form. However, if you subsequently change the form's **BackColor**, the slider component doesn't notice and there's no way to change the slider's background color from the Properties window. The only way to get a slider with the current background color is to throw away your existing slider and place a new one on the form.

- No control over background color at run-time. This is a far worse problem. Irrespective of whatever color you're able to persuade the slider control to adopt at design time, it will promptly ignore it at run-time, defaulting to whatever the current Windows button-face color happens to be. This is probably a shortcoming of Microsoft's OCX wrapper, since the same problem doesn't appear when using the Delphi VCL wrapper around the slider control.

- No control over the appearance of the thumb. Being able to control the appearance of the thumb allows the developer to produce a much more attractive user-interface. You might choose to implement the thumb as an application-supplied bitmap, or alternatively you might choose to vary the thumb's appearance according to its position on the track-bar. The thumb might progressively change color as it's moved along, or else you might want to draw a changing number on top of the thumb itself. Cute effects like this just aren't possible with the existing implementation.

- No control over the appearance of the tick marks. Although you can turn ticks on or off and decide on which side of the track-bar you want them to appear, the same arguments apply. Because there's no way of getting in on the action, you're stuck with the canned functionality which the control provides.

245

Achieving Flicker-Free Graphics

Having looked at the inherent limitations in using 'off-the-shelf' components, and having hinted at the advantages to be gained by giving your application a distinctive look and feel, let's now get stuck into the development of our own enhanced slider. The illustration shows an example of the control that we're going to put together in this chapter. It supports horizontal and vertical orientation, allows you to specify different border styles and it behaves like one of the latest Microsoft controls which 'highlight' themselves as the mouse moves over them.

Initially, we'll design our new control as a horizontal slider, and we'll add an **Orientation** property at a later stage—you'll see why this makes sense later.

However, before starting work on the control proper, let's begin by putting together a reusable class module which allows us to add flicker-free graphics to any control created with VB5 CCE. This module will be completely reusable and can easily be incorporated into any other control projects you develop.

What do we mean by flicker-free graphics? Well, here's the problem. Imagine that you're dragging the thumb of a slider control along the track of the control. Each time that the thumb moves a little, it has to be redrawn in its new position. But before we can do that, it's also necessary to redraw the part of the control where the thumb previously was, so that the thumb doesn't appear to be in the same place twice. If we did all this in 'real-time', using the ordinary graphic support built into Visual Basic, we'd see a lot of unpleasant flicker as the individual parts of the control were redrawn while the thumb was in motion. This doesn't sound very impressive!

A much better solution is to use an off-screen bitmap, sometimes also referred to as a memory bitmap. You can think of an off-screen bitmap as a blank sheet of paper the same size and shape as the control. When the appearance of the control changes (as when the thumb moves, or some property of the control is modified), a new image of the control gets drawn on to our blank piece of paper. When we're done drawing, we can just zap the entire image of the control on to the screen in one quick operation—this is called **blitting**. Because we've blitted the complete image of the control on to the screen instantaneously, the user never sees any flicker. Blitting an off-screen bitmap on to the screen is a very powerful technique, and the visual effect is much smoother as we shall see.

Blitting for Beginners

Before reading on, we'd encourage you once again to review the final version of the slider control source code, looking in particular at the way in which the **UserControl_Paint** routine initializes an object of type **MemDC** and then does all its painting by calling methods of this object. The information presented in this section is necessarily somewhat involved, and it would help you to see where we're heading before mapping out the route we use to get there!

In Windows, drawing operations (such as creating a line, a polygon, displaying a bitmap, or whatever) are always performed relative to a **device context**. Although this term may be foreign to Visual Basic developers, it's absolutely central to the Windows API. When drawing to the screen, you use a device context which 'points' at the physical display, but when creating an off-screen bitmap, you create a **memory device context**, select a memory bitmap into it, and then draw into that device context in the usual way. Rather than appearing on the screen, the drawing operations get stored up into the memory bitmap which you can blit on to the screen at a later time.

If you find this hard to understand, then don't worry—most Windows programmers have problems the first time they come up against this concept! As we mentioned earlier, you can think of a memory bitmap as a blank sheet of paper and in the same way, you can think of the memory device context (device context's are often called DC's for short) as a sort of printer into which you load your blank paper. Once you've 'printed' your drawing on to a bitmap, it can be blitted on to the physical display at whatever position you want. You can even blit the same bitmap many times at different locations.

The off-screen drawing code we've used here is based around a Visual Basic class module called **MEMDC.CLS**. Here's the **Initialize** routine for this class along with the declarations for the private variables that it uses:

```
'=====================================================================
' Private Data Members
'=====================================================================
Private btnFace As Long             ' color to use for the 3d face
Private btnHighlight As Long        ' color to use for the 3d highlight
Private btnShadow As Long           ' color to use for the 3d shadow
Private hMemDC As Long              ' memory DC
Private hCtlDC As Long              ' display DC for the control
Private hOldBitmap As Long          ' original bitmap for the memory DC
Private ControlWidth As Long        ' width of the control - PIXELS!
Private ControlHeight As Long       ' height of the control - PIXELS!
```

```
'=====================================================================
'   Name:       Initialize
'   Purpose:    Init the off-screen DC and set up private variables
'=====================================================================
Public Sub Initialize(CtlHdc As Long, CtlWidth As Long, CtlHeight As Long)
    If CtlHdc <> 0 And CtlWidth <> 0 And CtlHeight <> 0 And hMemDC = 0 Then
        ' Save width and height of the control
        ControlWidth = CtlWidth
        ControlHeight = CtlHeight
        ' Stash the control's device context - need for Blit()
        hCtlDC = CtlHdc
        ' Create the memory device context
        hMemDC = CreateCompatibleDC(hCtlDC)
        ' Create a bitmap, select into memory DC and stash old
        hOldBitmap = SelectObject(hMemDC, _
        CreateCompatibleBitmap(hCtlDC, ControlWidth, ControlHeight))
        ' Set up color metrics for 3D surface rendering
        btnFace = GetSysColor(COLOR_BTNFACE)
        btnHighlight = GetSysColor(COLOR_BTNHIGHLIGHT)
        btnShadow = GetSysColor(COLOR_BTNSHADOW)
    End If
End Sub
```

This routine will be called by the 'client' code (in this case, by the **UserControl_Paint** routine of the slider control). The first parameter, **CtlHdc**, is the device context for our user control. The class module needs to know the control's DC so that it can blit the memory bitmap on to the actual display when the drawing takes place. The other two parameters specify the width and height of the control. Again, this information is needed for when the blit takes place, but it's also needed so that the **MemDC** code can create an off-screen bitmap whose size corresponds to that of the control.

Maybe you're asking yourself why we can't do all this stuff inside the **Class_Initialize** routine that's called when Visual Basic creates an instance of a particular class? It would be terrific if you could do that, but unfortunately Visual Basic has no mechanism for passing parameters to the **Class_Initialize** routine. As you know, when you create an instance of a class in Visual Basic, you have to do something along these lines:

```
Set varName = New ClassName
```

It would be *really great* if you could pass parameters through the **New** function something like this:

```
Set varName = New ClassName (Tom, Dick, Harry)
```

You'd then receive these parameters inside your custom **Class_Initialize**. Unfortunately, this is pure fantasy on our part—Visual Basic won't let you do it. Maybe it'll be in version 6.0, but until then we're stuck with the idea of a separate routine that's called to do per-instance initialization *after* the object's constructor has been called.

The **Initialize** code stores the width, height and control DC information and then uses a Windows API routine, **CreateCompatibleDC**, to create a memory device context. In the next statement, the code calls another API routine, **CreateCompatibleBitmap**, to create the memory bitmap that will hold the control's image. This new bitmap is immediately selected into the memory DC (we're loading the printer with paper) and the bitmap that was previously in the DC is stored away. Finally, the code calls **GetSystemMetrics** three times to determine what colors Windows is currently using to draw buttons—we want our color scheme to be compatible with this.

> *Incidentally, you may be wondering why the two private definitions for* **ControlWidth** *and* **ControlHeight** *stress that these values are in pixels. When we were originally developing this control, the* **ScaleMode** *property for* **UserControl** *was originally set to "**Twips**" (the default) which meant that a couple of very large numbers were passed as width and height to the* **CreateCompatibleBitmap** *API call. In fact, we ended up asking the poor old Windows API for a 16 million color bitmap with dimensions of around 2000 by 1000 pixels! Amazingly, this call succeeded, but it sure slowed the machine down to a crawl! The moral of the story is—when working with the Windows API, make very sure that you pass pixel values to routines that expect them.*

Of course, Visual Basic can't call the Windows API without some help—our control project includes another file called **API.BAS** which contains definitions for all the API routines we've used. In order to save some space, we haven't included the code to **API.BAS** here; it's provided with the rest of the slider source code on the Wrox web site at: **http://www.wrox.com/books/0235/code/**

Using Our Memory DC

Once the memory device context has been set up, we can call methods of the new class in the usual way by simply appending a method name to the instance name of the class. Let's begin with **InvertRect**, which is the simplest drawing method in the class module.

```
'================================================================
' Name:      InvertRect
' Purpose:   Invert a designated rectangle
'================================================================
Public Sub InvertRect(ByVal nLeft As Long, ByVal nTop As Long, _
                      ByVal nWidth As Long, ByVal nHeight As Long)
    Dim rc As RECT

    rc.Left = nLeft
    rc.Top = nTop
    rc.Right = nLeft + nWidth
    rc.Bottom = nTop + nHeight
    API.InvertRect hMemDC, rc
End Sub
```

*Maybe you're wondering why we've prefixed the call to **InvertRect** with "**API.**" This is necessary because there's a name clash between the **InvertRect** routine defined in the **MemDC** module and the routine of the same name defined in the API module. If we didn't add the prefix, the compiler would assume we were talking about the **MemDC** version of **InvertRect** and complain that we weren't passing the right type of parameters.*

This method takes four parameters which specify the size and location of a rectangle within the memory bitmap—not on the screen. It takes these parameters, builds a **RECT** data structure, and calls a Windows API routine called **InvertRect** to do the real work. Notice that the **hMemDC** device context is specified as the first parameter to **InvertRect**. This is what directs the drawing operation into our memory DC and on to the memory bitmap. If we'd accidentally specified **hCtlDC** here (the device context for the on-screen control), then the method would invert a portion of the screen and the memory bitmap would remain unaffected.

To use this method, the 'client' code (the drawing code in the slider control) only needs to do something like this:

```
hdc.InvertRect (20, 20, 100, 100)
```

This assumes that **hdc** has been declared as a variable of type **MemDC**, that **New** has been used to create a new instance of the class, and that the **Initialize** method has been called to create the off-screen bitmap. We'll see how this works in a little while when we look at the control code proper. For now—trust us!

```
'================================================================
'   Name:      FillRect
'   Purpose:   Fast rectangle fill using ExtTextOut
'================================================================
Public Sub FillRect(ByVal nLeft As Long, ByVal nTop As Long, _
                    ByVal nWidth As Long, ByVal nHeight As Long, rgbColor As Long)
    Dim r As RECT
```

```
        If hMemDC <> 0 Then
            ' Set wanted background color
            SetBkColor hMemDC, rgbColor
            ' Init rectangle dimensions
            r.Left = nLeft
            r.Top = nTop
            r.Right = nWidth + nLeft
            r.Bottom = nHeight + nTop
            ' Write to memory DC using ExtTextOut
            ExtTextOut hMemDC, 0, 0, 6, r, "", 0, 0
        End If
    End Sub
```

The second routine in **MemDC's** repertoire of methods is **FillRect**. As the name suggest, this fills an area of the memory bitmap with the color specified as the final parameter. To this end, the **SetBkColor** routine sets the background color for the memory DC and the **ExtTextOut** routine is then used to quickly fill the designated rectangle with the wanted color.

What's this you're thinking? Why is a routine that prints text being used to do nothing except fill a rectangle? Well, the short answer is speed. The Windows API contains a perfectly good routine, **FillRect**, which can be used to fill a rectangle with a specified color. However, to use **FillRect**, you need to create a brush which has the color you want and when you've finished the drawing operation, you need to destroy the brush. Not only is **FillRect** less convenient for us, but it's a lot slower too. It turns out that using **ExtTextOut** to print no text at all is just about the fastest available way of filling a rectangle! If this strikes you as odd, you're certainly not alone. Welcome to the wild and wacky world of the Windows API!

```
'=================================================================
'    Name:        Rect3D
'    Purpose:     Draw a 3D shaded rectangle on our memory DC.
'=================================================================
Public Sub Rect3D(ByVal nLeft As Long, ByVal nTop As Long, _
                ByVal nWidth As Long, ByVal nHeight As Long, FX As Effect3D)
    Dim LR_color As Long
    Dim UL_color As Long

    If hMemDC <> 0 Then
        ' Set upper-left and lower-right color values as wanted
        Select Case FX
            Case Flat
                LR_color = btnShadow
                UL_color = btnShadow
            Case Raised
                LR_color = btnShadow
                UL_color = btnHighlight
            Case Recessed
                LR_color = btnHighlight
                UL_color = btnShadow
            Case Selected
                LR_color = btnHighlight
                UL_color = vbBlack
        End Select

        ' The rectangle is rendered using three calls to FillRect.
        ' It would probably be more efficient to draw a series of
        ' non-overlapping single-pixel lines directly with
```

```
            ' ExtTextOut, but this code seems adequate.

            Me.FillRect nLeft, nTop, nWidth, nHeight, LR_color
            nWidth = nWidth - 1
            nHeight = nHeight - 1
            Me.FillRect nLeft, nTop, nWidth, nHeight, UL_color
            nLeft = nLeft + 1
            nTop = nTop + 1
            nWidth = nWidth - 1
            nHeight = nHeight - 1
            Me.FillRect nLeft, nTop, nWidth, nHeight, btnFace

            ' The Selected style is simply a color inversion.
            If FX = Selected Then InvertRect nLeft, nTop, nWidth, nHeight
        End If
End Sub
```

The most complicated drawing method in the **MemDC** module is **Rect3D**. As with the other two rectangle-drawing methods, it takes four parameters which give the location and size of the rectangle. Additionally, the fifth parameter allows the caller to specify an effect which is applied to the rectangle. This parameter, an enumerated type, can take one of the values shown below.

```
Public Enum Effect3D
    Raised
    Recessed
    Flat
    Selected
End Enum
```

The **Raised** and **Recessed** styles draw the rectangle with either an elevated or sunken appearance while the **Flat** style simply draws a flat rectangle using Windows' button shadow color. Finally, the **Selected** style produces a much stronger effect by creating a dark black sunken rectangle. **Rect3D** does its stuff by calling the **FillRect** and **InvertRect** methods mentioned previously.

```
'==================================================================
' Name:     Blit
' Purpose:  Blit the memory DC on to the display
'==================================================================
Public Sub Blit()
    BitBlt hCtlDC, 0, 0, ControlWidth, ControlHeight, hMemDC, 0, 0, SRCCOPY
End Sub
```

Perhaps the most important **MemDC** method is **Blit**. For the sake of simplicity, this method takes no parameters. It simply takes the off-screen bitmap created by the other drawing methods and blits it on to the screen using the control's device context. This is why the class module needed to store the size of the control and the **hCtlDC** control context—this information is needed by the API-level **BitBlt** routine which quickly transfers a bitmap from one device context to another.

```
'==================================================================
'    Name:       Class_Terminate()
'    Purpose:    Clean-up code called when a class object is destroyed.
'==================================================================
Private Sub Class_Terminate()
    If hMemDC <> 0 Then
```

251

```
            ' Put back the old bitmap, and nuke the memory bitmap
            DeleteObject (SelectObject(hMemDC, hOldBitmap))
            ' Also need to nuke the memory DC itself
            DeleteDC hMemDC
        End If
    End Sub
```

The final piece of the **MemDC** jigsaw puzzle is the **Class_Terminate** routine which is called when the caller's **MemDC** object is destroyed. If you're familiar with object-oriented programming with Visual Basic, you'll know that you don't need to explicitly call the **Class_Terminate** routine. As soon as a class object of type **MemDC** goes out of scope, Visual Basic automatically destroys the object, calling the **Class_Terminate** routine to perform any needed clean-up.

In this case, the **Class_Terminate** code selects the old bitmap back into the memory device context (compare this with the code in the **Initialize** method) and immediately destroys the memory bitmap that we've been using to create the image of the control. The memory DC itself is also destroyed at this time.

> *You might wonder why we don't use the same off-screen bitmap and memory DC for the lifetime of the control. Why go to the trouble of recreating these objects each time the control needs to be repainted and destroying them when we've finished painting? Well, it would certainly be possible to do that, but each time we came to draw the control, we'd have to take care to erase whatever image was contained in the off-screen bitmap. To return to our 'blank sheet of paper' analogy, if we're going to keep using the same piece of paper, then we need to reach for the eraser each time we want to reuse it! In practice, creating device contexts and bitmaps are very rapid operations (providing the bitmaps are small), so it's really not a big issue.*

As a convenience, the **MemDC** module also provides three other member functions which enable the client code to obtain the standard Windows colors used for drawing buttons. By hanging this information off the **MemDC** class, we're providing this information at the point where it's most likely to be needed—while the button's image is being drawn.

```
'===================================================================
'    Name:        Get ButtonFaceColor()
'    Purpose:     Returns button face color for interested parties
'===================================================================
Public Property Get ButtonFaceColor() As Long
    ButtonFaceColor = btnFace
End Property


'===================================================================
'    Name:        Get ButtonHighlightColor()
'    Purpose:     Returns button highlight color for interested parties
'===================================================================
Public Property Get ButtonHighlightColor() As Long
    ButtonHighlightColor = btnHighlight
End Property


'===================================================================
'    Name:        Get ButtonShadowColor()
'    Purpose:     Returns button shadow color for interested parties
'===================================================================
Public Property Get ButtonShadowColor() As Long
    ButtonShadowColor = btnShadow
End Property
```

Getting in a State...

A while back, we mentioned the way that menu items pop-up in Visual Basic 5.0 as you move the mouse over them. The same thing happens with Internet Explorer 3.0's Coolbar buttons—as the mouse moves over the button, it changes from monochrome to color and displays a raised 'Click Me!' appearance.

From the outset, we thought it would be a great idea to put the same functionality into our slider control. If you think about it, this really means that the control has got to have four separate states. These are:

 Normal - The control is in its normal state.

 Disabled - The control has been disabled and displays itself in such a way as to indicate that it can't be used.

 Highlighted - The control hasn't been clicked, but the mouse is over it and some highlighting is being shown.

 Active - The mouse is being held down over the control, full highlighting is being shown, and the control is responding to mouse movement.

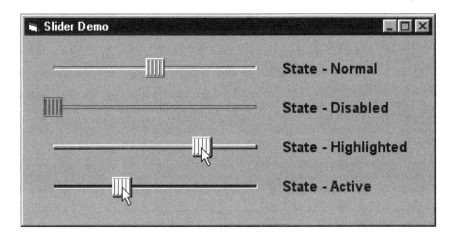

To put this in more concrete terms, take a look at the illustration shown above. Let us hastily point out that this screen-shot is a composite mock-up made from two other screen-shots. Most PCs are only fitted with one mouse, and ours isn't any different!

Going from top to bottom, you can see the normal state of the control on the top row. Next, we see the control in its disabled state. It has a flat, uninteresting look—which is pretty much what a disabled control is supposed to look like! On the third row, the mouse has moved over the slider which responds by highlighting the thumb and raising the track-bar. Finally, the bottom illustration shows what the slider looks like when the mouse is down and the thumb is being actively dragged backwards and forwards.

Incidentally, if you don't like the appearance of the slider, please realise that we're not graphics artists! Our job is to give you some guidance in writing controls, not teach you fine art. You'll no doubt have plenty of ideas of your own for how you want a slider to look.

Based on the above comments, we can define a private variable, **mControlState**, in our control source code:

```
Private Enum Control_State
    Normal          ' normal display, enabled
    Disabled        ' normal display, disabled
    Highlighted     ' mouse over control, no mouse down
    Active          ' mouse over control, mouse down and captured
End Enum
```

```
Private mControlState As Control_State      ' state of the control
```

At the same time, we may as well go ahead and set up the **Enabled** property. Most simple properties will be no more than wrappers around a private variable whose value directly reflects that of the property. In this respect, **Enabled** is slightly unusual because its value doesn't map directly on to **mControlState**. Instead, **Enabled** is False if **mControlState** equals **Disabled** and True otherwise. This is reflected in the code shown below.

```
Public Property Get Enabled() As Boolean
    Enabled = UserControl.Enabled
End Property

Public Property Let Enabled(ByVal NewEnabled As Boolean)
    If (UserControl.Enabled) <> NewEnabled Then
        UserControl.Enabled = NewEnabled

        If NewEnabled Then
            mControlState = Normal
        Else
            mControlState = Disabled
        End If

        PropertyChanged "Enabled"
        UserControl_Paint
    End If
End Property
```

It's vitally important that changes to the **Enabled** property get passed on to **UserControl** as shown above. If **UserControl** remains enabled, then the control can still receive the input focus through a *Tab* or mouse-click.

In addition to the **Let** and **Get** routines, we also need to ensure that the **Enabled** property gets properly saved through the **UserControl_WriteProperties** routine:

```
.WriteProperty "Enabled", UserControl.Enabled, True
```

and reloaded through the code in **UserControl_ReadProperties…**

```
UserControl.Enabled = .ReadProperty("Enabled", True)
If Not UserControl.Enabled Then mControlState = Disabled
```

Also, we must initialize the value of **mControlState** in **UserControl_Initialize**

```
mControlState = Normal
```

Keeping Things In Focus

As well as the four states mentioned earlier, the control can also receive the input focus, and it's customary for a control to show some change in its appearance when the focus is received. For simple controls, this might be nothing more than drawing a focus rectangle (a rectangle made up of dashed lines) around a control. For the slider control, we've chosen to indicate which slider has the focus by drawing it with a raised track, but of course you might have other ideas.

In order to keep track of whether or not we've got the focus, we need to declare another private variable, **mGotFocus**. This variable will be referenced later by the drawing code when deciding how to paint the control.

```
Private mGotFocus As Boolean       ' True if we've got the focus
```

To keep this variable updated with the true state-of-play, we have to write methods for **UserControl_GotFocus** and **UserControl_LostFocus**. These routines not only update the private variable, but also guarantee that the control is repainted as soon as the focus changes, so as to give immediate visual feedback to the user.

```
'================================================================
'    Name:        UserControl_GotFocus
'    Purpose:     Called when we get the focus.  Just remember the
'                 fact and repaint the control with focus
'================================================================
Private Sub UserControl_GotFocus()
    mGotFocus = True
    UserControl_Paint
End Sub


'================================================================
'    Name:        UserControl_LostFocus
'    Purpose:     Called when we lose the focus.
'================================================================
Private Sub UserControl_LostFocus()
    mGotFocus = False
    UserControl_Paint
End Sub
```

The **mGotFocus** flag also gets initialized inside **UserControl_Initialize:**

```
mGotFocus = False
```

Thumb Geometry

At this point, we've got a good foundation for proceeding with the real 'meat' of the control—the painting code and the routines necessary to keep track of the thumb position. However, before implementing any sort of control, it's a good idea to be very clear about the control's visual layout.

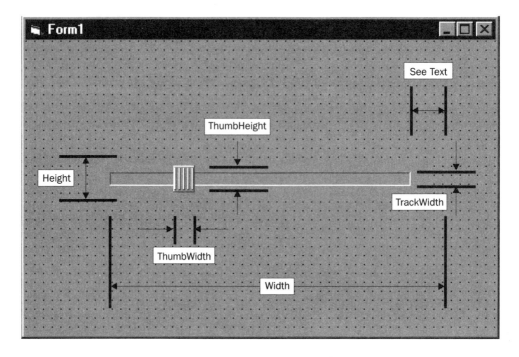

The annotated diagram above shows an enlarged slider control. Unlike the previous examples that you've seen, the **BorderStyle** property of this control has been set to **Raised** so that you can see the boundaries of the actual control. (We'll be showing you how to implement the **BorderStyle** property later.)

In this illustration, the **Width** and **Height** properties have their common and most obvious meaning, while it should come as no surprise to find that **ThumbWidth** and **ThumbHeight** define the width and height of the thumb. The width of the track-bar (the channel in which the thumb moves) is defined by the **TrackWidth** property. Strictly speaking, this property name is something of a misnomer since it applies whether the slider is horizontal or vertical, but we thought that **TrackBreadth** didn't sound quite so good!

Finally, there's the distance between the end of the track-bar and the edge of the control. This is determined by two properties, one of which is called **TrackIndent**. Here's how it works:

For Horizontal Sliders:
For a horizontal slider, the distance from the track-bar to the edge of the control is equal to **TrackIndent** plus half the width of the thumb.

For Vertical Sliders:
For a vertical slider, the distance from the track-bar to the edge of the control is equal to **TrackIndent** plus half the height of the thumb.

The reason that we use half the width (or half the height) in each case is so that the thumb can come right up to the end of the track-bar and 'overhang' it by half its width or height. This gives a much more pleasant effect than if the thumb were to stop dead as soon as its edge coincided with that of the track-bar. If you want to think of it another way, the **TrackIndent** property is the pixel distance between the edge of the control and the edge of the thumb when the thumb is at its furthest extent. The code inside the slider control automatically resizes the track-bar whenever the **TrackIndent** property is changed. As this property increases, the track-bar shrinks in length.

Adding a Property Quartet

By now, you should have a clearer idea of how the slider works. We'll continue by adding the above mentioned properties to our control. Firstly, we need to define a set of default values for the **TrackWidth**, **TrackIndent**, **ThumbWidth** and **ThumbIndent** properties. We do this by adding a number of private constants to the slider's code:

```
Private Const DEF_TRACK_WIDTH = 4    ' Default width of slider track
Private Const DEF_TRACK_INDENT = 4   ' Default indent for track
Private Const DEF_THUMB_WIDTH = 20   ' Default width of the thumb
Private Const DEF_THUMB_HEIGHT = 16  ' Default height of thumb
```

The four properties are implemented, in the usual way, through a set of private variables:

```
Private mTrackWidth As Integer     ' width of track
Private mTrackIndent As Integer    ' indent from control edge
Private mThumbWidth As Integer     ' width of the thumb
Private mThumbHeight As Integer    ' height of the thumb
```

In order to set these variables to their declared defaults, we must add the following code to the **UserControl_InitProperties** routine:

```
mTrackWidth = DEF_TRACK_WIDTH
mTrackIndent = DEF_TRACK_INDENT
mThumbWidth = DEF_THUMB_WIDTH
mThumbHeight = DEF_THUMB_HEIGHT
```

The four property variables need to be initialized in the **UserControl_ReadProperties** code:

```
mTrackWidth = .ReadProperty("TrackWidth", DEF_TRACK_WIDTH)
mTrackIndent = .ReadProperty("TrackIndent", DEF_TRACK_INDENT)
mThumbWidth = .ReadProperty("ThumbWidth", DEF_THUMB_WIDTH)
mThumbHeight = .ReadProperty("ThumbHeight", DEF_THUMB_HEIGHT)
```

And we need to write the properties in **UserControl_WriteProperties** so that the next time the developer loads the form, the properties end up with the same values they were saved with:

```
.WriteProperty "TrackWidth", mTrackWidth, DEF_TRACK_WIDTH
.WriteProperty "TrackIndent", mTrackIndent, DEF_TRACK_INDENT
.WriteProperty "ThumbWidth", mThumbWidth, DEF_THUMB_WIDTH
.WriteProperty "ThumbHeight", mThumbHeight, DEF_THUMB_HEIGHT
```

Finally, of course, we need to create the **Let**/**Get** routines for each of these four properties.

```
Public Property Get TrackWidth() As Integer
    TrackWidth = mTrackWidth
End Property
```

```
        Public Property Let TrackWidth(ByVal NewTrackWidth As Integer)
            If mTrackWidth <> NewTrackWidth And NewTrackWidth >= 2 Then
                mTrackWidth = NewTrackWidth
                PropertyChanged "TrackWidth"
                UserControl_Paint
            End If
        End Property

        Public Property Get ThumbWidth() As Integer
            ThumbWidth = mThumbWidth
        End Property

        Public Property Let ThumbWidth(ByVal NewThumbWidth As Integer)
            If mThumbWidth <> NewThumbWidth Then
                mThumbWidth = NewThumbWidth
                PropertyChanged "ThumbWidth"
                UserControl_Paint
            End If
        End Property

        Public Property Get ThumbHeight() As Integer
            ThumbHeight = mThumbHeight
        End Property

        Public Property Let ThumbHeight(ByVal NewThumbHeight As Integer)
            If mThumbHeight <> NewThumbHeight Then
                mThumbHeight = NewThumbHeight
                PropertyChanged "ThumbHeight"
                UserControl_Paint
            End If
        End Property

        Public Property Get TrackIndent() As Integer
            TrackIndent = mTrackIndent
        End Property

        Public Property Let TrackIndent(ByVal NewTrackIndent As Integer)
            If mTrackIndent <> NewTrackIndent Then
                mTrackIndent = NewTrackIndent
                PropertyChanged "TrackIndent"
                UserControl_Paint
            End If
        End Property
```

Bordering on Visible...

There are just a couple more properties that we need to add before we can create the actual drawing code for the control. In the previous section, we mentioned the **BorderStyle** property which allows you to specify a raised edge to the control. **BorderStyle** is an enumerated property and can take one of the four possible values given below:

```
Public Enum Border_Style
    Raised
    Recessed
    Flat
    None
End Enum
```

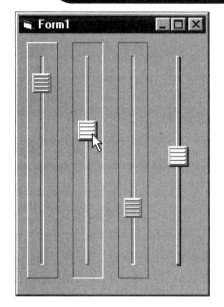

You've already seen examples of the **Raised** style and the **None** style (where you don't see the actual boundary of the control at all). The following illustration shows these two styles again, along with the other two for completeness. As you've no doubt figured out by now, these different borders are implemented through the **Rect3D** routine in the **MemDC** class.

Working from left to right, the first slider control has a **Raised** border style, the second has a **Recessed** style, the third has the **Flat** style and the fourth has its **BorderStyle** property set to **None**, meaning that you can't see the control boundary at all.

There's another reason why we've included this illustration: it highlights (pun strictly intentional) the difference between a highlighted slider and one that has the focus. In the picture, the second slider along is highlighted because the mouse is over it. However, it's the fourth slider which actually has the focus. This is signaled by the visual emphasis given to the track-bar and the highlighted thumb.

In addition to **BorderStyle**, the slider control also implements the familiar Visual Basic **BackColor** property which enables the developer to assign a particular background color to the control. Because we wanted the slider control to blend in with whatever Windows color scheme is in use, the **BackColor** property only applies if you have a **BorderStyle** equal to None. In all other cases, the control is filled with a color that's compatible with the way Windows draws control buttons.

Thus, if you happen to be using a **ControlStyle** of **Raised** and you then assign a value to the slider's **BackColor** property, the existing code will automatically set the **BorderStyle** to **None**. Similarly, if you're using a custom background color with a **ControlStyle** of **None**, assigning a different value to **ControlStyle** will cause the **BackColor** property to be ignored.

Maybe you won't like this way of doing things, but you need to realise that when developing an ActiveX control with VB5 CCE, you need to strike some sort of a balance between how a Visual Basic developer is expecting the control to behave, and the way in which a non-VB ActiveX control user is anticipating that things will work. As ever, if you don't like it—you're free to change it!

With all this in view, let's add the necessary code to implement the **BorderStyle** and **BackColor** properties. **BorderStyle** defaults to a value of **None** (it's our favorite style and at this point, we get to call the shots) so we need to add another constant definition to those already there.

```
Private Const DEF_BORDER_STYLE = None ' Default border style
```

As before, we also need a set of private variables to store the current values for the **BorderStyle** and **BackColor** properties. You'll have come across the way in which color properties are implemented through the **OLE_COLOR** type. In order to speed things up and eliminate the need to convert the background color into an RGB color every time we need to use it, we use two separate variables to hold the background color—one as an RGB long value for use with Windows API calls, and one as an **OLE_COLOR**.

```
Private mBorderStyle As Border_Style  ' border style for control
Private mBackColor As OLE_COLOR       ' background color
Private mBackColorRGB As Long         ' RGB version of the above
```

These variables get set to their default values in the **UserControl_InitProperties** routine, picking up the default background color from the **UserControl.Ambient** object in the usual way. **OleTranslateColor** is one of the various Windows API routines defined in the **API.BAS** code module—it maps an **OLE_COLOR** value on to an RGB color suitable for passing to a Windows API routine.

```
mBorderStyle = DEF_BORDER_STYLE
mBackColor = UserControl.Ambient.BackColor
OleTranslateColor mBackColor, 0, mBackColorRGB
```

As ever, we need to load the properties in **UserControl_ReadProperties**:

```
mBorderStyle = .ReadProperty("BorderStyle", DEF_BORDER_STYLE)
mBackColor = .ReadProperty("BackColor", UserControl.Ambient.BackColor)
OleTranslateColor mBackColor, 0, mBackColorRGB
```

And we need to write them back out in **UserControl_WriteProperties**:

```
.WriteProperty "BorderStyle", mBorderStyle, DEF_BORDER_STYLE
.WriteProperty "BackColor", mBackColor,_
                    UserControl.Ambient.BackColor
```

The associated **Let**/**Get** routines are given below. As discussed above, you can see that any assignment to **BackColor** forces **BorderStyle** back to **None**.

```
Public Property Get BorderStyle() As Border_Style
    BorderStyle = mBorderStyle
End Property

Public Property Let BorderStyle(ByVal NewBorderStyle As Border_Style)
    If mBorderStyle <> NewBorderStyle Then
        mBorderStyle = NewBorderStyle
        PropertyChanged "BorderStyle"
        UserControl_Paint
    End If
End Property

Public Property Get BackColor() As OLE_COLOR
    BackColor = mBackColor
End Property

Public Property Let BackColor(ByVal NewBackColor As OLE_COLOR)
```

```
        If mBackColor <> NewBackColor Then
            mBackColor = NewBackColor
            PropertyChanged "BackColor"
            OleTranslateColor mBackColor, 0, mBackColorRGB
            ' Setting BackColor forces BorderStyle to 'none'
            mBorderStyle = None
            UserControl_Paint
        End If
    End Property
```

Lights, Camera, Action!

And now for the moment you've been waiting for—time to paint the actual control. At this point, we've assembled all the various routines needed to render the control into the off-screen bitmap. The code to the **UserControl_Paint** routine is given below.

```
'================================================================
'    Name:          UserControl_Paint
'    Purpose:       Draw the control image on an off-screen
'                   bitmap and then blit directly on to screen.
'================================================================
Private Sub UserControl_Paint()
    Dim r As RECT
    Dim hdc As MemDC
    Dim Effect As Effect3D

    ' Init a memory device context for painting
    Set hdc = New MemDC
    hdc.Initialize UserControl.hdc, mWidth, mHeight

    ' First job is to draw the control background

    If mBorderStyle <> None Then
        hdc.Rect3D 0, 0, mWidth, mHeight, mBorderStyle
    Else
        hdc.FillRect 0, 0, mWidth, mHeight, mBackColorRGB
    End If

    ' Now we need to draw the slider "track"
    r = TrackRect

    If mGotFocus And (mControlState <> Active) Then
        Effect = Raised
        hdc.FillRect r.Left + 1, r.Top + 1, r.Right - r.Left, r.Bottom - r.Top, 0
    Else
        Select Case mControlState
            Case Normal
                Effect = Recessed
            Case Disabled
                Effect = Flat
            Case Highlighted
                Effect = Raised
            Case Active
                Effect = Selected
        End Select
```

```
        End If

        hdc.Rect3D r.Left, r.Top, r.Right - r.Left, r.Bottom - r.Top, Effect

        ' Next, draw the thumb
        DrawThumb hdc, ThumbRect

        ' Blit the image to the display
        hdc.Blit
    End Sub
```

As promised, this code kicks off by creating a new **MemDC** object and then using it for all drawing operations. If the border style isn't equal to **None**, then the **Rect3D** routine gets called to draw a raised, recessed or flat border around the control. If **BorderStyle** is None, then we just call **FillRect** to fill the control background with whatever **BackColor** has been set to.

There are a couple of important points to note here. Firstly, you may notice that we've passed a variable of type **Border_Style** (the **mBorderStyle** variable) to **Rect3D** which is expecting a parameter of type **Effect3D**. Basic is a language which has never been noted for strong type-checking and it will quite happily allow you to do this. If you tried to do something similar in Pascal, the compiler would rightly complain. The code works fine because we've arranged that the two enumerated types are equivalent as far as the first three possible values are concerned. In the fourth case (**Selected** versus **None**), **Rect3D** doesn't get called anyway. Yes, it's slightly naughty but it saves a lot of unnecessary messing about with **SELECT** statement and so forth.

Secondly, when you use off-screen bitmaps to implement your own controls, it's very important to ensure that the off-screen bitmap is completely initialized. What we mean by this is that you've got to ensure that you draw into every single pixel of the bitmap. When the bitmap gets created inside the **MemDC** class module, you'll recall that it's done through a call to the API routine **CreateCompatibleBitmap**. When you create a bitmap in this way (or indeed any other way), Windows doesn't clear the bitmap or pre-fill it with known pixel values. The image in the bitmap isn't guaranteed to be anything except garbage!

What this means is that if we were to create a slider control, and we neglected to fill in the entire background, we'd find that the control was surrounded with random dot patterns when blitted on to the screen. This, incidentally, is why we haven't incorporated a 'transparent background' option into the slider: using off-screen bitmaps is a great way of eliminating flicker, but it's not a universal panacea. To implement a transparent background capability, *and* use off-screen bitmaps, you'd have to somehow pre-initialize the off-screen bitmap with whatever background happened to be behind the control before drawing the control's own image into the bitmap. Over to you!

Let's Get Logical

If you look at the call to **hdc.Initialize** in the above **UserControl_Paint** code, you'll see that we've passed the control width and control height using a couple of new private variables, **mWidth** and **mHeight**. For now, you can think of these two variables as corresponding directly to the control's physical width and height. They get initialized in a private subroutine called **SetLogicalSize**:

```
    Private Sub SetLogicalSize()
        mWidth = UserControl.ScaleWidth
        mHeight = UserControl.ScaleHeight
    End Sub
```

This routine is called from **UserControl_InitProperties** and from the code in **UserControl_Resize**. You might wonder why we bother to store the control's current width and height in this way. Why not just reference the **ScaleWidth** and **ScaleHeight** fields in **UserControl** every time we need this information? The answer is that it's important to disassociate the actual physical size of the control (as supplied by **ScaleWidth** and **ScaleHeight**) from the *logical* size of the control obtained through **mWidth** and **mHeight**. The reason for this will become clearer when you read the section that deals with how to implement the **Orientation** property.

Returning to our discussion of the **UserControl_Paint** code, you'll see that this routine calls three other routines that we haven't discussed so far. These are:

TrackRect   Returns a bounding rectangle for the track-bar

ThumbRect   Returns a bounding rectangle for the thumb

DrawThumb   Draws the thumb at the specified position

Let's look at each of these routines in turn.

```
'=============================================================
'   Name:          TrackRect
'   Purpose:       Return a bounding rectangle for the track
'=============================================================
Private Function TrackRect() As RECT
    TrackRect.Left = (mThumbWidth \ 2) + mTrackIndent
    TrackRect.Right = mWidth - TrackRect.Left
    TrackRect.Top = (mHeight - mTrackWidth) \ 2
    TrackRect.Bottom = TrackRect.Top + mTrackWidth
End Function
```

TrackRect returns a **RECT** as its function result. It simply calculates the position of the track-bar rectangle based on the various quantities that we've discussed so far. The track-bar is horizontally and vertically centred in the control, and the distance from the track-bar to the left or right edge of the control is equal to **TrackIndent** plus half the width of the thumb. Similarly, the top and bottom of the track-bar is determined by whatever we've got left after subtracting the track-bar 'width' from the control's height.

If our slider control is going to be of any use, the thumb will need to be moveable. In order to keep track of the current thumb position, we introduce another private variable called **mThumbPos**.

```
Private mThumbPos As Integer    ' current pixel thumb position
```

It's the value of **mThumbPos** which determines the on-screen position of the thumb, *not* the other way around. Later, when we examine the mouse-handling code, we'll see that mouse events affect **mThumbPos** which *then* causes the thumb to be redrawn at a new position on the screen. With this particular slider control, the position of the thumb isn't a persistent property. In other words, the slider doesn't remember the thumb position when the form is closed. This is a reasonable design decision since we felt that in most applications, the programmer will want to see the thumb to some initial value before the form is displayed, For this reason, **mThumbpos** is initialized to zero in the **UserControl_Initialize** routine:

```
mThumbPos = 0
```

Having established **mThumbPos**, we can now make sense of the **ThumbRect** routine. Based on the foregoing discussion, you shouldn't have any difficulty understanding how it works.

```
'============================================================
'    Name:        ThumbRect
'    Purpose:     Return a bounding rectangle for the thumb
'============================================================
Private Function ThumbRect() As RECT
    ThumbRect.Left = mThumbPos + mTrackIndent
    ThumbRect.Right = ThumbRect.Left + mThumbWidth
    ThumbRect.Top = (mHeight - mThumbHeight) \ 2
    ThumbRect.Bottom = ThumbRect.Top + mThumbHeight
End Function
```

Finally, we come to **DrawThumb**. This is where you get to demonstrate your artistic abilities (or not, as the case may be) in coming up with a thumb which is just begging to be clicked. An enlarged view of the thumb from the vertical slider control is shown here. In order to give a bit more visual interest, we've incorporated a 'ridged' effect by making several calls to **Rect3D** on the surface of the thumb.

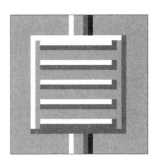

The complete thumb-drawing code is shown below:

```
'============================================================
'    Name:        DrawThumb
'    Purpose:     Routine to draw the default thumb
'============================================================
Private Sub DrawThumb(hdc As MemDC, r As RECT)
    Dim Effect As Effect3D
    Dim curLeft As Integer

    ' Draw drop-shadow if required
    If mControlState = Highlighted Or mControlState = Active Then
        hdc.FillRect r.Left + 1, r.Top + 1, r.Right - r.Left, r.Bottom - r.Top, 0
    End If

    If mControlState <> Disabled Then
        Effect = Raised
    Else
        Effect = Flat
    End If

    hdc.Rect3D r.Left, r.Top, r.Right - r.Left, r.Bottom - r.Top, Effect

    If mControlState = Highlighted Or mControlState = Active Then
        hdc.FillRect r.Left + 2, r.Top + 2, _
                    r.Right - r.Left - 4, r.Bottom - r.Top - 4, _
                    hdc.ButtonHighlightColor
    End If

    ' Decorate the thumb - if it's wide enough.
```

```
        curLeft = r.Left
        While r.Right - curLeft >= 4
            hdc.Rect3D curLeft + 1, r.Top + 2, 2, r.Bottom - r.Top - 4, Effect
            curLeft = curLeft + 4
        Wend
    End Sub
```

If the control is highlighted (mouse over it) or active, the thumb is drawn with an increased
degree of visual emphasis. If this is the case, the first part of the code draws a black 'drop-
shadow' behind the thumb using a call to **FillRect**. Next, **DrawThumb** draws the main body of
the thumb with a call to our old friend, **Rect3D**. This is drawn with a flat appearance if the
control is disabled. Next, the internal area of the thumb is filled with the current button highlight
color if visual emphasis is required. Finally, the code checks to see if there's room to draw one or
more ridges across the surface of the thumb and, if there is, **Rect3D** is repeatedly called to draw a
series of tiny 3D rectangles which are only two pixels wide. You can see this very clearly in the
enlarged view of the thumb above.

The Mouse Has Landed!

So far so good. We've now got a great-looking slider control (well, we think so anyway), but one
vital ingredient is missing. It doesn't yet respond to mouse events and is therefore totally useless.
It's time to add the mouse-handling code now. We'll start by adding one more private variable to
our code module.

```
Private mMouseLastPos As Integer   ' last recorded mouse position
```

This records the last mouse position that we were aware of and enables us to quickly determine if
the mouse has moved. You'll see how this works in a moment. For now, here's the code which
deals with mouse-down events:

```
'=============================================================
'   Name:         UserControl_MouseDown
'   Purpose:      Respond to mouse down.
'=============================================================
Private Sub UserControl_MouseDown(Button As Integer, _
                      Shift As Integer, X As Single, Y As Single)
    Dim InThumb As Boolean
    Dim InTrack As Boolean

    ' We're only interested if mControlState is Normal or
    ' Highlighted...  In theory, mControlState should be
        ' Highlighted at this point, but in practice, some mouse
    ' moves could have been lost because we haven't got the
    ' capture yet.

    If mControlState = Normal Or mControlState = Highlighted Then
        ' Figure out if mouse is over thumb or track
        InThumb = PtInRect(ThumbRect(), X, Y)
        InTrack = PtInRect(TrackRect(), X, Y)

        If InThumb Or InTrack Then
            ' If mControlState is Highlighted,
            ' then already got capture
            If mControlState = Normal Then API.SetCapture UserControl.hwnd
```

265

```
                ' Flag that we're active
                mControlState = Active
                ' If hit on track (but not thumb) then jump
                If Not InThumb Then MoveThumb (X)
                mMouseLastPos = X
                UserControl_Paint
            End If
        End If
    End Sub
```

Having received a mouse-down event, we need to figure out if we can handle it. If the control is currently disabled, then obviously any mouse-downs should be politely ignored. If the control state is **Active**, then this means that the mouse is already down and the thumb is being dragged around. Getting *another* mouse-down event at this time would indicate that something is seriously wrong with the logic of our control. Thus, we should only get a mouse-down when the control state corresponds to **Normal** or **Highlighted**. In principle, the control state should change to **Highlighted** as soon as the mouse moves over the control and the control state should always be **Highlighted** at the time the mouse-down occurs. However, it's possible to occasionally lose mouse-move events which means that a user who is quick with their mouse might be able to move the mouse over the control before we've noticed. Thus, to make the code bullet proof, we also need to accept a mouse-down when the control is **Normal**.

> *If you're worried about the idea of mouse events being overlooked, don't be. Once the slider knows that the mouse is doing something with it, it acquires the "capture" and this prevents any events we might be interested in from getting lost. We'll explain this in more detail shortly.*

Once the **UserControl_MouseDown** code has decided to look at the mouse-down event, it calls **ThumbRect** and **TrackRect** to determine where the mouse-down event occurred. Now you can see why we returned **RECT** structures as the function result—it makes the hit-testing code very neat and elegant. Mouse-downs within the control are ignored unless we've got a 'hit' on the thumb or the track-bar. In such cases, the code checks the control state and—if it's **Normal—** acquires the mouse capture. As we've just explained, it's more likely that the control state is **Highlighted**, which would imply that we've already got the mouse capture, so we don't try and acquire it again. All this will become clearer once we look at the **UserControl_MouseMove** code. Because we've got a mouse-down, we now change **mControlState** to **Active**. This will cause the control to be displayed in its active state next time that it gets repainted.

We wanted this slider control to work in such a way that if the user clicks on the track-bar (but not on the thumb), then the thumb will instantly jump to the 'clicked' position. This makes the control consistent with other sliders and allows the user to instantly move to an approximate position without doing a thumb-drag. Consequently, if the hit wasn't in the thumb, then the **MoveThumb** routine is called to move the thumb to the position given by the mouse X co-ordinate. Again, we'll be looking at **MoveThumb** shortly.

Finally, the code stores the current mouse X co-ordinate in **mMouseLastPos** and redraws the control to reflect the new state of play.

Why We Need a Mouse Trap...

Now's the time to explain what we mean by 'acquiring the capture'. As you'll no doubt appreciate, the internal operation of Windows relies heavily on messages. The window that receives mouse messages is normally the window that the mouse is moving over. However, this isn't always the case. For example, if you click the thumb on a push-button in a dialog, keep the mouse pressed down and then drag the mouse away from the button, the button will stay activated and continue to 'track' the mouse as you move it in and out of the push-button.

This is called 'acquiring the capture', or just 'capturing the mouse'. The window that currently has the mouse capture will *always* receive mouse messages, even when the mouse is nowhere near the window itself.

Now let's step back and think about our slider control. It should be clear that we need to capture the mouse in the same way. When the user clicks on the thumb, drags the mouse away from the slider and then drags the mouse back over the slider, we want to stay active the whole time. Ideally, we want to track mouse movement even when the mouse is over the other side of the screen from the slider control—always assuming, of course, that we're still active.

What might not be so obvious is the fact that we also need to capture the mouse when the control state is highlighted. In other words, the mouse might just casually be moved over our control, but we still need to capture the mouse for the time that it's over the slider. What's the reason for this? Well, imagine what would happen if the mouse was over the slider and was suddenly yanked away very rapidly. If we didn't have the capture, it would certainly be possible for the mouse to move out of the control without us getting any mouse-move events. The slider would think that the mouse was still over it and would continue to display itself as highlighted. This is obviously not a good thing. While developing the slider control, and before adding the mouse capture code, we found that this could indeed happen from time to time.

The bottom line is that if you're implementing a control which changes its state according to the position of the mouse, you really need to capture the mouse regardless of whether or not the user is actively dragging the mouse inside the control. If you don't, you risk missing mouse activity and leaving the control in an invalid state.

```
'==============================================================
'    Name:        UserControl_MouseMove
'    Purpose:     Track mouse movement within the control
'    Notes:       We have to capture the mouse for mControlState
'                     = Highlighted as well as mControlState = Active,
'                 otherwise we'll lose WM_MOUSEMOVE messages and
'                 stay highlighted when we shouldn't be!
'==============================================================
Private Sub UserControl_MouseMove(Button As Integer, _
                Shift As Integer, X As Single, Y As Single)
    Dim InThumb As Boolean
    Dim InTrack As Boolean

    ' Figure out if mouse is over thumb or track
    InThumb = PtInRect(ThumbRect(), X, Y)
    InTrack = PtInRect(TrackRect(), X, Y)

    Select Case mControlState
        Case Normal
            ' See if we've got a mouse-over. If so, get highlighted!
            If InThumb Or InTrack Then
                mControlState = Highlighted
                API.SetCapture UserControl.hwnd
                UserControl_Paint
            End If
        Case Highlighted
```

```
                If InThumb = False And InTrack = False Then
                    mControlState = Normal
                    API.ReleaseCapture
                    UserControl_Paint
                End If
            Case Active
                MoveThumb (X)
        End Select
End Sub
```

With all this in view, you should be able to understand the above code which handles mouse-move events. If **mControlState** is normal, this means that we've got a mouse-move when the control isn't yet highlighted. We respond by highlighting the control (but only if the mouse-move occurred within the track-bar or thumb) and calling the Windows API routine **SetCapture**, passing it the window handle of our control. This tells Windows to direct all subsequent mouse events to this control.

On the other hand, if the control state is **Highlighted** at the time we get the mouse-move, then we need to check if the mouse is now outside the active part of the control. (Bear in mind that now we've got the capture, the mouse could be outside the control altogether.) If it is, then we reset the control state to **Normal** and redraw the control. At the same time, **ReleaseCapture** gets called to release the mouse and restore normal mouse message processing.

> *One word of warning:* **GetCapture** *is a potentially dangerous routine. If you capture the mouse and then forget to release the capture when you should, then you can stop Windows from working properly. Windows 95 and Windows NT are relatively robust in such circumstances, but under older versions of Windows, it was easy to completely lock up the system by forgetting to release the mouse when you should! If you capture the mouse, take great care to ensure that it's released at the appropriate point in your code.*

The last bit of code in **UserControl_MouseMove** handles the situation when the control state is Active. In these circumstances, we just call **MoveThumb** to ensure that the thumb is following the current mouse position.

```
'============================================================
'    Name:        UserControl_MouseUp
'    Purpose:     Respond to mouse up.
'    Notes:       We should only respond to a mouse up message
'                 if mControlState is Active.
'============================================================
Private Sub UserControl_MouseUp(Button As Integer, _
                    Shift As Integer, X As Single, Y As Single)
    Dim InThumb As Boolean
    Dim InTrack As Boolean

    If mControlState = Active Then
        ' Figure out if mouse is over thumb or track
        InThumb = PtInRect(ThumbRect(), X, Y)
        InTrack = PtInRect(TrackRect(), X, Y)

        ' Note - if mouse is still inside control, then we
        ' switch state to Highlighted and keep the capture.
        ' If not, we switch state to Normal. Theoretically,
        ' the former should be true, but let's be defensive.

        If InThumb Or InTrack Then
```

```
                mControlState = Highlighted
        Else
                mControlState = Normal
                API.ReleaseCapture
        End If

        UserControl_Paint
        NotifyChange
    End If
End Sub
```

The final part of the mouse-handling puzzle is the code for mouse-up events which is shown above. A little bit of thought will convince you that we only need respond when the control state is active. If the control state is disabled, we won't receive the event, whereas if the control state is normal or highlighted, we shouldn't be receiving a mouse up event at this point.

If the mouse is inside the active part of the control (the thumb or track-bar) at the time the mouse-up is received, we switch the state to highlighted but keep the mouse capture. (As explained earlier, we need to have the capture for the **Highlighted** state.) If the mouse is released outside the control, then we can safely release the capture and set the control state to normal. Notice that in this latter case there's no need to move the thumb to its final resting place—the mouse-move code will already have ensured that it's there. However, we do need to notify the application program that the user has changed the slider's position—that's the purpose behind the call to **NotifyChange**. This will be explained is due course.

As promised, here's the code for **MoveThumb**. This routine's job is to move the thumb to a new pixel position in response to a mouse move. Internally, the routine checks to see that the mouse really has moved since it was last called. If it hasn't, then it just exits. This prevents the control from doing any more work than it has to and (in particular) ensures that we don't keep repainting the control because the mouse Y co-ordinate has changed when the X co-ordinate hasn't. Thanks to the **MemDC** code, our control is very quick at redrawing, but there's no sense in doing more painting than we have to!

```
'==========================================================
'   Name:        MoveThumb
'   Purpose:     Move the Slider thumb
'==========================================================
Private Sub MoveThumb(MouseX As Integer)
    Dim maxPos As Integer

    If MouseX <> mMouseLastPos Then
        ' Thumb is centred around mouse location, so subtract
        ' half thumb width & normalise
        mThumbPos = MouseX - (mThumbWidth \ 2) - mTrackIndent
        ' Pin the thumb at either end of travel
        If mThumbPos < 0 Then mThumbPos = 0
        maxPos = mWidth - mThumbWidth - (2 * mTrackIndent)
        If mThumbPos > maxPos Then mThumbPos = maxPos
        ' Now redraw and remember old position
        UserControl_Paint
        mMouseLastPos = MouseX
        ' Notify application that thumb is changing
        NotifyChanging
    End If
End Sub
```

Another important job of the **MoveThumb** code is to 'pin' the thumb at either end of the track-bar. We don't want the thumb to fall off the end of the track! The code ensures that the thumb position is within the prescribed limits, repaints the control, and remembers the current X mouse co-ordinate for next time round. Additionally, it calls **NotifyChanging** each time the thumb moves. This, in conjunction with **NotifyChange**, will be described presently.

Getting into Position

At this point, our slider control is almost useful! It now responds to mouse movements and we can happily while away the hours dragging the thumb backwards and forwards. Once the novelty has worn off, we need to add what is perhaps the control's most important property: **Position**. It's the **Position** property which gives the thumb's current position to the application, and the same property enables the application to set an initial value for the thumb.

Of course, what the application *doesn't* want to know is the absolute pixel position of the thumb - that would be of no use to man nor beast. Instead, we must allow the application to impose its own interpretation on the thumb position. We do this through two other properties called **Max** and **Min**. From the viewpoint of the application, the thumb can be anywhere between the **Max** and **Min** position - it's our responsibility to convert this arbitrary scale into an absolute pixel position for the thumb.

Let's begin by adding the **Max** and **Min** properties to the control.

```
Private Const DEF_MIN = 0        ' Default minimum value
Private Const DEF_MAX = 100      ' Default maximum value
```

Many slider-type controls opt for a default scale of 0..100, and we'll adopt the same convention here. The above private constants allow us to specify initial, default values for the private member variables, **mMin** and **mMax**, which are defined below:

```
Private mMin As Integer          ' Minimum value for control
Private mMax As Integer          ' Maximum value for control
```

We need to ensure that these variables receive their correct default values, and the correct place to do this is in the **UserControl_InitProperties** routine:

```
mMin = DEF_MIN
mMax = DEF_MAX
```

In the usual way, these properties must be retrieved in **UserControl_ReadProperties**...

```
mMin = .ReadProperty("Min", DEF_MIN)
mMax = .ReadProperty("Max", DEF_MAX)
```

...and written in **UserControl_WriteProperties**...

```
.WriteProperty "Min", mMin, DEF_MIN
.WriteProperty "Max", mMax, DEF_MAX
```

Most importantly, we need to write **Let**/**Get** routines for both **Max** and **Min**:

```
Public Property Get Min() As Integer
    Min = mMin
End Property

Public Property Let Min(ByVal NewMin As Integer)
    If mMin <> NewMin And NewMin <= mMax Then
        mMin = NewMin
        ' Changing mMin invalidates thumb position
        mThumbPos = 0
        PropertyChanged "Min"
        UserControl_Paint
    End If
End Property

Public Property Get Max() As Integer
    Max = mMax
End Property

Public Property Let Max(ByVal NewMax As Integer)
    If mMax <> NewMax And NewMax >= mMin Then
        mMax = NewMax
        ' Changing mMax invalidates thumb position
        mThumbPos = 0
        PropertyChanged "Max"
        UserControl_Paint
    End If
End Property
```

Rather than re-scaling the current thumb position when **Min** or **Max** change, We've taken the easy way out and reset the thumb to zero whenever the application assigns to **Max** or **Min**. In practice, this is perfectly acceptable since it's extremely unlikely that an application would want to modify these parameters 'on the fly'. Typically, the application would create a new control, set **Max** and **Min**, and then set an initial value for **Position** before allowing the user to interact with the control. The code also contains a couple of small 'sanity-checks' to ensure that **Max >= Min**.

Now that we've established boundaries for the **Position** property, we can implement **Position** itself. As we mentioned elsewhere, this property is not persistent, so we don't have to set up private variables, read and write the property or any of that stuff. However, we do need to create **Let**/**Get** routines for **Position** so that it can be accessed from the outside world.

The **Get** routine simply calls another routine, **PositionFromThumb**, which converts the current thumb position into the range of values established by **Min** and **Max**.

```
Public Property Get Position() As Integer
    Position = PositionFromThumb(mThumbPos)
End Property

Public Property Let Position(ByVal NewPosition As Integer)
    ' Firstly, pin the position to the Min, Max bounds
    If NewPosition < mMin Then NewPosition = mMin
    If NewPosition > mMax Then NewPosition = mMax
    ' Has anything changed?
    If PositionFromThumb(mThumbPos) <> NewPosition Then
        mThumbPos = ThumbFromPosition(NewPosition)
        UserControl_Paint
```

```
                NotifyChange
        End If
    End Property
```

Just as the mouse-move code needs to limit the thumb to the track-bar, the **Let** code for the **Position** property needs to 'pin' any incoming integer so that it lies between **Min** and **Max**. Having done this, **PositionFromThumb** is called to see if the new **Position** value differs from the old. If it does, a new position for the thumb is calculated with **ThumbFromPosition** (which converts a position value into an absolute pixel position), and the thumb is relocated. The control is then repainted and **NotifyChange** is called to indicate that a change in thumb position has taken place.

```
'==============================================================
'    Name:        PositionFromThumb
'    Purpose:     Given a thumb location, calculate Position
'==============================================================
Private Function PositionFromThumb(ByVal Thumb As Double) _
            As Integer
    Dim TRange As Double            ' T(hi) - T(lo)
    Dim PRange As Double            ' P(hi) - P(lo)

    TRange = mWidth - mThumbWidth - (2 * mTrackIndent)
    PRange = mMax - mMin
    PositionFromThumb = ((Thumb / TRange) * PRange) + mMin
End Function


'==============================================================
'    Name:        ThumbFromPosition
'    Purpose:     Given a Position, calculate thumb location
'==============================================================
Private Function ThumbFromPosition(ByVal Pos As Double) As Integer
    Dim TRange As Double            ' T(hi) - T(lo)
    Dim PRange As Double            ' P(hi) - P(lo)

    TRange = mWidth - mThumbWidth - (2 * mTrackIndent)
    PRange = mMax - mMin
    ThumbFromPosition = ((Pos - mMin) / PRange) * TRange
End Function
```

The code above shows the two routines **PositionFromThumb** and **ThumbFromPosition** which map an absolute position on to a pixel thumb position, and vice versa, respectively. If your high-school mathematics isn't up to this, don't worry about it—it took us a while to get it right too!

Telling the Boss

Life is good. The slider now works as advertised and it's a lot more useful than it was before adding the **Position** property. But with the code as it stands, an application would have to keep reading the value of **Position** to see whether things have changed. That would obviously make the slider cumbersome to use in circumstances where you want something to change (a color perhaps, or the position of some screen element) as the slider is moved.

To address these difficulties, we want to add events to our control so that the application will be notified immediately. For maximum flexibility, we add two events:

Changed - Tells the application that a change has been made

 Changing - Triggered whenever the thumb moves while the mouse is down.

By responding to one or both of these events, the application can elect to be notified only after a change has taken place or else be continually updated while a thumb drag is underway.

Adding these events to the control is very easy. First, we declare two new **Public** events in the slider source code:

```
' notify application of position change
Public Event Changed(Pos As Integer)
' notify applicaton that position is changing
Public Event Changing(Pos As Integer)
```

Next, we add two private variables. These variables ensure that we don't send an event notification unless we really have got something new to say. Imagine, for example, that you have a very 'coarse' range set up on the slider (say, 0..4 for the sake of argument) and that the slider's length is such that the thumb can move a total distance of 100 pixels. This means that the thumb could potentially be moved 20 pixels before the **Position** property actually changes. These private variables remember the last sent position, and prevent a notification being sent when **Position** hasn't actually changed.

```
Private mLastChangePos As Integer    ' last Change position sent
Private mLastChangingPos As Integer ' last Changing position sent
```

We also need to set these variables in the **UserControl_Initialize** property. By giving them invalid values, we ensure that we get an initial trigger.

```
mLastChangePos = -1    ' use an invalid value to get a trigger
mLastChangingPos = -1  ' ditto
```

Last but not least, here's the code for **NotifyChanging** and **NotifyChange**. These routines call **RaiseEvent** to generate the wanted event. As a convenience to the application program, the current **Position** value is passed as a parameter to the event call in both cases. This saves the application from having to read **Position** for itself once the notification is received.

```
Private Sub NotifyChanging()
    If Position <> mLastChangingPos Then
        RaiseEvent Changing(Position)
        mLastChangingPos = Position
    End If
End Sub

Private Sub NotifyChange()
    If Position <> mLastChangePos Then
        RaiseEvent Changed(Position)
        mLastChangePos = Position
    End If
    ' Since there's been a change, the "Changing" event
    ' should get a hit too
    NotifyChanging
End Sub
```

273

The Lazy Man's Guide to Control Orientation

An **Orientation** property may or may not be appropriate to the control you're developing. This property allows a control to be oriented in a horizontal or vertical fashion. Obviously, it doesn't make sense for a text edit box or a push button, although it might make sense to build a label control that can display text vertically for the purposes of decoration. In the case of the slider control, the **Orientation** property is essential.

How do we go about implementing the **Orientation** property? Firstly we need to define a new enumeration type like this:

```
Public Enum Orientation_Style
    Horizontal
    vertical
End Enum
```

This ensures that our new property will have these human-readable names when it shows up in Visual Basic's Properties window—or anywhere else the control might be used. We need to define a private variable of this type and we also need to add the necessary code to ensure that it's set up with a default value. We chose to make the slider horizontal by default—you'll understand why later.

```
Private Const DEF_ORIENTATION = Horizontal    ' Default orientation
```

```
Private mOrientation As Orientation_Style     ' Current orientation
```

Having done this, we must remember to initialize the value of **mOrientation** inside the **UserControl_InitProperties** procedure, and save and restore the value of this flag in the **UserControl_ReadProperties** and **UserControl_WriteProperties** routines:

```
mOrientation = DEF_ORIENTATION
```

```
mOrientation = .ReadProperty("Orientation", DEF_ORIENTATION)
```

```
.WriteProperty "Orientation", mOrientation, DEF_ORIENTATION
```

With these preliminaries over, we can then write the **Let** and **Get** routines for the new **Orientation** property like this:

```
Public Property Get Orientation() As Orientation_Style
    Orientation = mOrientation
End Property

Public Property Let Orientation(ByVal NewOrientation As _
                          Orientation_Style)
    Dim Temp As Integer

    If mOrientation <> NewOrientation Then
        ' Swap width and height
        Temp = Height
        Height = Width
        Width = Temp
        mOrientation = NewOrientation
        SetLogicalSize
```

```
            UserControl_Paint
      End If
  End Property
```

Looking at the above **Let** routine, you'll see that when the orientation changes, the code simply swaps the current values for the control's **Width** and **Height** properties. If you run this code, you'll see that the control's overall size does indeed change, but the actual drawing of the control gets hopelessly messed up.

The reason for this should be pretty obvious—although we've resized the control, the actual drawing code doesn't yet 'know' how to draw a vertical slider. A lot of code needs to be changed; the code for drawing the track-bar, the thumb drawing code and all the mouse hit-testing code needs to be rewritten to cater for vertically-oriented sliders. It sounds like a depressing amount of extra work—effectively all of the existing code needs to be duplicated to cater for the case where a vertical slider is being used. Surely there must be an easier way of doing this?

Just-In-Time Co-ordinate Skewing!

Well yes, there *is* a sneaky way of doing this. Although some additional code is required, it's far less than would be needed if we were implementing the vertical orientation drawing code in a more orthodox manner. Our scheme works by fooling the slider control into thinking that it's horizontal all the time. In this way, we can go ahead and just use the existing drawing code for the horizontal slider that we've already developed. However, when it comes to actually drawing the control's image on to our off-screen bitmap, any co-ordinates we've used are "skewed" right at the last minute. At the time of writing, it seems to be highly fashionable to refer to your latest brainchild as 'Just In Time', so with tongue firmly in cheek, we've referred to our co-ordinate mapping strategy as 'Just In Time Co-ordinate Skewing'.

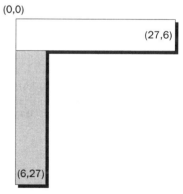

So what exactly do we mean by 'skewing'? To see how this works, look at the following illustration.

In this diagram, you can see two slider controls superimposed over one another. Both of them share a common origin where the x and y co-ordinates are both zero. If you pick any arbitrary point in the horizontal slider, you can map it to the equivalent point in the vertical slider simply by swapping x and y. Thus, (27,6) becomes (6,27), (3,19) becomes (19,3) and so forth.

In practice, things are somewhat more complicated than this (as you'll soon see) but in essence, that's all there is to co-ordinate skewing. Fooling the slider into thinking that it's horizontal all the time is pretty simple. The **SetLogicalSize** routine (which previously just stashed the control's width and height) now needs to look like this:

275

```
Private Sub SetLogicalSize()
    If mOrientation = Horizontal Then
        mWidth = UserControl.ScaleWidth
        mHeight = UserControl.ScaleHeight
    Else
        mWidth = UserControl.ScaleHeight
        mHeight = UserControl.ScaleWidth
    End If
End Sub
```

This gives the control the same logical width and height irrespective of orientation. Next, we need to skew the various x, y co-ordinates used to draw the image of the control. The big question, of course, is where does this skewing operation take place?

As it turns out, we're well placed to add co-ordinate skewing to our slider control because all the drawing code is routed through the **MemDC** class module which takes care of maintaining our off-screen bitmap. Thus, the logical place to do the skew is inside the **MemDC** module. But this means that **MemDC** needs to be aware of whether or not skewing should take place, i.e. whether or not we're using a vertical slider control. In order to keep this class module as general purpose as possible, without building any Slider-specifics into it, we simply added a new parameter to the **MemDC**'s **Initialize** method like this:

```
Public Sub Initialize (CtlHdc As Long, CtlWidth As Long, _
                    CtlHeight As Long, Optional Skew As Boolean = False)
```

The call to **hdc.Initialize** in the slider control's **UserControl_Paint** method now looks like this:

```
hdc.Initialize UserControl.hdc, mWidth, mHeight, mOrientation = vertical
```

This code ensures that the **Skew** flag is set to True when the slider control has a vertical orientation. Incidentally, this is the only change we had to make to the **UserControl_Paint** method in order to support vertical orientation. Some small changes are required in other routines.

What happens to the **Skew** parameter that gets passed to the **hdc.Initialize** code? The answer is that it gets stored into a private, Boolean variable called **XYSkew**. At the same time, another private variable called **SkewCount** (an integer) is initialized to zero.

```
... 'MedDC Initialize method
' Stash the skew value
XYSkew = Skew
SkewCount = 0
' Stash the width and height of the control
If Not XYSkew Then
    ControlWidth = CtlWidth
    ControlHeight = CtlHeight
Else
    ControlWidth = CtlHeight
    ControlHeight = CtlWidth
End If
...
```

The above code (part of the **Initialize** routine) is crucially important. You'll recall that the **MemDC** code works by creating a memory device context and an accompanying off-screen bitmap.

276

The size of this bitmap must exactly match the display surface of the control. Thus, the code inside **MemDC** really *does* need to know what are the true dimensions of the control. Unlike the higher-level code in the control itself, we can't pretend here that the slider is horizontal when it's actually vertical. This is the reason for the slightly odd-looking assignments to the **ControlWidth** and **ControlHeight** variables; these members must be initialised to the true width and height of the control so that the off-screen bitmap has the correct dimensions.

There are three **MemDC** routines that actually draw something on to our off-screen bitmap. These are **FillRect**, **InvertRect** and **Rect3D**. All three of these routines need to conditionally 'skew' their input parameters according to the state of the **XYSkew** variable. As well as swapping over the (x, y) co-ordinates, it's also necessary to exchange the width and height parameters which are passed to these routines. This should be obvious, since the width of any rectangle that gets drawn for a horizontal slider is going to end up as the height of a rectangle in a vertical slider—and vice versa.

Thus, the three aforementioned routines need to swap their (x, y) co-ordinates and their Width, Height co-ordinates if the **XYSkew** variable is set to True. Simple? Well no, not quite..

Fun with Re-entrancy

If you look back at the code for the **MemDC** class and, in particular, the code for the three interface routines mentioned earlier, you'll see that the **Rect3D** routine actually calls the **FillRect** and **InvertRect** routines to do its stuff. Do you see the problem? Imagine that we've got a vertical slider control whose paint code calls **Rect3D** to draw a three-dimensional rectangle. Internally, **Rect3D** examines the **XYSkew** variable and maps its input co-ordinates so as to be appropriate for a vertical slider. It then calls **FillRect** to do some work. Because **FillRect** is also an interface-level routine, it also examines **XYSkew** and skews its input co-ordinates, not knowing that they've already been adjusted by its caller! The resulting mess could turn into an interesting debugging exercise.

There are many different solutions to this sort of programming problem, one of which might be to distinguish between interface routines (which skew) and internal, private routines (which don't). The private routines would effectively be duplicates of the public routines but without the skewing code. However, this is not a very elegant solution since it means that whoever writes **Rect3D** (or any new public routines you might care to add) has got to take great care to call only private routines. Worse, it leads to a lot of unnecessary code duplication.

Another possible solution is to append an **Optional** parameter to the end of each interface-level routine. This parameter would tell the routine whether or not to skew its input parameters. External to the class module, callers of the interface-level routines would omit the optional parameter causing it to default to True. Within the class module, public routines would call other public routines and pass a value of False to ensure that no further skewing takes place. Although this approach would work, it's still inelegant because it messes up the interface to the class and exposes functionality that we really don't want to be exposed.

The solution we have adopted uses a different approach and explains the purpose behind the **SkewCount** variable you saw earlier. Every public, interface-level routine in the **MemDC** class module begins with the following statement:

```
SkewBegin nLeft, nTop, nWidth, nHeight
```

Similarly, every public routine ends with this statement:

```
    SkewEnd
```

Now here's the code for these two new routines:

```
Private Sub SkewBegin (nLeft As Long, nTop As Long, _
                       nWidth As Long, nHeight As Long)
    Dim Temp As Long
    SkewCount = SkewCount + 1
    If SkewCount = 1 And XYSkew Then
        Temp = nLeft
        nLeft = nTop
        nTop = Temp
        Temp = nWidth
        nWidth = nHeight
        nHeight = Temp
    End If
End Sub

Private Sub SkewEnd()
    SkewCount = SkewCount - 1
End Sub
```

You'll notice that each time **SkewBegin** gets called, it increments **SkewCount**. Only if this variable is set to 1 (in other words, this is the *first* call to **SkewBegin**) do the parameters get skewed. For any other calls to the routine, **SkewCount** gets incremented and nothing else happens. Similarly, **SkewEnd** does nothing except decrement this internal counter. When the number of calls to **SkewBegin** is balanced by the number of calls to **SkewEnd**, this counter drops back down to zero. Thus, **Rect3D** can call **SkewBegin** and then invoke **InvertRect** which again calls **SkewBegin**. The second call to **SkewBegin** is effectively ignored.

This approach is elegant and simple. Provided that every interface-level routine religiously calls **SkewBegin** and **SkewEnd** at the appropriate point, we've achieved our objective of allowing one interface-level routine to easily call another without cluttering up the public interface with unnecessary detail and—most importantly—without skewing the input parameters more than once.

More Thumb Fun

As we've seen, only a few simple alterations to the **MemDC** module are needed in order to support the **Orientation** property. However, this isn't the end of the story. Back at the ranch, there are a few more changes to the actual control code that are required. Unlike the **MemDC** alterations, these changes *are* slider-specific and really depend on the sort of control that's being implemented.

Although the drawing code will now show a nice-looking vertical slider, it suffers from the problem that the thumb will be at the top of the slider when the **Position** property is set to zero. This is because we've effectively rotated our slider clockwise through 90 degrees. Thus, a thumb which starts off on the left will end up at the top. Unfortunately, the user will expect a vertical slider's thumb to be at the bottom and rise as the **Position** property is increased.

We could correct this by revisiting our co-ordinate skewing code in the **MemDC** module and applying another transformation to the y co-ordinate. Specifically:

```
y = ControlHeight - y
```

However, this would reduce the generality of the **MemDC** code, and while it might be appropriate for the slider, it might not be a good idea for some other control. In the most general case, the **Initialize** call to **MemDC** should have a parameter which unambiguously specifies what transformation to apply—whether to do horizontal flipping, whether to do vertical flipping and whether or not to swap the *x* and *y* axes. In time honored tradition, this 'deluxe' version of the **MemDC** is left as an exercise to the reader, but the amount of work involved is relatively minor.

In the case of our slider control, we've avoided the problem by adding some logic to the **ThumbRect** routine:

```
Private Function ThumbRect() As RECT
    If mOrientation = Horizontal Then
        ' If it's a horizontal Slider, then zero is on the left
        ThumbRect.Left = mThumbPos + mTrackIndent
    Else
        ' If it's a vertical Slider, then zero is at the bottom
        ThumbRect.Left = (mWidth - mThumbWidth - _
                (2 * mTrackIndent) - mThumbPos) + mTrackIndent
    End If

    ThumbRect.Right = ThumbRect.Left + mThumbWidth
    ThumbRect.Top = (mHeight - mThumbHeight) \ 2
    ThumbRect.Bottom = ThumbRect.Top + mThumbHeight
End Function
```

When the **mOrientation** variable indicates that the slider is vertical, the **ThumbRect** routine now calculates an enclosing rectangle for the thumb which starts from the other end of the track-bar. In this way, we get the effect we want and the thumb sits at the bottom of the slider when **Position** is zero.

The changes we've discussed so far relate to the appearance of the slider on the screen—the control's 'output', so to speak. But what about the 'input'? Just as the output parameters need to be skewed when using a vertical slider, the mouse parameters need to be skewed in the same way. If anything, this is easier to do than for the output side. There are three routines which receive mouse input:

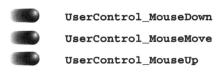

           UserControl_MouseDown

           UserControl_MouseMove

           UserControl_MouseUp

For each of these three routines, the x, y co-ordinates need to be swapped over on entry to the routine. We simply added the following code to the beginning of these three routines.

```
If mOrientation = vertical Then
        Dim Temp As Single
        Temp = X
        X = Y
        Y = Temp
End If
```

*Strictly speaking, this is a bit naughty. The X, Y parameters to each of these three methods are passed by reference (the Visual Basic default calling convention) which means that we're actually modifying the value of the parameters in whatever ActiveX glue code it is that calls the **UserControl** methods. However, no harm results because Microsoft's glue code makes scratch copies of any parameters it passes to the **UserControl** methods.*

There's one other change needed before the mouse will correctly track the thumb in a vertical slider. Just as we needed to reverse the 'sense' of the thumb, making it start from the other end of the track-bar, we have to make a corresponding change to the **MoveThumb** routine which takes the mouse X co-ordinate (which, of course will be the mouse Y co-ordinate when the slider is vertical).

```
If MouseX <> mMouseLastPos Then
        ' Thumb is centred around mouse location, so subtract
          ' half thumb width & normalise
     mThumbPos = MouseX - (mThumbWidth \ 2) - mTrackIndent
      If mOrientation = vertical Then mThumbPos = mWidth - _
          mThumbWidth - (2 * mTrackIndent) - mThumbPos
```

Armed with these changes, everything now works well apart from one minor cosmetic detail. If the user of our control happens to change the **ThumbWidth** property while the slider is vertical, they'll see that it's actually the thumb's height that changes! Similarly modifying the **ThumbHeight** property will alter the width of the thumb. This happens, of course, because of the way in which we've swapped the *x, y* axes in order to implement the vertical slider.

The necessary changes to the **Get/Let ThumbWidth** code are given below. For reasons of space, we haven't listed the changes to the **ThumbHeight** code but you should be able to infer what's necessary from the code below.

```
Public Property Get ThumbWidth() As Integer
    If mOrientation = Horizontal Then
        ThumbWidth = mThumbWidth
    Else
        ThumbWidth = mThumbHeight
    End If
End Property

Public Property Let ThumbWidth(ByVal NewThumbWidth As Integer)
    If mOrientation = Horizontal Then
        If mThumbWidth <> NewThumbWidth Then
            mThumbWidth = NewThumbWidth
            PropertyChanged "ThumbWidth"
            UserControl_Paint
        End If
    Else
        If mThumbHeight <> NewThumbWidth Then
            mThumbHeight = NewThumbWidth
            PropertyChanged "ThumbHeight"
            UserControl_Paint
        End If
    End If
End Property
```

And that's really it as far as the **Orientation** property is concerned. Although this has been quite a lengthy explanation, it's an important topic because it develops a strategy for creating an arbitrarily complex control while minimizing the amount of work necessary to support horizontal and vertical representations of that control.

Making the Slider 'Keyboard-Aware'

Almost all controls respond to the keyboard as well as the mouse, and there's no good reason why our slider control shouldn't do the same. Before implementing the keyboard handling code, let's clearly identify how we want the control to behave.

Firstly, the slider should respond to the left, right, up and down cursor keys, moving the thumb position a small amount each time that a key is pressed. Secondly, we want the slider to move by a larger amount when the *PageUp* and *PageDown* keys are used. Finally, it would be great if the slider also responded to the *Home* and *End* keys, jumping to the beginning or end of the track respectively.

Which Way Is Up?

This question isn't perhaps as stupid as it sounds. If you've tried out Microsoft's ActiveX wrapper for the COMCTL32 slider control, you'll know that when used vertically, the zero position corresponds to the *top* of the control and the position of maximum travel is at the bottom. This is the opposite way round to the way our slider works.

If you think about it, the correct 'sense' of the thumb in a vertical slider depends to a large extent on what you're using the slider control for. Imagine a 'Sound Studio' application where you're setting up a number of vertical sliders which control quantities such as Bass, Treble, Volume and so forth. In this case, the user would reasonably expect to increase the controlled quantity by moving the thumb up towards the top of the screen.

Now imagine an application which displays a small preview window for some document. Alongside the preview window is another vertical slider which allows the user to control his position in the document. As the user pulls the thumb down towards the bottom of the screen, the controlled quantity (in this case, the position within the document) increases—the reverse situation to the previous example.

One way of getting around this would be to introduce a new property, **ReverseThumb**. This property would reverse the relationship between the thumb and the **Position** property. You could use it to make a vertical slider work in an appropriate way for your application and you could even use it to reverse the mapping of the thumb in a horizontal slider. We haven't gone down this route because it would needlessly complicate the code, and there's another approach which is both simpler and more versatile.

SmallChange and LargeChange

By introducing two new properties, **SmallChange** and **LargeChange**, we can get a lot more flexibility for very little extra code. **SmallChange** stores a value which is added or subtracted from the **Position** property each time that a left, right, up or down keystroke is received. **LargeChange** stores another value which is added or subtracted from **Position** whenever a *PageUp* or *PageDown* keystroke is received.

For each of the possible keys mentioned, here's what the code does:

Key	Horizontal Slider	Vertical Slider
Cursor Up	Ignored	Position = Position + SmallChange
Cursor Down	Ignored	Position = Position - SmallChange
Cursor Left	Position = Position - SmallChange	Ignored
Cursor Right	Position = Position + SmallChange	Ignored
Page Up	Position = Position + LargeChange	Position = Position + LargeChange
Page Down	Position = Position - LargeChange	Position = Position - LargeChange
Home	Move thumb to start (left)	Move thumb to start (bottom)
End	Move thumb to end (right)	Move thumb to end (top)

As you know, the slider control defaults to a **Min** value of 0 and a **Max** value of 100. By default, the **SmallChange** property takes a value of 1 and **LargeChange** takes a value of 10. This means that whenever you use the up/down/left/right keys, **Position** gets incremented or decremented by 1. When you use the *PageUp* and *PageDown* keys, **Position** is incremented or decremented by 10. If desired, anyone using the controls can set **SmallChange** and/or **LargeChange** to zero which effectively disables the corresponding keys.

Now here's the cunning bit: by setting the **SmallChange** and **LargeChange** properties to negative values, we can independently reverse the sense of the above mentioned keystrokes. In other words, if you want the cursor up key to reduce value of **Position**, then assign a negative value to **SmallChange**. With these simple changes and bearing in mind that the developer is free to put his or her own interpretation on the value of the **Position** property, we've got a very flexible approach.

To add the keyboard handling code to the slider, we first need to implement the new **SmallChange** and **LargeChange** properties:

```
Private Const DEF_SMALL_CHANGE = 1      ' Default small change value
Private Const DEF_LARGE_CHANGE = 10     ' Default large change value

Private mSmallChange As Integer    ' delta for small Slider changes
Private mLargeChange As Integer    ' delta for large Slider changes
```

The following code needs to be added to the **UserControl_InitProperties** routine:

```
mSmallChange = DEF_SMALL_CHANGE
mLargeChange = DEF_LARGE_CHANGE
```

Also, we need to load the new properties in **UserControl_ReadProperties**...

```
mSmallChange = .ReadProperty("SmallChange", DEF_SMALL_CHANGE)
mLargeChange = .ReadProperty("LargeChange", DEF_LARGE_CHANGE)
```

...and stash them away in **UserControl_WriteProperties**

```
.WriteProperty "SmallChange", mSmallChange, DEF_SMALL_CHANGE
.WriteProperty "LargeChange", mLargeChange, DEF_LARGE_CHANGE
```

The **Get** and **Let** properties for the two new properties are equally straightforward. It's not necessary to redraw the control after modifying one of these properties because they have no direct effect on the control's appearance.

```
Public Property Get SmallChange() As Integer
    SmallChange = mSmallChange
End Property

Public Property Let SmallChange(ByVal NewSmallChange As Integer)
    ' For maximum versatility, there are no restrictions here.
    ' Setting SmallChange to 0 will disable left/right/up/down
    ' cursor keys.  Setting SmallChange < 0 reverses the 'sense'
    ' of cursor keys.
    mSmallChange = NewSmallChange
End Property

Public Property Get LargeChange() As Integer
    LargeChange = mLargeChange
End Property

Public Property Let LargeChange(ByVal NewLargeChange As Integer)
    ' For maximum versatility, there are no restrictions here.
    ' Setting LargeChange to 0 will disable PgUp/PgDn cursor keys.
    ' Setting LargeChange < 0 reverses the 'sense' of PgUp/PgDn.
    mLargeChange = NewLargeChange
End Property
```

Finally, once the **SmallChange** and **LargeChange** properties are implemented, we can write the **KeyDown** handler for the control. There are some restrictions here on which method we can use. The **KeyPress** method isn't available as it only supports the ASCII character set, whereas we're interested in the non-ASCII keys such as *PageUp*, *PageDown* and so forth. Similarly, the **KeyUp** method is a bad choice because it doesn't support the PC keyboard's ability to auto-repeat keys which are held down. If you hold down a key and it auto-repeats 50 times, you'll see only one **KeyUp** event! Fortunately, multiple **KeyDown** events *are* generated while a key is held down.

The code for our **UserControl_KeyDown** handler is given below:

```
'================================================================
'    Name:      UserControl_KeyDown
'    Purpose:   Respond to whatever keypresses we're interested in.
'    Notes:     Can't use KeyPress, 'cos it only deals with ASCII
'               Can't use KeyUp because it ignores auto-repeat.
'================================================================
Private Sub UserControl_KeyDown(KeyCode As Integer, Shift As Integer)

    ' We shouldn't get a keydown unless we've got the focus and
    ' are enabled.  Therefore, we only need to check that we're
    ' not currently active.  Trust me - I'm a doctor.....:-)

    If mControlState <> Active Then
        Select Case KeyCode
            Case vbKeyLeft
                If mOrientation = Horizontal Then _
```

```
                                Position = Position - mSmallChange
                  Case vbKeyUp
                     If mOrientation = Vertical Then _
                                Position = Position + mSmallChange
                  Case vbKeyRight
                     If mOrientation = Horizontal Then _
                                Position = Position + mSmallChange
                  Case vbKeyDown
                     If mOrientation = Vertical Then _
                                Position = Position - mSmallChange
                  Case vbKeyPageUp
                     Position = Position + mLargeChange
                  Case vbKeyPageDown
                     Position = Position - mLargeChange
                  Case vbKeyHome
                     Position = mMin
                  Case vbKeyEnd
                     Position = mMax
               End Select
          End If
     End Sub
```

Summary

You might be wondering why we haven't added tick-marks to the slider, and why there's no facility to allow an application program to supply its own drawing code for the slider thumb. Well, this is where you come in! We hope we've provided the material to get you fired-up and enthusiastic enough to continue enhancing the control for yourself.

In this chapter, we've worked through the development of a 'from the ground up' control which doesn't use any subsidiary components. Along the way, we've looked at various useful techniques such as:

 Drawing into an off-screen bitmap to improve repainting performance and minimize flicker.

 The importance of capturing the mouse to prevent loss of mouse events.

 A simple way to add an **Orientation** property to arbitrarily complex controls by 'virtualizing' the painting process for one orientation only.

All these techniques have involved using the Windows API to a greater or lesser extent. We want to encourage you to dig deeper into the API. The more you do so, the better the controls that you'll be able to build. Good luck and have fun!

Distributing Controls

By now you've created at least a few controls with the VB5 CCE. You're probably proud enough of your creations that you want to share them with others. There might be developers out there who could use your control to add that key feature to their application or web page; they might even pay you for it! Or you've developed the controls to make your programming easier, and you're distributing them to end-users as part of an application that you've authored. Whatever your motivation, without some way of installing your control on other machines, you'll be the only one to have the pleasure of seeing it or using it.

Fortunately, Visual Basic makes it easy to distribute controls in any of these situations. This chapter introduces and compares the different choices an author has when distributing a control; we talk about how to use the Setup Wizard application (that ships with the VB5 CCE) to create setup media for all of these options, and we cover some of the important issues facing control authors in the Internet world.

In this chapter you'll learn:

- How to choose between different ways of distributing your control.
- What the Setup Wizard is and how it works.
- How to create a setup program to distribute your control to other developers.
- How to use the Internet Setup Wizard to make your control available in a web page.
- Why code safety on the Internet is important and how to apply it to your control.
- The differences between design-time and run-time licensing.

Control Distribution Choices

Developers using Visual Basic 3.0 had one choice when they'd completed their project—make an executable and distribute it. The number of required files was usually small; in simple cases, a tool like the Setup Wizard wasn't even necessary. Distribution complexity increased somewhat when Visual Basic 4.0 gave the ability to create in-process and out-of-process ActiveX code components (formerly known as OLE servers). Today, with the full version of Visual Basic 5.0, developers have even more options. They can create executables, ActiveX code components, ActiveX controls, and ActiveX documents; furthermore, each of these products brings its own characteristics to the mix.

Since this is a book about creating controls with VB5 CCE, we'll focus on the specific options available to a control author. Believe me, there are plenty to keep us occupied.

Users of Controls

Who uses a control? As a Visual Basic developer you might say 'me', and you'd be correct. The people using your application could answer the question the same way: they're also control users. Visual Basic 4.0 was the first widely used host for ActiveX controls. Visual Basic developers provided the first market for control vendors. Today, many more applications and development environments can use controls. This is good news for you since, having reached this point in the book, you're no longer just a Visual Basic programmer, you're also a control vendor yourself. Controls can also be hosted inside a C++ or MFC application, inside Office 97 applications, and even inside web pages.

Before we explore the different options, we'll review a few key concepts. The following terms have been defined earlier in this book, but they're so important to this discussion that we'll reiterate them here. A **control developer**, or **control author**, is someone who develops a control for use in other applications. After a control has been authored, it can be used by **developers** working in any environment that supports ActiveX controls. Finally, the person who installs an application or views a web page which uses controls is the **end-user**.

As you'll see shortly, the way you distribute a control depends largely on what type of person will use your control. You won't follow exactly the same procedure when you're targeting developers as you will when you're distributing a control in a web page. Also, even when you've decided what type of user will use your control, there are additional factors that need to be considered. We'll talk first about distributing to developers and then to end-users.

Licensing is an important issue for a control author. A control is no use to a developer if it can't be used as a part of their application. However, end-users that find a control installed on their machine as a result of setting up an application or browsing to a web page shouldn't be able to use that control in their own applications or web pages. We'll cover this later in the chapter, so for now just understand that you can create a control that requires licensing information. Also, that there is a difference between licensing your control for design-time use and licensing your control for use in a run-time environment (like a compiled application or web page).

Distributing to Application Developers

Controls are most commonly distributed to developers (and end-users) as files with an `.ocx` extension. However, Visual Basic developers can also directly use the source code for a control, so you can also distribute the `.ctl` files. There are advantages to both approaches, and each requires a different method of distribution.

OCX Files

The traditional way of distributing a control to developers is via a setup program that installs the compiled OCX file and all additional files, and then registers the control. The Setup Wizard can generate this setup program automatically, and we'll cover this later in the chapter.

Controls distributed in OCX files can be used in any ActiveX control container. Since they are separate components, they can be upgraded independently of the applications that use them. When you distribute an OCX file independently of an application, you also need to distribute any required support files. Again, we'll come back to this later in the chapter.

CTL (and CTX) Files

If the developers using your control are only going to be using Visual Basic, you may want to consider distributing the source code for your control rather than the compiled version. With this method there is no need for a setup program; you simply provide the CTL and CTX files that hold the source code and binary information for your control. CTL files are text files that hold the source and property information for the control; CTX files contain any binary information such as the toolbox bitmap. Developers add the control to their project via the Project | Add User Control menu item.

With this method, developers don't need to distribute any additional files with their application, and they needn't worry about version problems since the correct version is compiled into the application.

If your developers are going to modify the control, you will need to distribute the source code for your control rather than the compiled version. This will also be the case if you developed and used the control in an application that you yourself wrote, testing only the functionality that you used—and now you'd like to distribute it so that others can use the control. Since you haven't fully tested every aspect of the control, distributing the source is good practice because it allows developers using the control to fix problems without contacting you for help.

Distributing to End-Users

Most controls distributed to end-users are packaged in OCX files. It's also possible to compile the control into an application, if the application is written with VB 5.0, and the source code is available.

The usual questions facing someone distributing controls to end-users relate to the packaging of the OCX file and its dependent files, and the way this block of files is delivered to and installed on the end-user's machine. We'll talk about the two most common distribution mediums for VB5 created controls—in a Visual Basic application, and as part of a web page.

In a Visual Basic Application

Even though VB5 CCE can't create executables, and the Setup Wizard that ships with the CCE can't create setup programs for executables, we'll still talk briefly about this topic so that you can compare it to distributing a control within a web page.

Controls that are a part of an application need to be installed and registered on each user's machine. Installing a control to be used by an application is a lot like installing a control for development use. The same OCX and dependency files are copied to the machine, and the control is registered. In fact, if the control doesn't support design-time licensing, then what actually happens during the installation process may be exactly the same. For controls that do require a design-time license, a key step is missing during an end-user installation: no licensing information is added to the registry. Because of this, no development environment can use the control.

Distributing a VB authored control with a VB application is easy. When the Setup Wizard is run to generate the setup program for the application, it detects each control used by the application, and automatically includes the OCX file and any dependencies in the files to be distributed. The control is registered as part of the installation process on the end-user machine. The VB 5.0 Setup Wizard recognizes required files for VB controls automatically. Don't forget that the version of the Setup Wizard included with the Control Creation Edition of VB 5.0 can't generate setup programs for executables; this is a feature reserved for the other editions of VB.

In a Web Page

As we've said, ActiveX controls need to be present and installed on an end-user machine to run. So what does this mean where the Internet and web pages are concerned? Someone browsing to your page shouldn't be expected to manually locate and install a control. Fortunately, a key part of Internet Explorer 3.0—called the Internet Component Download Service—handles all the details for us. All we need to be concerned with, as a control developer, is how to package the control and ensure that it can't do any harm to a user's machine.

To create a set of files to be downloaded by IE, we use the Setup Wizard again. Given a path to the project file for the control, the wizard will compress the file into a CAB (short for cabinet) file that can be digitally signed and placed on a web server. When a user views your page, Internet Explorer will automatically download, uncompress, verify, and install controls inside CAB files generated by the Setup Wizard. The wizard even parcels out the common dependency files so that they will only be retrieved and installed if necessary. Since Microsoft provides these files on one of their web sites, all you have to put on your web server is the compressed file for your control. CAB files for VB authored controls are often less than 20K in size! The required support files, like **MSVBVM50.DLL**, are often significantly larger, but these files only need to be downloaded once. If this sounds complicated, don't worry, we'll cover it all in much more detail later in the chapter.

Introducing the Setup Wizard

By now, I hope that our repeated references to the Setup Wizard have raised your curiosity about this tool. The Setup Wizard is, indeed, a very powerful and important part of most of our distribution tasks, and we'll be covering it in more detail in the rest of this chapter. Before we do this, though, let's give it a proper introduction.

The Setup Wizard that ships with the CCE can create setup programs for controls built with VB5 CCE. The full version of the Visual Basic 5.0 Setup Wizard can generate setup programs for all kinds of projects that Visual Basic can produce. Whether you're distributing a control, an ActiveX code component, an ActiveX document, or the old standby, an executable, the Setup Wizard is there to help. Although additional steps exist for certain types of projects, the general routine always stays the same. The Setup Wizard first prompts for a project file, and then inquires about how the distribution files should be packaged and where they should be placed after they have been created: on a local or network directory, or on a series of floppy disks. After this initial information is collected, you'll notice a pause (or not, depending on the speed of your computer) while the Setup Wizard determines what additional files your project needs. When this step is complete, the wizard will confirm that the file list is complete and allow you to add or remove any files. Finally, after the wizard has gathered the information it needs, it generates the files, and the Setup Wizard is complete.

How are Dependent Files Managed?

As controls and applications become more complicated, they can either grow in size or place portions of executable code into separate files. Since much of the same code is executed by any Visual Basic project, it makes sense to only package the code that a developer writes, and to leave the rest to supporting files. These supporting files are essential for the operation of the project, and without them the application or component can't run.

There can be many dependencies for a Visual Basic project. This is good or bad news, depending on your point of view. The last thing control developers want is to force their users to download megabytes of files if they already exist on the machine. But it also means that someone, or something, needs to remember which files are needed. This can make distributing a project, at least in theory, more difficult. How do you know which files need to be distributed? One of the most important tasks of the Setup Wizard is managing file dependencies. The VB 5.0 Setup Wizard uses DEP files to accomplish this.

The DEP File

All dependency information for a control is contained in the control's DEP file. This file is the key to Visual Basic 5's handling of dependent files. The file itself is just a text file that contains one or more sections for each file needed by the control, as well as the default installation location of each file, minimum version necessary, and how the component accomplishes any necessary registration.

To get an idea of how a DEP file is laid out, here's the text from a DEP file that was generated for the Card control we built in Chapter 8.

```
[Version]
Version=1.0.0.2

[MSVBVM50.DLL <0009>]
Register=$(DLLSelfRegister)
Dest=$(WinSysPath)
Date=10/25/1996
Time=10:30:08
Version=5.0.34.24
CABFileName=MSVBVMb5.cab
CABDefaultURL=http://activex.microsoft.com/controls/vb5
CABINFFile=MSVBVMb5.inf
Uses1=

;Lots more info in here!

[CARDS32.DLL <0009>]
Register=
Dest=$(WinSysPath)
Date=8/9/1996
Time=0:00:00
Version=4.0.1371.1
CABFileName=
CABDefaultURL=
CABINFFile=
Uses1=
```

The structure of the file is just like an initialization (**.ini**) file. The first section relates to the version of our control, the rest of the sections are each for a single dependent file. We've shown two of them here: the main runtime support file of VB itself, and the cards DLL which we encapsulated. Notice that the VB runtime file has already been built into a cabinet file for Internet download and placed on the Web by Microsoft. Also, an information (**.inf**) file has been specified which would tell a browser how to install the dependent file. We will look at little more at this later.

After you've finished authoring a control, you should always create a DEP file for the control. This isn't hard—you don't have to track down the file dependencies or information yourself because the Setup Wizard can do it for you. All you have to do is run the Setup Wizard, specify the path to the control's project file, select the Generate Dependency File option on the Select Project and Options step, and let the Setup Wizard do the rest of the work. You can choose between creating a dependency file and a setup program for your control, or just dependency file itself.

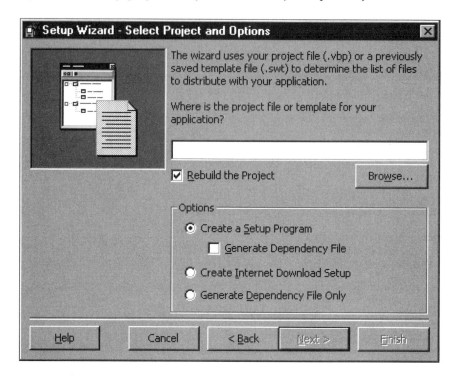

So how does the Setup Wizard know what files your control needs? VB provides an ace in the hole: the **VB5DEP.INI** file. When you instruct the Setup Wizard to create a dependency file for your component, it checks the **VB5DEP.INI** file first, to determine the base requirements for any VB-created control. After this, it checks for dependency information (again in the form of DEP files) for any controls or components that the authored control contains. The aggregation of these requirements is what makes up the dependency file for your control.

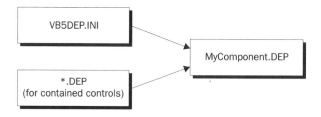

If someone tries to use the Setup Wizard to make a setup program for an application that uses your control, and you haven't provided a DEP file, then the Setup Wizard won't be able to include any dependencies for your control, and the setup program that it generates will probably fail. When the Setup Wizard can't find dependency information for a file, it displays a dialog to that effect. Don't put any control developers through the hassle! Make a DEP file.

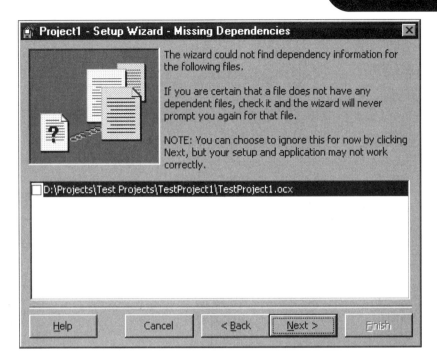

Without DEP files, the Setup Wizard won't operate correctly. You don't need to understand exactly what each line in each DEP file means, especially in the initial stages of learning how to create and distribute controls, but having a feel for how they work will be helpful. Many of the lines are self explanatory.

Conventional Distribution

You have a grasp of the options that a control author has when deciding how to distribute a control, from the first section of this chapter. However different these choices may be, the Setup Wizard provides a fairly constant process to accomplish all of its tasks. For example, a control author creating a distribution program for a single control completes exactly the same steps as an application developer distributing an entire application that may contain any number of controls. The Setup Wizard does different things internally for both cases, but what the tool user sees does remain relatively constant. The Internet Setup Wizard that creates compressed archives for web distribution of a control is the sole case where these things aren't the same, but we'll look at this in a later section.

Control developers need to create conventional setup programs with the Setup Wizard in two cases. To be specific:

 When distributing a control for development use

 When distributing a control in an OCX file as part of a Visual Basic application.

Note that when a control is compiled into an application, no additional files need to be distributed— the control's source code is included in the application's executable file.

First, we'll cover each step of the Setup Wizard in detail, and then we'll talk about how the licensing support your control may have can affect your setup.

A Setup Wizard Walk-through

Before we get into important details about the procedure of generating a setup program, we'll show how the Setup Wizard is used, step-by-step. To do this, we'll create a setup program for a control.

In this example, we'll be using the address control that you developed in Chapter 5. If you'd like to follow along on your machine, you can use your project files, or make a copy of the files available from the Wrox web site.

Starting the Wizard

When you first use the Setup Wizard, you'll see an introductory screen. This will appear each time, if you don't check the checkbox labeled Skip this screen in the future. For now, just click the Next button.

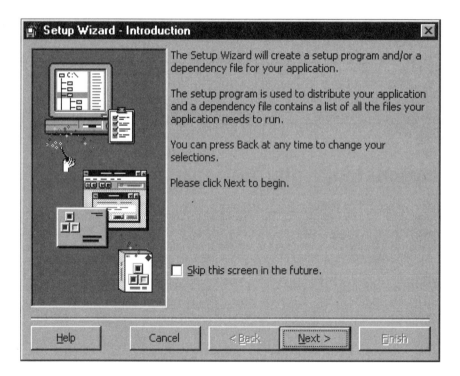

Select Project and Options

In the first real step of the wizard, you have to make two important selections: which project to use when creating setup media, and what kind of setup media to create. The project file should be selected by entering the path and name of the .vbp file, or by choosing from the file dialog displayed when the Browse... button is clicked.

The version of the Setup Wizard that ships with the Control Creation Edition of VB 5.0 can only build
setup programs for ActiveX control projects. Attempting to create a setup program for a non-control project
causes the error 'The Control Creation Edition of the Setup Wizard only builds setups and downloads for
VB created ActiveX controls'.

If the Rebuild the Project checkbox is checked, the Setup Wizard will start up VB 5.0 and recreate
the project. This can be handy, saving you the trouble of restarting VB and compiling the control
before continuing. However, if you know that the OCX file for your project includes all the recent
changes you've made, uncheck the box.

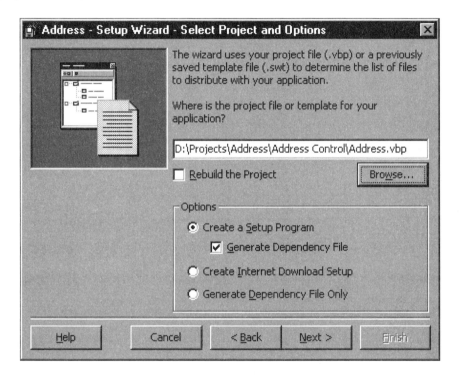

The type of distribution can be selected using the Options frame. The default selection, Create a
Setup Program, should be selected to create a setup program that will run off a series of floppy
disks or a network drive. This is the conventional way to distribute a control or application and
works with applications, ActiveX code components, and ActiveX controls. The Create Internet
Download Setup option, on the other hand, works only with controls, and is used to generate a
package of files to support a control on a web page. We'll cover this option in detail, later on in
this chapter.

Checking Generate Dependency File causes the Setup Wizard to create both a setup program and
a dependency (DEP) file for the project or control. If you'd like to forego the creation of a setup
program and just generate a DEP file, choose the Generate Dependency File Only option.

In this example, we'll enter the path to the address control's project file in the file text box and
leave the default option, Create Setup Program, selected. The control's OCX file was created
previously, so the Rebuild The Project checkbox should be unchecked. Finally, since it's always a
good idea to create a dependency file for a control, we'll remember to check the Generate
Dependency File checkbox. After completing these steps, choose the Next button to continue.

295

Distribution Method

There's only one choice to make in this section of the wizard: how should the Setup Wizard format the files it generates? To answer this question, think about how your users will install your application.

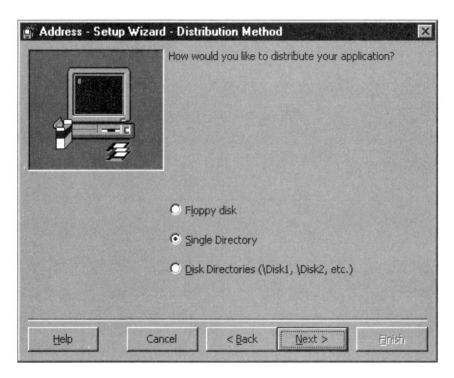

If your users will be connecting to a network share and running **SETUP.EXE**, you should leave the default option of Single Directory selected. With this option, the Setup Wizard will copy the files it generates to a single directory. This option also works well if you'll be distributing the setup program and files over the Internet. In this case, after the wizard has finished, run PKZIP or another compression program on the directory that the Setup Wizard has used. This generates a single file that can be placed on a web or FTP server.

The Floppy Disk and Disk Directories options both cause the Setup Wizard to generate files so that they can be copied on to multiple disks for distribution. The difference lies in where the wizard will copy files that it generates. Selecting Floppy Disk causes the wizard to manually prompt you to insert the actual master diskettes in sequence, while if you choose Disk Directories, the wizard will copy files to a series of subdirectories on the hard disk, called Disk1, Disk2. This last option is useful if your users will be connecting to a share and copying files to floppy disks for installation on a machine that doesn't have network access.

We'll choose the single directory default selection here, although you can pick any of the three options. Only the next step of the wizard changes—depending on the choice made in this step.

Single Directory (also Floppy Disk or Multiple Directories)

This step in the setup wizard allows you to specify the options that relate to your choice of distribution method. This screen is different for the single directory, floppy disk, and multiple directories options. If you've chosen Single Directory, the wizard just needs to know the path to the directory where it can place the files it creates.

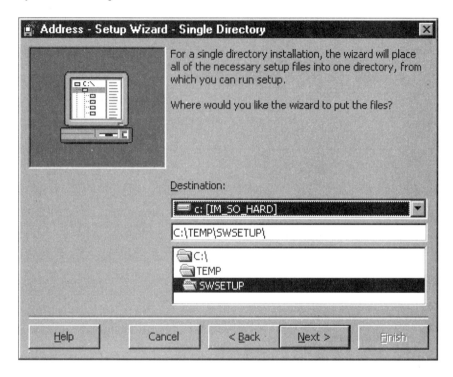

The Floppy Disk dialog asks for a drive letter and disk size, and the Disk Directories option leads to a screen that asks for the disk size and a path.

In this case, we'll just accept the default directory of `c:\temp\swsetup\`.

ActiveX Components

The next screen lists all of the ActiveX code components (formerly known as OLE servers) that the Setup Wizard has detected your project uses. The Setup Wizard can only detect code components accessed via early-binding—so late-bound components must be added manually. In your VB code, early-bound components are declared as **ProjectName.ClassName**, while late-bound components are just declared as **Object**. If your control uses any ActiveX code components that aren't shown, be sure to add them with the Add Local... button so that the Setup Wizard will include them.

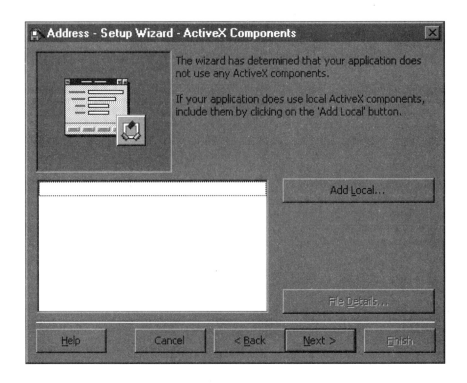

We aren't using any ActiveX code components in our control, so we'll leave this section blank and press Next to continue.

Confirm Dependencies

The Confirm Dependencies step lists any dependency files detected by the Setup Wizard that are required for the control to work. You should check each component's licensing agreement to make sure that redistribution of the files with a control is allowed. If you know that the some controls or files listed will already be present and registered on your client machines, you may want to uncheck the box next to each of these controls. Be *very* certain you know that your user's machines will have the controls or files before you uncheck any of these check boxes. Unless you have fine control over the machines where your control will be installed (as you may in a corporate environment), it's a good idea to provide all files that your control needs.

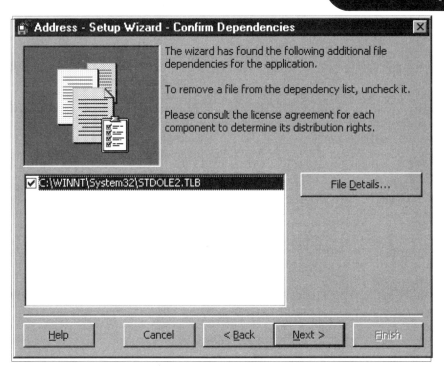

Although the **STDOLE2.TLB** file must be installed for a control to work, the reference here is actually not needed. The Setup Wizard has included it because it was referenced in the References dialog for our control project. **STDOLE2.TLB** will always be included in our setup files because it's required by the VB virtual machine (**MSVBVM50.DLL**).

In our case, we'll go ahead and leave the reference checked. It's always a good idea to remove unneeded references in the References dialog during control development when testing the project—and not during the Setup Wizard. Why? If you remove a reference while testing your control, the control won't work correctly if that reference is necessary. If you remove a required reference while using the Setup Wizard, you won't know anything is wrong until your user has installed the control and finds that it doesn't work. When in doubt, leave the files listed by the Setup Wizard alone. Click Next to move along to the next step.

The Working Setup Wizard

Before the next dialog appears, the wizard will pause for a few seconds, and show a few messages to explain what's happening. This is when the Setup Wizard does most of its work. As the Processing: VB Runtime Required Files and Processing: Detected Project Files messages flash upon the screen, the Setup Wizard is using the **VB5DEP.INI** and any project or control dependency files to generate a complete list of all required files.

Depending on your control, you may receive a message asking about property pages and using the control in a design environment other than Visual Basic. If you know that the control will only be used by developers inside Visual Basic then you may answer no to this prompt. Otherwise, it's a good idea to allow the Setup Wizard to include the property page DLL so that developers in other environments will be able to see your property pages.

299

File Summary

After all this work, the Setup Wizard displays the result: a list of every file that it thinks is necessary for this control to work on a machine that doesn't have Visual Basic installed. Additional files can be added by using the Add... button, and files can be removed from the setup by unchecking their checkbox. Pressing the File Details... button displays a dialog with specific information about the currently selected file, such as installation and version information. If you'd like to modify the installation location for a file, it can be done through the File Details dialog. The Summary Details... button shows a single dialog with information that relates to the entire project, like the number of files and total number and size of all the included files.

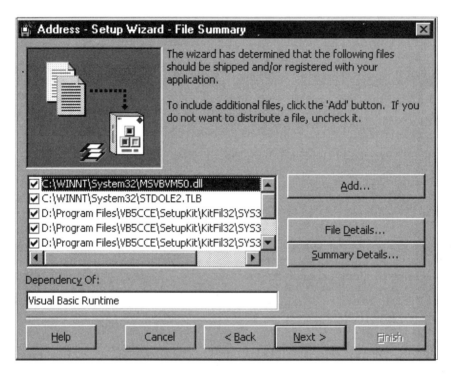

The Dependency Of: dropdown box is an interesting part of the File Summary dialog: it shows why each file was included. For example, in our demonstration, if we select **STDOLE2.TLB**, we see that the file is a dependency of the VB Virtual Machine (the Visual Basic Runtime entry) and that it is referenced in our OCX (Reference in <path to OCX>). If we'd removed the reference to **STDOLE2.TLB** back in the design environment, the Setup Wizard would have still included **STDOLE2.TLB**, because it's needed by the Visual Basic runtime.

Once we've examined everything we want to, we can press Next to move on to the last step in the wizard.

Finished!

You've made it, the Setup Wizard has all the details about your project it needs. Now you just need to press the Finish button, and let the wizard compress and copy the files to the location you specified.

If you've used Setup Wizard with previous versions of VB then you may expect to be able to save the installation options as a template. Unfortunately, this feature isn't implemented in the CCE version of the Setup Wizard.

After the wizard has compressed the files and copied them to your directory or floppy disks, the process of creating distribution media is complete. Your users can now install the control on their machines and use it in their applications.

Design-Time Licensing and The Setup Wizard

You can prevent unauthorized developers from using your control in other projects by requiring that your control use licensing information to operate. In this case, the control will not allow itself to be used in a development or runtime environment if that licensing information is not available. It's easy to create a VB 5.0 control that requires licensing information to operate—you just need to set the Require License Key checkbox on the General tab of the Project Properties dialog.

When a developer attempts to use a licensed control in a design-time environment like Visual Basic, the licensing information that has been entered into the registry some time earlier (like during installation) is used to create the control. When the application that uses this control is compiled, the licensing information in the registry is compiled into the application. After this application has been installed on an user's machine, the control uses the information from the compiled executable when it is created, rather than using information from the registry. This means that licensing information is added only to the registry on developers' machines. Application users only have the OCX file installed, and the appropriate licensing information comes from the compiled executable.

Licensed controls are used somewhat differently in web pages, since there's no compiled application for the licensing information to come from. We'll discuss the distribution of licensed controls for runtime use within web pages a bit later.

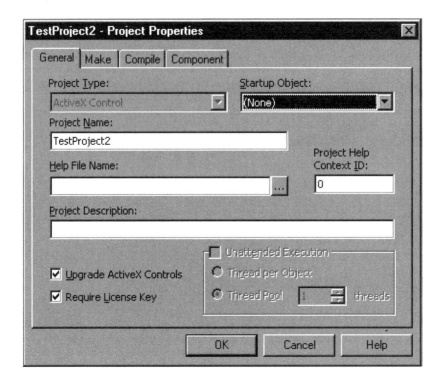

While including licensing support in a control makes it more difficult for developers to use your control without proper consent, it also adds some complexity when distributing the control to developers or end-users. When a control that includes licensing support is compiled, Visual Basic creates a **.vbl** file in addition to the **.ocx** file. This **.vbl** file includes all the information that needs to be in a developer's registry to enable design-time use of the control.

When the Setup Wizard detects that it's generating a setup program that involves a licensed control, it displays a dialog to that effect:

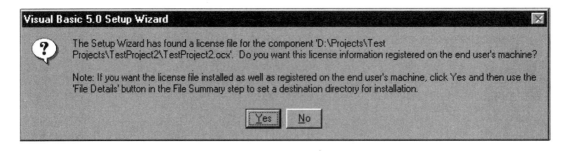

If you're distributing this control for development use, you should answer yes and allow the Setup Wizard to add the information in the **.vbl** file to the registry on the developer's system when installing the control.

By default, the information from the **.vbl** file will be registered, but the **.vbl** file itself will not be installed on a machine during setup. This prevents developers who are using your control from distributing the licensing information it needs separate from their compiled applications.

If you'd like to install the **.vbl** file, select the **.vbl** file in the File Summary dialog and change the text of the Destination Directory combo box from (Do Not Install This File) to a path on the user's machine. In most cases there's no need to do this, because the information will have already been added to the developer's registry during the setup of the control.

Distributing a Control with a VB 5 Application

Although this is a book on the VB5 CCE, we'll mention a few things about distributing a control as part of an application built with VB 5.0. The Setup Wizard is used almost identically when distributing an application as it is when distributing just a control.

Remember that the Control Creation Edition of VB 5 can't create stand-alone applications or setup programs for stand-alone applications. The other editions of VB 5 are able to create stand-alone applications.

To create a setup program for an application with the VB 5 Setup Wizard, simply select the **.vbp** file in the Select Project and Options dialog, and complete each step of the wizard. Ensure that the Confirm Dependencies screen includes a line for each control used in the project—both those authored with VB 5 and those authored without. If you're creating the setup program for the application on the same machine that you used for authoring the control, the Setup Wizard will ask about the licensing file, as in the above screenshot. In this case, be sure not to register the license file because the licensing information is already compiled into your executable. Remember, if you answer yes, then users who install your application will be able to use the control in their own applications.

Web Distribution

In addition to the stand-alone executables, controls can also be used within web pages. The ease with which you can create a control with VB 5 CCE, and the ability to view this control over the World Wide Web, is an extremely powerful combination. Browsers like Internet Explorer have mechanisms for downloading and installing controls. The Setup Wizard can create a package of files to be downloaded by a browser and makes this process as easy as creating a conventional setup program.

An Internet Download Walk-through

The Setup Wizard needs to answer a different set of questions when its output will be a file to be automatically downloaded by a web browser. As you might expect, if the Create Internet Download Setup option in the Select Project and Options dialog is chosen, then the Setup Wizard will make different inquiries.

In this example, we'll again be using the address control that you developed in Chapter 5. If you'd like to follow along on your machine, you can use your project files, or download them from the Wrox web site.

When you start the wizard, you get the same introductory screen as before. Clicking **Next** will move you on to the **Select Projects and Options** screen. This dialog is, again, the same as before, but this time we're going to create a CAB file so that our control can be used in a web page.

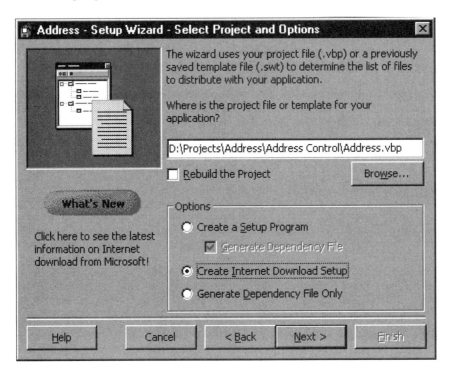

Select the **Create Internet Download Setup** option. A graphic and text will then appear to the left of the options frame. If you click on this graphic and text, you'll automatically jump to the Visual Basic home page on the Microsoft web site. For now, though, just press the **Next** button to continue

Internet Distribution Location

The files that the Internet Download portion of Setup Wizard generates are placed at a location that you specify in this step. These files can be placed on a local drive or on a network drive. If you have access to a directory that is served by a web server, you may want to place your files there to make it easier to test your setup when it is complete. Alternatively, the files can always be copied to a web server later.

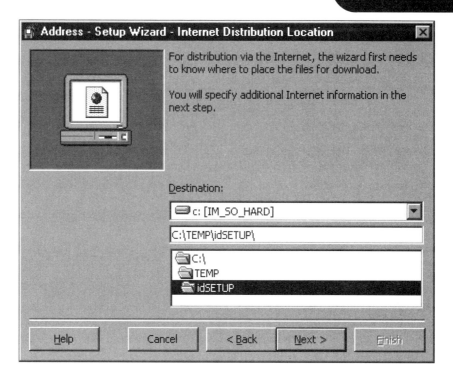

Choose your directory and press Next to continue.

Internet Package

When you distribute an application on floppy disks, or on a network share, you commonly provide every possible file that a user may need. For example, any application or ActiveX control authored with Visual Basic 5 requires that the Visual Basic Virtual Machine (**MSVBVM50.DLL**) be installed and registered. Conventional setup programs usually include this file, even though every user who has a VB 5 control or application on their machine already has the file correctly installed.

Since download times are an extremely important consideration in an Internet or intranet situation, the Setup Wizard provides a way to include just the custom files in an Internet Download setup, and to include references to common files. This way, files that are already on a user's machine aren't downloaded unless they are needed. In fact, you don't even have to provide these files on your web site—a special area exists on the Microsoft site that will always contain the most up-to-date versions of these files, digitally signed by Microsoft and available free for download. If your web application will be run in an environment where access to the Internet is not always available, you can download and host the common files on a machine on your network.

This dialog allows you to choose where the common files will be downloaded from—if they aren't already present on an user's machine. The default Download from the Microsoft web site setting causes the link in the generated CAB file to point towards Microsoft's web site. If you choose Use Alternate Location, then you should also provide a path (in UNC or URL format) where the files can be found. If you select this option and leave the path text box blank, the common files should be placed in the same directory as the CAB file the Setup Wizard generates.

For demonstration purposes, we'll choose the default selection.

This dialog also includes a button that provides access to a very important part of the Internet Download Setup Wizard. Don't press Next yet; instead, press the Safety button to display the Safety dialog.

Safety

Security for ActiveX controls is provided via two mechanisms: digital signatures and control marking. We'll discuss both of these topics, in depth, later in this chapter. This Setup Wizard dialog handles the control marking aspect of control safety: it allows you to mark your VB 5 control as 'safe-for-scripting', 'safe-for-initializing', or both.

Our control is safe-for-scripting and safe-for-initializing. The control is safe-for-scripting because after it's embedded on a web page, a script author can't do any harm to a client machine with script code. They can set the address, read the address, call methods, etc., but they can't cause the control to do anything harmful to the machine, like write to the hard drive or indiscriminately change registry settings. Along the same lines, the control is 'safe-for-initializing' because none of the values that can be set with **PARAM** tags in HTML can be set in such a manner that they cause the control to do anything damaging to the end-user's machine. We'll discuss these concepts in more detail later in the chapter.

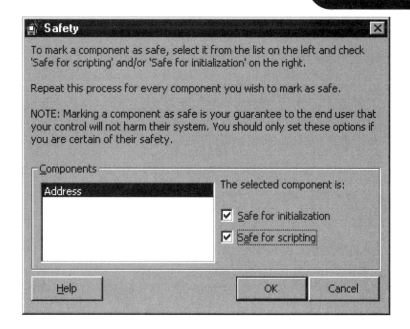

Since there is only one control in our project, it's already selected. If the OCX file exposed more than one control, each control could be selected and have its safety properties set individually. For our control, we'll check the Safe for initialization and Safe for scripting check boxes, and then press OK to return to the Internet Package dialog. Now we can press Next to continue.

ActiveX Components

This dialog serves the same purpose whether you are creating files for download by a web browser or generating a conventional setup program. Any ActiveX code components used by the control should be listed here. If they're not, use the Add Local... button to add them to the project.

The address control doesn't use any code components, so we'll just press Next to move along to the next step.

Confirm Dependencies

Since the address control doesn't have any dependencies to confirm, the Setup Wizard will skip this step in our demonstration. However, controls with dependencies, like controls that contain other ActiveX controls, will cause this dialog to be displayed.

File Summary

After the ActiveX Components or Confirm Dependencies steps, there will be a slight pause as the Setup Wizard uses **DEP** files, and the information that it has gathered so far, to determine what files need to be included in the **CAB** file it will soon generate. It will then display the File Summary dialog.

This again displays a list of files that the Setup Wizard has detected are needed by this control. Additional files can be added by using the Add... button, and information about a single file, or the entire list of files, can be determined, respectively, from the File Details... and Summary Details... buttons. The Dependency Of: combo box shows where the demand for each file originated.

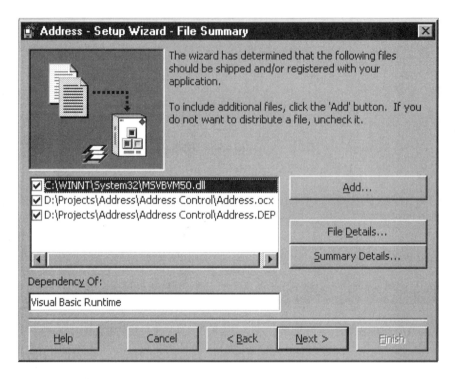

As you may have noticed, although we're creating setups for the same control in both demonstrations, the number of files listed in the File Summary step for the conventional setup is much higher than in the Internet Download setup. This is because many of the files that the Setup Wizard includes when generating a conventional setup program are updates to system files that VB 5 controls use. For example, the **OLEAUT32.DLL** and **OLEPRO32.DLL** DLLs are system files. With the Internet Download setup, since users that will view your controls need to have Internet Explorer 3.01 (or a newer version), the system files that are needed are already present on the user's machine, because Internet Explorer has installed them.

Finished!

This dialog is displayed when the Setup Wizard has collected all the information it needs. Press the Finish button to tell the Setup Wizard to generate the files for the Internet Download setup.

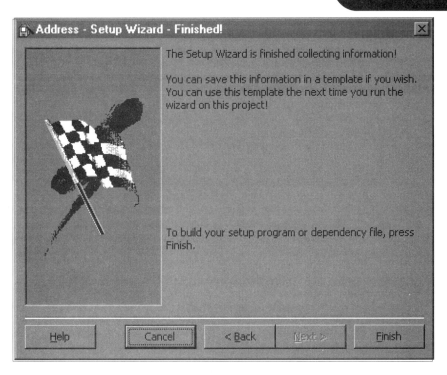

Before you place the CAB and sample HTM files for your control or group of controls on a web server, you should digitally sign your CAB file so that it can be safely downloaded. For more information on this topic, see the Digital Signatures section later in this chapter.

Files Generated by the Internet Setup Wizard

When you use the Setup Wizard in the conventional manner to generate a set of distribution disks, the wizard will compress and copy each file to the disks or distribution directory. In contrast, the Internet Setup Wizard creates a single CAB file that includes references or the files themselves for everything that should be distributed. In addition to the CAB file, the Setup Wizard also generates files that can provide more information or be used to customize the setup.

The Setup Wizard creates a sample HTML file with code that shows how the control should be used in a web page. The CAB file and this file are placed in the distribution directory specified during the Setup Wizard process. If you're not using an HTML editor that can handle ActiveX controls, you can cut and paste the **OBJECT** tag from this file into any pages where you'd like to place your control.

Any files that were compressed or used during the creation of the CAB file are placed in a directory named **Support**. The Setup Wizard creates this directory beneath the distribution directory. For a simple control that doesn't require any dependencies other than the Visual Basic virtual machine, this directory will contain three files: the OCX file itself, an INF file, and a DDF file. Any other files that were compiled into the CAB file will also be placed here.

309

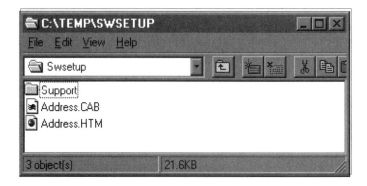

The INF file is a setup **inf**ormation file. It holds all information about where the control should be installed, lists any additional files that are necessary for proper operation, lists where these files should be installed, and explains how the control should be registered. The Setup Wizard uses the Diamond file compression utility to create the CAB file. Information needed by this tool to create the CAB file resides in the DDF file that the Setup Wizard generates. DDF files are similar to **.vbp** project files in Visual Basic or **makefile**s in the C/C++ world.

The INF and DDF files can be used if you'd like to modify the setup of your control, or if you need to regenerate the CAB file manually without the aid of the Setup Wizard.

Understanding INF and DDF Files

The contents of a cabinet file are specified in the DDF file. This is used as the input to the Diamond tool, which ultimately creates the CAB file. The DDF file contains the cabinet name, the names of the components to be included, and the name of the INF file which will control the installation on the client:

```
.OPTION EXPLICIT
.Set CabinetNameTemplate=MyFormula.cab
.Set Cabinet=on
.Set Compress=on
MyFormula.ocx
MyFormula.inf
```

What we see above is the minimum required for a DDF file. It includes the **.OPTION EXPLICIT** directive which aids in the debugging process by identifying errors in variable names. Although not mandatory, this line of code should be standard in all your files. Next it defines the name of the cabinet file you want to create. The **.cab** extension *is* mandatory. The next directives tell Diamond that we do want to create a cabinet file, and that we would also like it to be compressed. Lastly, we just list the files we want to include in the cabinet file (including a path if they're not in the same folder as the DDF file).

Comments can, and should, be added to DDF files by using a semi colon as the first character. This is especially useful if you intend making your own modifications.

```
;An example of a comment in a .DDF file
```

The DDF file can be used as a convenient checklist for what entries need to be in the INF file.

Structure of an INF File

The INF file consists of directives for the installation of the components being downloaded. It needs to be specified in the DDF file and included in the CAB file. It's also important to remember that a CAB (and therefore a DDF file) can only reference one INF file.

The INF file includes the location of the component and its **CLASSID**. Other optional parameters can include the version number and the destination directory (i.e. the complete directory path where the component should be installed on the client machine). Here's a simple example:

```
[Add.Code]
MyFormula.ocx=MyFormula.ocx
MyFormula2.ocx=MyFormula2.ocx
MyFormula.dll=MyFormula.dll

[MyFormula.ocx]
file=thiscab
clsid={7823A620-9DD9-11CF-A662-00AA00C066D2}

[MyFormula2.ocx]
file=http://www.myserver.com/objects/MyFormula2.cab
clsid={132WRR13-551Q-1S44-3551-199WR6739VB1}

[MyFormula.dll]
file=http://www.myserver.com/libraries/MyFormula.dll
clsid={572QGD13-591A-1S27-8410-194TL4881N41}
```

The first section defines the components to be installed, giving a section name where more information about each one will be found. By default, the file name is used for this. Within each section, you specify the location of the file to be installed, and its **CLASSID** for the registry.

Notice how the location is specified. The component can be in the same cabinet as the INF file (which will normally be the case), in a different cabinet file (which would then be automatically downloaded and unpacked) or any other web location specified by the URL. If you are installing on an intranet, using a source location on the server, you can specify the normal path to the files you want to install.

Extra parameters can be added to the INF file to define the file version required and the destination directory of the downloaded component. The **FileVersion** parameter allows you to specify the minimum version of the component that is required for the application to run successfully. If the client system doesn't have at least this version of the component registered and installed, the newer version will be downloaded.

```
FileVersion=4,70,0,1161
```

The default destination for downloaded components is the **Windows\Occache** directory. However, this can be overridden by using the **DestDir** parameter, which can be either **\Windows** or **\Windows\System**. To install components in the **\Windows** directory, you use a value of **10**, and to install in **\Windows\System** you use **11**.

The following example INF file specifies how two particular files will be installed. The first one, **MyFormula.ocx**, will be installed into the client's **\Windows** directory from a remote web server, but only if the version already installed on the client machine is less than **4,70,0,1161**. Then it

311

will install the file **MyFormula2.OCX** from the local server's **G:\isdept\cust\controls** directory into the **\Windows\System** directory, but only if it doesn't already exist on the client machine.

```
[Add.Code]
MyFormula.ocx=MyFormula.ocx
MyFormula2.ocx=MyFormula2.ocx

[MyFormula.ocx]
file=http://myserver.com/cabs/MyFormula.cab
clsid={7823A620-9DD9-11CF-A662-00AA00C066D2}
FileVersion=4,70,0,1161
DestDir=10

[MyFormula2.ocx]
file=file://G:\isdept\cust\controls\calc2.ocx
clsid={132WRR13-551Q-1S44-3551-199WR6739VB1}
DestDir=11
```

Creating the CAB File

The last task is to create the CAB file using the Diamond tool. This is found in the **/Setupkit/ KitFil32** folder of your VB5 CCE installation folder. It's a command line argument driven program, which combines the files specified in the DDF (the components to be downloaded and the controlling INF file) into a single compressed cabinet file. From the command line you type:

```
diantz.exe /f filename.ddf
```

where `filename` is the name of the DDF file you created earlier. That's all there is to it. After you've created your CAB file, you need to digitally sign it before placing it on your web server. We'll discuss this next.

Digital Signatures and Code Signing

If a user can't be confident that the control you've placed on your web page won't harm their machine, they may decide not to download it. Signing your code with a unique digital signature is a very important way to assure users that your control won't do any damage to their machine.

Code signing is complementary to a common method of security on the web known as 'sandboxing'. Sandboxed code doesn't have access to parts of the operating system that could be used to do dangerous things. For example, any operation that uses the file system might be prohibited—so that malicious code couldn't reformat the hard drive or fill it with garbage. Java applets, and the scripting languages VBScript and JavaScript, all use sandboxing to provide security.

Sandboxed code provides safety, but it greatly limits what developers can do with a language or environment. Signed code guarantees reliability in a different way. A user can be sure that signed code was written or certified by the person or organization that signed the code, and that the code hasn't been modified since it was signed. The digital signature provides a sort of electronic 'shrinkwrap' for the code—someone who purchases software in a store knows that the company on the box created the software and that the disks or CD inside haven't been tampered with, and a digital signature provides this same assurance for code downloaded over the Internet.

Digital signature technology has been developed, tested extensively, and codified into published standards by academia and industry over the last 30 years. Microsoft's implementation of these standards is called Authenticode. Internet Explorer uses Authenticode to verify downloaded software.

This section discusses the open technology that makes digital signatures work and gives instructions on how a control author can obtain code signing credentials and sign and test the download of signed code. If you're not interested in how code signing works, but just want to sign your CAB file, skip the next section and start reading at the section named *Obtaining Software Publishing Credentials*.

How Digital Signatures and Code Signing Work

The open standards that make code signing possible involve things called one-way hash functions and public/private key cryptography.

A hash function is a mathematical function that, given an input of any length, produces an output string of fixed length, called a digest, that identifies the input. A one-way hash function is a hash function with the additional property that the conversion is very easy to compute in one direction, and nearly impossible in the other. A real-world example of a one way hash function is a glass window: once the window is broken into a thousand pieces, no one is going to put it back together. When signing a block of code, the code is first run through a one-way hash algorithm, producing a digest. Authenticode can use either the SHA or MD5 algorithms. SHA, which stands for **S**ecure **H**ash **A**lgorithm, was developed jointly by the National Institute of Standards and Technology and the National Security Agency for use with digital signatures. MD5 is another one-way hash algorithm design that works well with digital signatures. MD stands for **M**essage **D**igest. Both of these are publicly known algorithms that have been tested extensively and are very secure.

After the hash algorithm has been used to produce a digest, the developer encrypts the digest with their *private key*. Public/private key cryptography is one of the most commonly used cryptography systems in the world today. The system revolves around two keys: one that a person keeps private and one that is made public. Bits encrypted with the private key can only be decrypted with the public key, and, in reverse, bits encrypted with the public key can only be decrypted with the private key. Signing a document with your private key ensures that everyone will be able to read it, while signing your document with someone else's public key means that only they will be able to decrypt it (because they are the only one with the corresponding private key).

OK, so now you know some of the technical background behind digital signature technology, how do you actually sign your code? After using an automatic process to generate a private/public key pair, and obtaining a certificate from a Certificate Authority (CA)—explained further in the next section—you use tools provided in the ActiveX SDK to sign the code. This process places the encrypted digest and certificate (that contains your public key) in a reserved space in the file that's being signed. We'll talk about this, in detail, in the next couple of topics.

When signed code is downloaded, the application (Internet Explorer in this case) calls the **WinVerifyTrust** API function. This function handles the verification process. First, the certificate is extracted from the signed file and checked with the certification authority. Then the digest is decrypted using the public key included in the certificate. **WinVerifyTrust** uses the same hash function with the actual code and generates a new digest, which is compared with the decrypted digest. If they match, then the code was signed with the correct public/private key pair and hasn't been tampered with since it was signed. Any mismatch indicates a problem, and **WinVerifyTrust** will return a failure. The application that called the API function can then take whatever action it desires.

Obtaining Software Publishing Credentials

Individuals and commercial companies can obtain software publishing credentials from certificate authorities. At this early stage in the game, Verisign Inc. is the only authority offering IDs on a wide basis. Verisign has set up a special web site specifically for this task; the URL is **http:// digitalid.verisign.com**. Obtaining credentials for yourself or your company is a simple matter of browsing to this site, clicking the link that advertises digital IDs for software publishers and then following the on-line instructions.

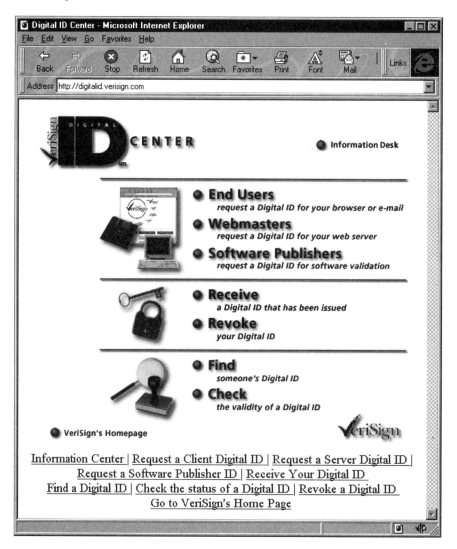

After entering personal or company information and creating a public/private key pair, you'll submit your public key to the certificate authority. The private key resides only on your machine, in a file with a **.pvk** extension. After verifying your information, which can take from minutes to days, depending on the certificate you are requesting, Verisign will reply to the email address you provided in your information with a URL from where you can obtain your ID. Verisign provides the ID in a file with a **.spc** extension. It's very important that you keep these files confidential. If someone were to obtain your credentials they could cause many problems for you by circulating a malicious control or application under your name.

Signing a Control With Your Credentials

Once you have your **.pvk** and **.spc** files from Verisign, you can sign the CAB file you generated with the Setup Wizard. The ActiveX SDK includes a wizard utility called **SIGNCODE.EXE** that walks you through the process of signing code.

The ActiveX SDK can be downloaded from the Microsoft site. At the time of writing, the URL for the SDK is **http://www.microsoft.com/intdev/sdk**. After downloading the SDK, follow the instructions on the web site to install the files. The application we're interested in is called **SIGNCODE.EXE** and should reside in the **INETSDK/BIN** directory. This wizard provides an easy-to-use front end for some of the command line utilities in the same directory.

After passing the introductory screen, the wizard asks for information about the file you'd like to sign. In the first text box, enter the name of the CAB file or PE (portable executable) file—like an EXE or OCX, that you'd like to sign. The wizard asks What would you like to call this program? Whatever is entered on this line will be the title of the certificate that's displayed when a program using **WinVerifyTrust** checks the validity of this file. In the last box, enter a filename or URL where people curious about what they'll be installing can find more information. This can be a web page on the Internet, or a file location or web page on an intranet. When you've entered your information, press Next to continue.

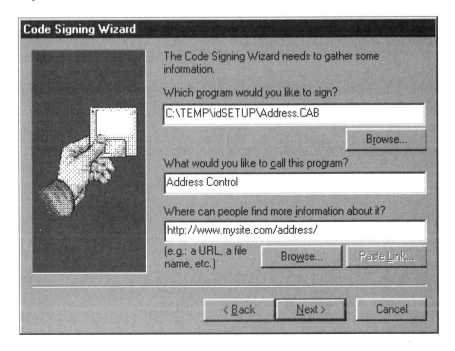

315

The next step of the wizard asks where your software publishing credentials and private key reside. Enter the paths to these files in the text boxes. The current Authenticode implementation allows you to choose from either the MD5 or SHA 1 hash algorithm. Unless you know your cryptography and have a special preference, the default MD5 algorithm is fine. That's all the information the wizard needs. Then press Next to continue.

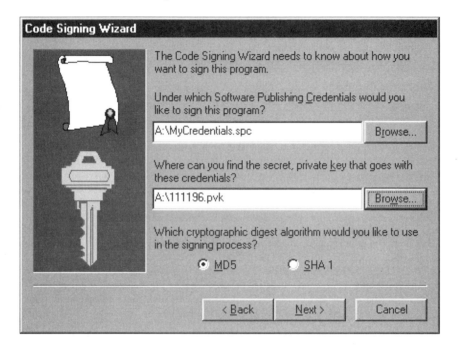

The wizard then presents the information that was entered in the previous two steps so that it can be reviewed for accuracy. If everything is OK, press Next one last time and then press the Sign button to sign your code. If the wizard is successful, you'll see the following dialog:

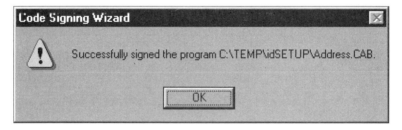

That's it! You code is signed. Now there's just one last thing to take care of before you can throw your control out for all the world (or your company) to see. You need to test it to make sure your control really was compressed and signed successfully.

Testing Signed Code

There are a couple of easy ways to test that the steps you've followed to create your signed CAB file have been successful. The ActiveX SDK includes a useful tool to check digital signatures, and Internet Explorer itself can be used to test download of code.

Before you check the CAB file itself, you should make sure that the digital signature was applied correctly. The ActiveX SDK installs a utility called **CHKTRUST.EXE** in the **INETSDK\BIN** directory. This command line utility calls the **WinVerifyTrust** API function on the file you specify. Since this is exactly what Internet Explorer or any other Authenticode enabled application will do to check a signature, the results you'll get from **CHKTRUST** will be the same results your users get from IE. To use this utility, first start an instance of the command prompt, and then enter **CHKTRUST** followed by the filename of the CAB file to check and a **-c** parameter to indicate that the file is a CAB file. For example, to check a file named **Address.cab**, that resided in a directory called **Projects**, you'd type something like this on the command line:

```
D:\Projects> d:\inetsdk\bin\chktrust -c address.cab
```

If you've successfully signed the CAB file, you'll see a certificate displayed. **CHKTRUST** can also be used to test the signatures on Java class files and PE (portable executable) files. When testing other file types, you shouldn't use the **-c** parameter. Instead, type **chktrust /?** to print a list of the possible file types and their command line switches and then use the appropriate option.

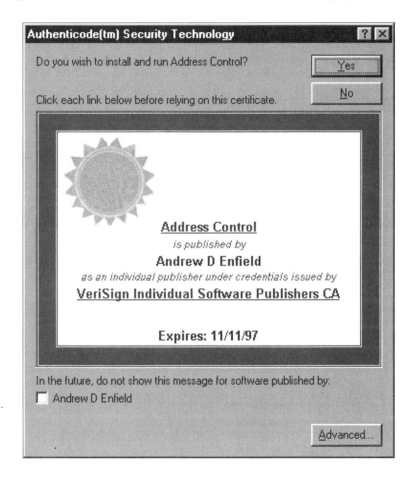

When the signature has been verified, you should check that the code has been compressed without problem, and that the control will be installed correctly when downloaded. When Internet Explorer encounters an **OBJECT** tag with a COM class ID in the HTML that it's parsing, it checks to see if the object is already registered and resident on the machine. If it is, IE just creates an instance of the object with standard OLE calls. Only when the object isn't on the machine is it downloaded and installed.

This justifies our method of checking the basic integrity of the CAB file: we unregister the control on our development machine. This removes the registry information and makes Internet Explorer think that the control doesn't exist on the machine.

To unregister a VB 5 created control (or most other controls), use this syntax:

```
regsvr32 -u ControlName.ocx
```

Controls created with Visual Basic 5 export functions called **DLLRegisterServer** and **DLLUnregisterServer**. The **RegSvr32** program simply loads the OCX and calls one of these functions—it's up to the OCX itself to add or remove its registry information.

After unregistering the OCX, browse to the page that the Internet Setup Wizard created. This page contains only an **OBJECT** with a **CODEBASE** attribute tag that refers to the control packaged in the CAB file. If the control has been signed, you should see the Authenticode certificate. Depending on the size of your control, you may see the Installing Components message in the status bar of the browser or it may flash by too quickly to be visible. Then your control should be visible in the browser itself.

As a last step, you should check your download code from other machines by browsing to an HTML page that contains the object. Even if you have the guts to try to simulate this on your development machine, it's difficult to remove all the files you think will be downloaded with your control. And if you make a mistake while in the midst of this delicate process, you may wreck your installation of VB or even of Windows. The easiest and most painless way to discover errors in the files that are included in your setup is just to fire up Internet Explorer on other people's machines and see if your control is downloaded, installed, and instantiated by IE.

Marking Controls: Scripting and Initializing Safety

The authenticity provided by a digital signature is great if the control or server doesn't already reside on your machine. Any downloaded code can be verified, and only installed if the author is known and trusted. But what if the code is already installed on your machine? No digital signatures are ever checked. For this situation, and to enhance the safety that controls can provide, there are the concepts of scripting and initializing safety.

Controls should only be marked as safe-for-scripting if they can guarantee that no script code can use them to do anything damaging to a user's machine. A control that simply displays graphical information is safe for scripting, while a control that writes strings to a registry location that can be specified in code is most certainly not safe. This doesn't necessarily mean that safe-for-scripting controls can't use the registry or file system—it just means that they can't use it in an unsafe manner. A control that used the registry to track information internally can still be safe, as long as a script author can't use this ability to harm the machine.

Safe-for-initializing controls are similar to controls that are safe-for-scripting. These controls pledge that, no matter what the initialization values received from **PARAM** statements in HTML, they won't harm an end-user's machine. A control that allows an HTML author to set its background color with a **PARAM** tag is safe-for-initializing; one that writes the character X to a file the number of times specified in a **PARAM** tag is not.

It's important that your control be marked as safe-for-scripting or safe-for-initializing (assuming of course, that it is indeed thus safe). Users of Internet Explorer who have not changed their security settings from the default values won't be able to see your control if it's not marked safe and your page contains script code and/or initialization values.

Wait, you might be thinking, does that mean that a non-safe control can be viewed, without problem, if the page doesn't contain script code or initialization values? Yes, this is correct. Internet Explorer only complains about a non-safe control if the page that it's on contains script code (for controls not marked safe-for-scripting) or **PARAM** tags (for controls not marked safe-for-initializing). If a page contains no script code, then that page can't cause a non safe-for-scripting control to do any damage. Likewise, a control that isn't safe-for-initializing can't do any harm if no **PARAM** values are specified.

If your control is unsafe, it shouldn't be marked as safe. Doing so can possibly make you liable for any damage that the control causes. Users with the default security setting of High will receive a dialog saying that potentially unsafe code hasn't been displayed, with instructions to see the on-line Help for information on how to view this code. People with security set to Medium will see warning dialogs and will be able to selectively choose which code Internet Explorer uses.

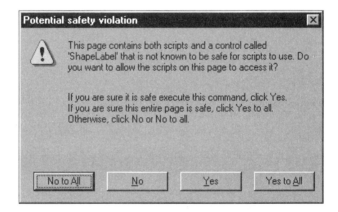

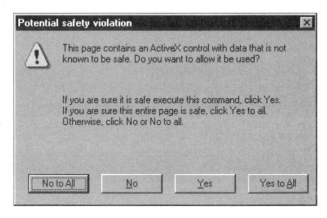

Controls can mark themselves as safe-for-scripting or safe-for-initializing by implementing the IObjectSafety interface or by adding keys to the registry. VB 5 controls marked with the Internet Setup Wizard use the registry. When you use the Internet Setup Wizard's Safety dialog to mark your control, the wizard adds the appropriate lines to the INF file that is compiled into the CAB. These lines are merged into the registry when the control is installed.

Control Licensing on Web Pages

The last important topic we need to cover is how licensed controls are handled on the World Wide Web. Controls with licensing support require licensing information before they will create an instance of themselves. Registry keys with this licensing information are created when a developer installs a product that contains licensed controls for development use. The development environment uses this registry information to create the control at design-time. When an application that uses licensed controls is created, the licensing information is compiled into the application; the application then uses this information to create the controls at run-time.

Where does this leave web pages that use licensed controls? The licensing information can't be compiled into a web page, since web pages aren't compiled. The simplest solution would be to add it to the web page itself, in plain text. This isn't a good solution because it would make copying the licensing information extremely easy, and so would allow people who haven't properly licensed the control to use it for development.

The solution that Internet Explorer uses is to expect the licensing information necessary for control creation to be put in a separate file with a `.lpk` extension, which resides on the web server and isn't downloaded in its entirety to the local machine. Microsoft has provided an application called **LPK_TOOL.EXE** to make creating these license information files easy. This application installs with the ActiveX SDK into the same directory as the code-signing tools: **INETSDK\BIN**.

LPK_TOOL is easy to use. The left list box contains all the ActiveX controls registered on the machine. To create a license package, just select each control on your page and press the Add button to copy it to the right list box. When you've listed all the controls, press the Save & Exit button to create the LPK file and exit the application. That's all there is to it.

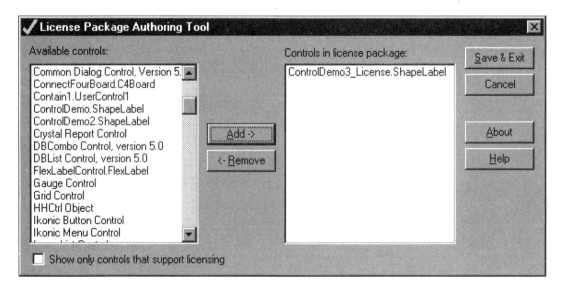

Once you've created the license package file, you just need to modify your HTML document so that each control that needs licensing information references the license package file. To do this just add a single **PARAM** tag with the name **LPKPath** to each **OBJECT** tag, like this:

```
<OBJECT
    classid="clsid:42DA39C7-42A8-11D0-BB2F-F4E08F000000"
    id=ShapeLabel
    codebase="ControlDemo3.CAB#version=1,0,0,0">
    <PARAM NAME="LPKPath" VALUE="LPKfilename.LPK">
</OBJECT>
```

To make it harder to improperly refer to an LPK file that you didn't create yourself, the LPK file must exist in the same directory as the HTML file that references it. Once you've created the license package file, modified your HTML, and placed the file on your web server along with your HTML and CAB files, you're all set. People who browse to your page will be able to see the licensed controls you've included on the page.

Summary

This chapter has covered the distribution of controls in several different situations. We have taken a detailed look at the Setup Wizard and how it can be used to create setup programs and Internet download packages for controls that are authored with Visual Basic 5, and we have discussed several other related issues.

The important points to note are as follows:

- Distribution mechanisms depend on whether the control is being distributed to developers or end-users, and whether it is going to be used in a VB application or downloaded from a web page.

- All dependency information for a control is contained in the control's DEP file.

- The Setup Wizard can be used for both conventional distribution and web distribution.

- You can prevent unauthorized developers from using your control in other projects by requiring that your control use licensing information to operate.

- Code safety on the Internet is important. You should digitally sign your controls and mark them safe-for-scripting and/or safe-for-initializing.

Index

Index

Instant HTML Programmers Reference

Author: Steve Wright
ISBN: 1861000766
Price: $15.00 C$21.00 £13.99

This book is a fast paced guide to the latest version of the HTML language, including the extensions to the standards added by Netscape and Microsoft. Aimed at programmers, it assumes a basic knowledge of the Internet. It starts by looking at the basics of HTML including document structure, formatting tags, inserting hyperlinks and images and image mapping, and then moves on to cover more advanced issues such as tables, frames, creating forms to interact with users, animation, incorporating scripts (such as JavaScript) into HTML documents, and style sheets.

The book includes a full list of all the HTML tags, organised by category for easy reference.

Instant VBScript

Authors: Alex Homer, Darren Gill
ISBN: 1861000448
Price: $25.00 C$35.00 £22.99

This is the guide for programmers who already know HTML and another programming language and want to waste no time getting up to speed. This book takes developers right into the code, straight from the beginning of Chapter 1. The first object is to get the programmer to create their own 'reactive' web pages as quickly as possible while introducing the most important HTML and ActiveX controls. This new knowledge is quickly incorporated into more complex examples with a complete sample site built early in the book.

As Internet Explorer is the browser that introduced VBScript, we also take a detailed look at how to use VBScript to access different objects within the browser. We create our own tools to help us with the development of applications, in particular a debugging tool to aid error-trapping. Information is provided on how to build your own controls and sign them to secure Internet download. Finally we take a look at server side scripting and how with VBScript you can get the clients and server communicating freely. The book is supported by our web site which contains all of the examples in the book in an easily executable form.

Wrox Press
http://www.wrox.com/

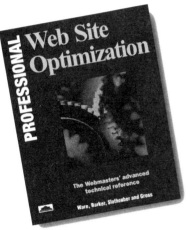

Professional Web Site Optimization

Authors: Ware, Barker, Slothouber
and Gross
ISBN: 186100074x
Price: $40.00 C$56.00 £36.99

OK, you've installed your web server, and it's working fine and you've even got people interested in visiting your site - too many people, in fact. The real challenge is just starting you need to make it run faster, better and more flexibly.

This is the book for every webmaster who needs to improve site performance. You could just buy that new T-1 you've had your eye on, but what if the problem is really in your disk controller? Or maybe it's the way you've designed your pages or the ISP you're using.

The book covers web server optimization for all major platforms and includes coverage of LAN performance, ISP performance, basic limits imposed by the nature of HTTP, IP and TCP. We also cover field-proven methods to improve static & dynamic page content from database access and the mysteries of graphic file manipulation and tuning.

If you've got the choice between spending fifteen thousand on a new line, or two hundred dollars in new hardware plus the cost of this book, which decision would your boss prefer?

Professional Visual C++ ISAPI Programming

Author: Michael Tracy
ISBN: 1861000664
Price: $40.00 C$56.00 £36.99

This is a working developer's guide to customizing Microsoft's Internet Information Server, which is now an integrated and free addition to the NT4.0 platform. This is essential reading for real-world web site development and expects readers to already be competent C++ and C programmers. Although all techniques in the book are workable under various C++ compilers, users of Visual C++ 4.1 will benefit from the ISAPI extensions supplied in its AppWizard.

This book covers extension and filter programming in depth. There is a walk through the API structure but not a reference to endless calls. Instead, we illustrate the key specifications with example programs.

HTTP and HTML instructions are issued as an appendix. We introduce extensions by mimicking popular CGI scripts and there's a specific chapter on controlling cookies. With filters we are not just re-running generic web code - these are leading-edge filter methods specifically designed for the IIS API.

WROX

Register Instant Visual Basic 5 ActiveX Control Creation and sign up for a free subscription to The Developer's Journal.

A bi-monthly magazine for software developers, The Wrox Press Developer's Journal features in-depth articles, news and help for everyone in the software development industry. Each issue includes extracts from our latest titles and is crammed full of practical insights into coding techniques, tricks, and research.

Fill in and return the card below to receive a free subscription to the Wrox Press Developer's Journal.

Instant Visual Basic 5 ActiveX Control Creation Registration Card

Name _____

Address _____

_____

_____

City _____ State/Region _____

Country _____ Postcode/Zip _____

E-mail _____

Occupation _____

How did you hear about this book? _____

☐ Book review (name) _____

☐ Advertisement (name) _____

☐ Recommendation _____

☐ Catalog _____

☐ Other _____

Where did you buy this book? _____

☐ Bookstore (name) _____ City _____

☐ Computer Store (name) _____

☐ Mail Order _____

☐ Other _____

What influenced you in the purchase of this book?

☐ Cover Design

☐ Contents

☐ Other (please specify) _____

How did you rate the overall contents of this book?

☐ Excellent ☐ Good

☐ Average ☐ Poor

What did you find most useful about this book? _____

What did you find least useful about this book? _____

Please add any additional comments. _____

What other subjects will you buy a computer book on soon? _____

What is the best computer book you have used this year?

_____

Note: This information will only be used to keep you updated about new Wrox Press titles and will not be used for any other purpose or passed to any other third party.

WROX

WROX PRESS INC.

Wrox writes books for you. Any suggestions, or
ideas about how you want information given in
your ideal book will be studied by our team.
Your comments are always valued at Wrox.

Free phone in USA 800-USE-WROX
Fax (312) 465 4063

Compuserve 100063,2152.
UK Tel. (0121) 706 6826   Fax   (0121) 706 2967

———— *Computer Book Publishers* ————

NB. If you post the bounce back card below in the UK, please send it to:
Wrox Press Ltd. 30 Lincoln Road, Birmingham, B27 6PA